Praise for *Philip K. Dick and Philosophy: Do Androids Have Kindred Spirits?*

"Life sometimes imitates art, and we're heading toward many of the technologies and scenarios imagined by Philip Dick, one of the most iconic and philosophical writers in science fiction. *Philip K. Dick and Philosophy: Do Androids Have Kindred Spirits?* is a nice, accessible guide to many metaphysical and ethical issues waiting in our future."

—PATRICK LIN, co-editor of *Robot Ethics* and co-author of *What Is Nanotechnology and Why Does It Matter?*

"*Philip K. Dick and Philosophy: Do Androids Have Kindred Spirits?* is an intelligent, exciting, and highly entertaining read that will be valued by all thoughtful Dick fans as well as philosophers. The original and thought-provoking chapters assembled by Dylan Wittkower explore a vast range of philosophical topics and display the breadth and depth of Dick's writing with great style."

—MARYA SCHECHTMAN, author of *The Constitution of Selves*

"Philip K. Dick was one of the twentieth century's most penetrating writers concerned with the human condition. Mortality and self-knowledge obsessed him, and his work on these topics is some of the most thoughtful we have seen. Amazingly, Dylan Wittkower has managed to assemble a collection of thinkers who not only understand Dick but whose explanations will help the rest of us understand him better."

—JOSEPH C. PITT, author of *Thinking About Technology*

"For anyone who's ever wondered if they might be a replicant, *Philip K. Dick and Philosophy: Do Androids Have Kindred Spirits?* is required reading. As these writers show, some of the deepest questions that we confront—questions about identity, free will, and our place in the universe—are perfectly illustrated by the memorable characters populating Dick's fictional worlds, from the Nexus-6 androids, to the Precogs, to the customers of Rekal, Inc."

> —AMY KIND, contributor to *Star Trek and Philosophy* and *Battlestar Galactica and Philosophy*

"Some minds reflect this age, others incubate the next. Humanity is about to stumble into a new, perhaps terrifying age. Thanks to the incisive chapters Dylan Wittkower has assembled in *Philip K. Dick and Philosophy: Do Androids Hve Kindred Spirits?*, we may not do so blindly."

> —R. SCOTT BAKKER, author of *The White-Luck Warrior*, *Disciple of the Dog*, and *Neuropath*

"An advanced degree in Dick-ology, an essential book for anyone wishing to discover the shocking depth of Philip K Dick's ideas."

> —DAVID GILL, publisher, *Total Dick-Head* blog

"Dylan Wittkower has assembled a fantastic collection of chapters analyzing the deep themes of Dick's stories, including the elusiveness of free will, the ambiguous nature of personhood, and the uncertain reliability of knowledge. *Philip K. Dick and Philosophy: Do Androids Have Kindred Spirits?* is a real treat for fans of both Dick's stories and the movie adaptations."

> —ERIC J. SILVERMAN, author of *The Prudence of Love*

Philip K. Dick
and Philosophy

Popular Culture and Philosophy® Series Editor: George A. Reisch

For full details of all Popular Culture and Philosophy® books, visit www.opencourtbooks.com.

Popular Culture and Philosophy®

Philip K. Dick and Philosophy

Do Androids Have Kindred Spirits?

Edited by
D.E. WITTKOWER

OPEN COURT
Chicago and LaSalle, Illinois

Volume 63 in the series, Popular Culture and Philosophy®, edited by George A. Reisch

To order books from Open Court, call toll-free 1-800-815-2280, or visit our website at www.opencourtbooks.com.

Open Court Publishing Company is a division of Carus Publishing Company.

Library of Congress Cataloging-in-Publication Data

Philip K. Dick and philosophy : do androids have kindred spirits? / edited by D.E. Wittkower.
     p. cm.—(Popular culture and philosophy ; v. 63)
    Includes bibliographical references and index.
    ISBN 978-0-8126-9734-6 (trade paper : alk. paper)
    1. Dick, Philip K.—Criticism and interpretation. 2. Philosophy in literature.
  3. Science fiction, American—History and criticism. I. Wittkower, D. E., 1977-
    PS3554.I3Z794 2011
    813'.54—dc22

                        2011021040

Table of Precognitions

Through a Screen Darkly

01
Hollywood Doesn't Know Dick

ETHAN MILLS

Some of the biggest Hollywood blockbusters of the last few decades have been based on the work of Philip K. Dick—*Blade Runner, Total Recall, Minority Report, The Adjustment Bureau,* just to name the biggest and most block-busting of them.

Like many Dick fans, I was dazzled by some of these movies before I ever picked up Dick's short stories and novels. But when I found the original stories, I noticed something was amiss. I felt like Deckard, Quail, or Anderton: something weird was going on. And it wasn't just that 'the book is better than the movie', as that pretentious friend is always telling you. This wasn't just a matter of details or minor plot points. Something essential had been lost in translation from print to film.

But what is this "something"? Could there be some Hollywood conspiracy out to get Dick's loyal readers? Would it be safer to stay in the theater or on my couch enjoying the movies? And who the hell do I think I am, anyway, going around uncovering plots involving dead science-fiction writers and Hollywood studios?

But I couldn't stop investigating. So I grabbed my trench coat, put on a brooding face, and went in search of my bounty.

My investigation revealed that, since Hollywood began plundering Dick's work, fans have complained about everything from Deckard's lack of uncertainty about his humanity in *Blade Runner* to the sappy nonsense at the end of *Minority Report.* You might chalk this up to the lameness of studio executives out to make a quick buck, but my investigation has

3

revealed that this reflects a deeper tension between two philosophical views about the human condition.

We Can Conceive It for Ourselves Wholesale

One of these philosophical views is what I call the "Holly-worldview." Some worldviews give a place for genuine free will, unconstrained by cause and effect, while others decry this as an illusion and claim that human actions—including our decisions, thoughts and feelings—are subject to cause and effect like everything else. Whether your worldview is philosophically well founded or whether it's the result of false memories implanted by Rekall, Inc., worldviews are like assholes: everyone has one.

According to the Holly-worldview good defeats evil, free will secures the triumph of the human spirit and our heroes discover knowledge of reality and virtue (all before the credits roll). The Holly-worldview says that the universe is a nice place, although you have to defend it against the occasional villain. Movies must have happy endings. Villains must be punished and heroes must learn valuable lessons. It probably wouldn't hurt, either, if the heroes find true love.

Opposed to this, there's the Dickian worldview: a universe of paranoia, ignorance, and lack of true freedom. Dick's heroes think someone's out to get them. And they're right. They consider the possibility that everything they think they know is wrong. They only occasionally discover the truth. Dick's heroes wonder if they make any genuinely free decisions. They accept that they don't. The Dickian worldview says that the universe is generally hostile to our Hollywood aspirations. A "happy ending" for Dick is often overcoming a small obstacle while coming to accept some inevitable—and possibly depressing—fact about our place in the universe.

My guess (based on meticulous armchair sociology) is that most Americans prefer the Holly-worldview, which explains why Hollywood alters Dick's original vision. Are there good reasons to support the Holly-worldview or should philosophical bounty hunters retire it? Let's think about a way to answer that by investigating how Dick challenges two tenets of the Holly-worldview: free will and knowledge.

Free Will at the Box Office

Despite my complaints, I think *Minority Report* is a pretty cool movie. The cinematography is beautiful. The high-tech stuff is sleek and shiny (Apple products: still cool in 2054!), but there's enough gritty stuff to seem real. Tom Cruise, despite his antics off-screen, does a great job playing Anderton. Steven Spielberg is the most successful director in Hollywood for good reason. Screenwriters Jon Cohen and Scott Frank added a compelling back-story for Anderton and linked the movie to debates about civil liberties and pre-emptive action going on when the movie was released in 2002.

I'm fine with all that. My complaints are philosophical.

In the short story, "The Minority Report," the Precogs predict that Anderton will murder Leopold Kaplan, a retired General. Of course, in true Dick fashion, there's a conspiracy: the military wants to put Precrime out of business. The philosophically interesting part is that there are three minority reports. Each Precog has a slightly different prediction incorporating different data. The last prediction included the data that Anderton knew of the earlier predictions. The first and last Precog predictions said that Anderton would kill Kaplan, which created an illusion of a majority report, although they disagreed about details. Anderton does kill Kaplan exactly as the last Precog vision predicted and he does so fully conscious that he is saving Precrime and preventing a military coup. Anderton is content with this state of affairs and neither he nor his loyal wife complain one bit as he accepts his punishment of exile to the colonies in the outer solar system.

In Spielberg's movie, *Minority Report*, Anderton's supposed to kill some random guy named Leo Crow. Anderton steals one of the Precogs, Agatha. When Anderton goes to interrogate Crow, Agatha tells Anderton, "You still have a choice. The others never saw their future." Crow claims he murdered Anderton's son six years earlier, which drives Anderton to want to murder Crow. There was no minority report. He is going to kill Crow. Agatha feebly gasps, "You can choose." Anderton doesn't kill Crow after all in an apparent triumph of free will (human dignity is saved later when Anderton gets Precrime shut down).

The Adjustment Bureau involves a similar shift from story to film. In Dick's story, "Adjustment Team," an employee at a real estate company, Ed Fletcher, learns that our lives are "adjusted" by a team of shadowy men (and at least one shadowy dog). When the team catches him, Fletcher agrees that these adjustments are all for the greater good and says he won't tell anyone about the Adjustment Team. They let him go and even send a fake vacuum-cleaner salesman to distract his wife from asking questions about where he's been.

In George Nolfi's movie, *The Adjustment Bureau*, a politician named David Norris (Matt Damon) learns about a group of guys in Mad Men outfits who continually change the course of events to go according to the Plan (unfortunately, no dogs are involved). Things get supernatural when it turns out that the Adjustment Bureau employees may be angels who work for the Chairman, a ridiculously thinly disguised metaphor for God. Things get Hollywood when an Adjustment Bureau employee named Harry (Anthony Mackie) helps David and Elise (Emily Blunt) to be together even though it goes against the Plan. Their love teaches the Chairman a lesson, whereupon they are granted freedom from the Adjustment Bureau's meddling in a triumph for both romance and free will.

In each case, the short story exemplifies the Dickian worldview, in which real free will is doubtful, while the movie insists on the Holly-worldview in which the heroes' free will secures our human dignity. Maybe the screenwriters thought the original stories were too hard to tell in movie form, but I suspect a clash between the Dickian worldview and the Holly-worldview is the real culprit. The Dickian worldview wouldn't work in a Hollywood movie (meaning less box office revenue). This isn't just an economic matter, but a philosophical point. People don't like their belief in free will questioned. But why not? And why on Earth (or Mars) would Dick question something as obvious as free will?

Determinism's Bounty on Free Will

Dick's doubts stem from a view known as determinism. Determinism is frequently and incorrectly confused with fate, or the idea that some beings (usually supernatural) are controlling your life. The movie, *The Adjustment Bureau*, is really about fate, since the Chairman dispatches men with magic Moleskine notebooks to tinker with our lives. The movie is a mess, philosophically speaking, but it seems as if humans have free will that angels continually work to circumvent.

On the other hand, determinism is a non-supernatural theory that says that, given the way things are now, there is only one possible future. The story, "Adjustment Team," is determinist: if they make certain adjustments, then the consequences they predict will necessarily occur. They're not quashing the free will we would otherwise have as in the movie, they're setting up the "if" side of an "if-then" sentence.

Another way to explain determinism is that every event in the universe is determined by the laws of nature. This makes sense. Stuff doesn't just randomly happen. It follows a predictable order. If it didn't, science—and even more sadly, science fiction—would be a waste of time. If John Anderton didn't think the laws of physics were regular enough that the force created by igniting gunpowder would cause a bullet to fly out of the barrel of his gun, he wouldn't have bothered to want to shoot anybody.

Where things get weird is applying determinism to every event in the universe, even human actions. Anderton's actions are events in the universe (aren't they?). Suppose you knew everything about Anderton: his past, his current brain states, his tendencies, what he ate for lunch, and so forth. If you knew all that, couldn't you predict his actions? Don't we predict each other's actions all the time?

You might say that our predictions aren't always correct, but a determinist would reply that this is due to a lack of knowledge. We're talking about reality here. Just because we don't know what the causes are doesn't mean they're not there. If hypothetically you could know everything about Anderton and predict his actions like a Precog, doesn't it make sense that his actions are the inevitable result of the sum total of all the causes leading up to those actions? Why would you think he could have done otherwise? Where is there room for this mysterious "freedom"? Think carefully about these questions. I promise if you really understand determinism, it will blow your mind.

Like cheese, determinism comes in hard and soft varieties. Hard determinists rule out freedom and moral responsibility. If you weren't in control of your choices, but rather your choices were caused by everything from your brain states to the bad noodles you ate, you're no better off than an android with false memories. You're not really in control, so blaming or praising you in any moral sense would be like blaming the sands of Mars for being red.

Soft determinists, on the other hand, think determinism and freedom are compatible (hence, they're also called compatiblilists). David Hume, for example, points out that if we didn't predict people's behavior, the very idea of laws would be ridiculous. If we didn't think stop signs would cause people to stop, why have them? If Precrime laws didn't stop murder, how would Anderton have a job?

Soft determinists think our usual notion of free will is unnecessarily bizarre. You don't need free actions to spring from some uncaused cause. This is actually a pretty mysterious idea. What's the difference between an uncaused cause and stuff just randomly happening? We don't say that a computer running a random number generator is free. You don't want your decisions to be random, you want them to be yours. The soft determinist alternative says that a free action has the right kind of cause: it is unconstrained and flows from your character. Anderton's choice to run was caused, but it wasn't caused by someone else, it was caused by Anderton's character (meaning his general tendencies as a person). His character was in turn caused by lots of things. No uncaused cause is needed.

Most people besides philosophers seem to think that we need the traditional idea of free will to secure the basis of morality and human dignity, making determinism a big threat. I disagree. I think soft determinism gives us all the freedom we really need. More people would agree with me if they read Philip K. Dick carefully enough. I'll give some reasons for all this later, but first let's look at another aspect of the Dickian worldview.

Skepticism for Fun and Profit

Philosophical skepticism starts with a simple question: How do you know stuff you think you know? How do you know other people—or androids—have minds? How do you know the world exists outside your mind? How can you tell real memories from fake ones, real people from androids? The idea that you don't know the answers to such questions is called philosophical skepticism. The Holly-worldview says that we can know the answers. But Dick has his doubts.

Blade Runner is an awesome movie. It was groundbreaking in its day and it's still amazing thirty years later. As with *Minority Report*, my complaints are philosophical.

In the US theatrical cut, there's a happy ending in which Deckard drives into the countryside with Rachael. There's little indication that it's possible Deckard could be a replicant. How un-Dickian.

The existence of the Director's Cut (1992) and Final Cut (2007) indicates that director Ridley Scott wasn't happy either. He removed the happy ending and added a weird unicorn dream sequence, which many people—including Scott himself—see as an indication that Deckard is really a replicant. The closest we get to anything explicit is when Rachael asks Deckard if he's taken the Voigt-Kampff test himself, but he's asleep and doesn't hear her.

On the other hand, Dick's novel, *Do Androids Dream of Electric Sheep?*, quite explicitly raises the question of whether Deckard might be an android. In Chapter 9, the android Luba Luft tells Deckard directly, "You must be an android." She presses the issue asking if his memories of taking the Voigt-Kampff test are false or if he could be an android who killed a human and took his place. He explicitly denies all this and refuses to take the test, leaving the question of his humanity unresolved not only for readers but for himself. Nonetheless, most people think the novel supports the idea that Deckard is human, since he's eventually able to feel empathy for living creatures. This is something androids apparently can't do, as when the android Pris remorselessly mutilates a spider.

I'm not so easily convinced. Once Luft brings up the android possibility so explicitly, there's no way to rule it out. This is why philosophical skepticism is such a problem: any evidence you appeal to can be called into question. Sure, Deckard can feel empathy, but how do we know he's not a new model of empathic android? Sure, he thinks he can tell a Nexus-6 from a human with the Voight-Kampff test, but does he really know that this test itself is accurate? Give all the evidence you want. Some smug skeptic will give you reason to doubt that it's evidence at all. This leaves us with an inability to know one way or the other whether Deckard is human or android.

Unlike most people, I think the novel is more properly skeptical than even the Director's or Final Cuts. Scott obviously wants us to believe that Deckard really is a replicant, thus giving an answer to the question of whether Deckard is a replicant. On the other hand, Dick brings up both the android and the human possibilities in such a way that any possible evidence is entirely compatible with both possibilities. The question of whether Deckard is human or android can't really be answered by any evidence, not by origami unicorns and not by empathy boxes. The inability to give any satisfactory answer is what skepticism is all about.

Dick pushes skepticism to dizzying extremes in the novel *Ubik*. *Ubik* is one seriously weird book and my favorite Dick novel. There are psychic agencies competing with each other's Precogs and anti-Precogs. There's "half-life" in which you can talk to the dead who exist in suspended animation. Even the characters' outfits are crazy: for example, "fuchsia pedal-pushers, pink yakfur slippers, a snakeskin sleeveless blouse, and a ribbon in his waist-length dyed white hair."

Philosophical skepticism appears in full force in the second half of the book. The characters are unsure about almost everything: what year it is, why consumer products are regressing into older products, why the money in their wallets is changing and why people are randomly disintegrating. They don't even know if they themselves are alive or dead. They receive a message apparently from their dead boss: "ALL OF YOU ARE DEAD. I AM ALIVE."

Dick wrote a screenplay for *Ubik* and a movie is supposed to be on the way. I hope they treat it with care. I'd hate to see *Ubik*'s wild skepticism domesticated by the Holly-worldview.

What's So Bad about Determinism?

Many people consider a world of determinism and skepticism depressing, but Dick suggests it's not so bad. People are afraid of determinism and skepticism because they hold the Holly-worldview. Such fears are less reasonable once this worldview loosens its grip on us.

Dick is a soft determinist, since he thinks freedom and determinism are compatible. In the story, "The Minority Report," Anderton realizes his action was determined, but he is nonetheless free and responsible, since his action was unconstrained and flowed from his character. This explains why Anderton is untroubled by the fact that he acted exactly as the last Precog predicted. Dick's point is that we shouldn't worry about determinism even if the Precogs did exist. He even suggests that if you like what the Adjustment Team is doing, there's no reason to be upset by their meddling. In making these points, Dick joins a distinguished list of philosophers including the ancient Stoics, Baruch Spinoza, David Hume, John Stuart Mill, and Daniel Dennett. This group has diverse views on other matters, but they all agree with Dick that determinism is nothing much to worry about.

What's So Bad about Skepticism?

Skepticism is usually thought of as a bad thing. Dick's paranoia, for instance, grows out of his skepticism—you never know when they're out to get you. Even if you're not as paranoid as Philip K. Dick, skepticism can make you pretty upset. We like to think of ourselves as people who know things. You're probably reading this book to learn something about Dick and philosophy, that is, to know more stuff. If skepticism were true, there would be a tragic mismatch between how you think of yourself (someone who knows stuff) and how you really are (someone who knows very little). And that would be almost as upsetting as Dickian paranoia!

But maybe skepticism isn't all bad. In Chapter 16 of *Do Androids Dream of Electric Sheep?*, Rachael asks Deckard, "Have you ever made love to an android before?" She implores Deckard, "Don't pause and be philosophical, because from a philosophical standpoint it's dreary. For us both." Maybe this dreariness is a result of skepticism, but I'd say it's a result of the belief that Rachael isn't a real woman. She tells him not to dwell on it. Dick rarely gives voice to the wisdom of his female characters (genius that he was, he was a pretty sexist writer, more likely to describe a woman's body than her thoughts). I think Rachael is on to something.

In modern times skepticism is a problem, but for ancient Greek skeptics such as Sextus Empiricus, skepticism wasn't a problem. It was the solution. In the ancient world, skepticism was a way of life. The key to happiness is to suspend judgment on philosophical matters, to give up wanting to know those things, since that desire causes mental disturbance. Suspending judgment is like saying, "I neither confirm nor deny those allegations." In order to suspend judgment, Sextus Empiricus suggests that you find equally powerful arguments for and against a particular view on philosophical topics such as cause and effect, the existence of God, etc. Ancient skeptics would say we should find both the pro and con arguments on whether Deckard is an android or whether the characters in *Ubik* are alive or dead. Doing so leads to suspension of judgment and ultimately to mental tranquility.

I think there were similar skeptics in ancient India such as Nāgārjuna and Jayarāśi (although my interpretations here are controversial among people who study Indian philosophy). Like their Greek counterparts, Nāgārjuna and Jayarāśi thought the key to happiness was to give up wanting to know the answers to philosophical questions.

But they were a little more radical. Instead of using equally powerful arguments to suspend judgment, they used philosophy to uproot the very impulse to do philosophy. They did this by demonstrating that all answers to a philosophical question lead to unwanted consequences such as internal contradictions. They used this method, for example, to point out the inherent flaws in theories advocated by philosophers in ancient India about the means of knowledge. Nāgārjuna was a Buddhist who saw this as leading to non-attachment to philosophical views (even Buddhist views). Jayarāśi was a non-religious philosopher who thought he could destroy any philosophical basis of religion in order to live a happy, down-to-earth sort of life. They would agree that when it comes to Deckard's humanity or the alive-or-dead? issue of *Ubik*, you should find contradictions in all theories on the matter. By doing so, you'll stop worrying about it.

Greek and Indian skeptics see their philosophical practice as part of a way of life. Most Dick fans are bothered by questions such as whether Anderton has free will or whether Deckard is an android. But ancient skeptics would use their arguments to get us to stop trying to believe anything about these and other philosophical issues. They want to replace all the angst, worry and dogmatic attachment that philosophy can create with a bemused shrug. Greek skeptics describe it like this: imagine the puzzling feeling you would have if asked about whether the number of stars in the sky is odd or even, and then try to cultivate that feeling about every philosophical issue. The way of life described by skeptics in ancient Greece and India is very strange. I couldn't do it all the time. Few people could. Nonetheless, the lesson of ancient skepticism is that sometimes the best way to stop worrying is to stop wanting what you worry about.

A Happy Ending?

Dick didn't think skepticism was a way of life, but he provides some of what we need to deal with our fears. We can take his paranoia and fear as cathartic (even if he didn't). Once we get over it, we just might be better off. Determinism may be true. We may not know some of the things we want to know. But this isn't much to worry about after all.

I should come clean and say that neither Dick's nor my investigations have discovered any definitive answers on these issues. I doubt anybody will solve the problems of skepticism and freedom versus determinism anytime soon, but Dick's philosophical journeys help us face our fears to tackle these questions in an honest and open way. Good philosophy, like good science fiction, rarely gives us the answers we want. It usually leads to more questions. But maybe a little philosophical bounty hunting can retire a few of our unfounded fears.

02
A Quintessence of Dust

ROSS BARHAM

Ask any self-respecting SFer, 'What's a replicant?', and straight off they'll be able to tell you that it's a *genetically engineered android created for slave labor by the Tyrell Corporation*. Now, what's remarkable about this isn't so much that they'll all have seen Ridley Scott's 1982 cult classic, *Blade Runner*—I mean, who hasn't? Rather, it's that such a concise response can tell us so much. Look at it this way: if we divide up the information in terms of the four Aristotelian types of 'cause', we get the following:

1. *Efficient Cause*—replicants are genetically engineered by technicians working for the Tyrell Corporation;

2. *Material Cause*—replicants consist of bio-mechanical matter;

3. *Formal Cause*—replicants are modeled on humans and designed by the Tyrell Corporation; and,

4. *Final Cause*—replicants are intended to closely resemble humans for the purpose of slave labor.

And yet if you were to ask, 'What makes us human?', you'll find that only the first three categories are readily answerable (and then, mostly only thanks to recent advances in science):

1. *Efficient Cause*—individual humans are created as a result of procreation by human parents, whereas human

beings collectively evolved from ancestral species via a combination of random genetic mutations and adaptive natural selection;

2. *Material Cause*—humans consist of biochemical matter (mainly water);

3. *Formal Cause*—humans are formed anatomically according to the blueprint of their inherited DNA.

When it comes to the fourth way of enquiring after what it is to be human—*what is our point or purpose?*—the answer is not at all clear. But it is and remains one of the central questions of philosophy. What's more, it's also the central theme to both the movie *Blade Runner* and the Philip K Dick novel on which it was based, *Do Androids Dream of Electric Sheep?* These two iconic works give us quite distinct visions of a futuristic bounty hunter, Rick Deckard, grappling with his conscience as he sets about 'retiring' a handful of replicants that have gone rogue. But each offers us something important and profound both about what it is to be a human . . . and what it's not.

Show Me What You're Made Of

In philosophy we like to treat everything as systematically as possible. So a common approach when attempting to address the fourth and 'final' cause of what it is to be human is to offer an exhaustive list of all the characteristics that are seemingly unique to us as a species. This is a method we also picked up from Aristotle. He felt that if a thing has a final cause then it should be identifiable by the fact that it is unique to it. So, as far as Aristotle could tell, the purpose of humans is to live a life according to reason, because it seemed to him that only we are capable of reasoning.

Since Aristotle's time, numerous contenders have been suggested as being equally significant to what essentially it is to be human. Some of the more promising prospects include: *rationality*, *agency*, *morality* and *love*. Buckets of ink have been spilt over the centuries both in defense and criticism of these concepts, but the film *Blade Runner* in particular takes a different and rather unique tack (and not only for using celluloid rather than ink); *Blade Runner* dramatically pits man against replicant—one-by-one rejecting these various contenders for what essentially makes us human.

Blade Runner plainly shows rationality as failing to meet the grade for what makes us human. Roy Batty, the leader of the rogue replicants, easily checkmates the designer of his 'brain' (or CPU) at a game of chess, and later even taunts Deckard for acting irrationally under pressure. Nor does agency seem to make the final cut: from the very outset of the film, the replicants have an agenda of their own that wasn't programmed into them by the Tyrell Corporation, simply by virtue of the fact that they have rebelled from their off-world enslavement.

The question of morality is a more subtle matter, for as Captain Bryant—Deckard's supervisor—explains:

> The replicants were designed to copy human beings in every way except their emotions. The designers reckoned that after a few years they might develop their own emotional responses. You know, hate, love, fear, anger, envy.

But while the rogue replicants are certainly emotional and empathetic, these basic building blocks of morality definitely haven't come together to make android saints: Leon's brutal shooting of Deckard's predecessor, Holden, is an obvious case in point. Rather, *Blade Runner* makes what philosophers call a *reductio ad absurdum*, to show that if morality was the defining trait of humans, then Deckard—the film's ostensibly human protagonist—might not then be fully 'human' because of the morally ambiguous nature of 'retirement' as perhaps just a euphemism for murder. Again, Roy jeers at Deckard: "I thought you were supposed to be good. Aren't you *the good man?*"

And finally, although *Blade Runner* is in many ways a typical Hollywood love story with many parallels to Shakespeare's *Romeo and Juliet* (boy meets girl; girl turns out to be an enemy robot; boy sacrifices everything for girl even though their fate is ultimately doomed . . .), the movie nonetheless pulls back from fully endorsing this much celebrated and almost sacrosanct human capacity for love. Firstly, with respect to Deckard and Rachael's relationship, the question is never whether she can love *him*, but whether he can truly love *her*; as Gaff—the police officer seemingly assigned to supervise Deckard's progress—puts it: "It's too bad *she* won't live, but then again, who does?" And secondly, although Roy and Pris are seemingly in love with one another, when Roy sincerely mourns Pris's retirement by kissing her softly on the lips, her tongue is initially seen to protrude from her mouth, but afterwards has retracted; such a gratuitous detail cannot but distract and alienate the audience from fully endorsing love as sufficient for humanity.

Have You Ever Retired a Human by Mistake?

Blade Runner then clearly takes a negative approach to the question of what it is to be human—telling us what it's not, rather than what it is. The point it makes is that many of the individual attributes and characteristics that we take to be essential to our humanity, while perhaps necessary, nevertheless fall short of being sufficient. This is a sentiment shared also by contemporary Australian philosopher, Raimond Gaita. He argues that philosophers have long been misguided in hoping that we might ever successfully settle what is essential to being human using the blackboard-list style of method recommended by Aristotle some two millennia ago. Rather, Gaita claims that no other concept or concepts could ever successfully recapture what is essential to a 'human'. He illustrates this point with an example of a racist woman that he knows personally (here called 'M'):

> M unhesitatingly attributes to the Vietnamese all that makes up the raw material for philosophical accounts of morality. She knows that the Vietnamese are persons according to most accounts of that concept. No doubt crosses her mind that they are self-conscious, rational, with thoughts and feelings, and are able to reflect critically on their desires, thoughts and feelings.[1]

And yet, as Gaita points outs, unfortunately M remains a racist nonetheless. In light of "how little these theories achieve," then,

---

[1] Raimond Gaita. *A Common Humanity* (Text, 1999), pp. 259–260.

Gaita concludes that 'human' ought to be regarded as an irreducible concept, and in doing so, tips his hat to French philosopher Simone Weil, who wrote, while working for the Resistance in Nazi-occupied France:

> There exists an obligation towards every human being for the sole reason that he or she is a *human being*, without any other condition requiring to be fulfilled, and even without any recognition of such an obligation on the part of the individual involved.[2]

That is to say, a human—*any* human—is deserving of our moral respect, no matter how smart, free, moral or loving they happen to be (or not to be). But while *Blade Runner* endorses this view only implicitly, there are a number of instances in *Do Androids Dream of Electric Sheep?* that more explicitly emphasize the significance of the concept 'human being'. For instance, the character of J.R. Isidoro is a 'chickenhead', meaning that the radioactive dust that blankets Earth has deteriorated his intelligence, and his social standing along with it. Isidore, however, is fortunate enough to have retained employment: "his gloomy, gothic boss accepted him as *human* and this he appreciated." His boss is able to see past society's prejudice against chickenheads; he realizes that being human is not a simple matter of intelligence. Further, when Deckard vidphones the office after having retired almost all of the rogue replicants, his secretary informs him:

> "Inspector Bryant has been trying to get a hold of you. I think he's turning your name over to Chief Cutter for a citation. Because you retired those six—"

> "I know what I did," he said.

By cutting her off at this point—before she refers to the retired replicants as 'androids' (or worse, 'skin-jobs')—Deckard implies that, like it or not, he has come to view the moral standing of the androids in a new light. He doesn't go so far as to call them 'human' as such, but it is nevertheless suggested that he no longer considers the line separating us from them as so clearly

---

[2] Simone Weil, *The Need for Roots* (Routledge, 2002), p. 5.

demarcated: "So much for the distinction between authentic living humans and android constructs," Deckard reflects.

But to say that 'human' is an irreducible concept is not merely to say '*a human is a human is a human is a human, and that's all there is to it*', for, while the reductive analytic approach of identifying necessary and sufficient conditions may not have succeeded, the philosophical fields of phenomenology and existentialism have other ways to productively explore what we mean by even an irreducible concept such as 'human' appears to be. Indeed, many of these are in keeping with the methods and strengths of *Do Androids Dream of Electric Sheep?*, for while Dick may not have written typical academic philosophical works, nonetheless the world, characters, situations, and imagined *zeitgeist* his writing evokes all speak volumes about what makes us human.

The Lung-less, All-Penetrating Masterful World-Silence

German philosopher Martin Heidegger, wrote in his essay, "The Question Concerning Technology," that technology is a double-edged sword, with both the power to save, but also the danger of potentially alienating us from the world, each other, and ultimately even our own selves. The imagined reality of *Do Androids Dream of Electric Sheep?* illustrates this to perfection: a handful of humans are virtually the only remaining life form on Earth; their emotional lives are self-selectively controlled by mood organs, and their spiritual needs are artificially assuaged by "black empathy boxes"; an inane TV host named Buster Friendly is the only source of culture; animals are bought from out of catalogues; a blanket of pollution that was initially made in the service of progress has long since made the planet inhospitable; the entire enterprise of human civilization appears to have critically failed. These factors—disturbing enough by themselves—all coalesce to produce in the Earth's few remaining inhabitants, a profound and alienating awareness of the ever-encroaching, yawning, "silence of the world." As Deckard's desolate wife confides in him:

". . . I heard the building, this building; I heard the—" She gestured.

"Empty apartments," Rick said.

Even the chickenhead Isidore has developed his own idiosyncratic take on the Second Law of Thermodynamics to account for it:

> Kipple is useless objects. When nobody's around, kipple reproduces itself. It always gets more and more. No one can win against kipple, except temporarily and maybe in one spot, like in my apartment. But eventually I'll die or go away, and then the kipple will again take over. It's a universal principle operating throughout the universe; the entire universe is moving toward a final state of total, absolute kipple-ization.

Dick's vision of such a future sees us deeply estranged from the world which once was our home. Our constant misuse of technology, both in the past and the present, finds us staring into the face of unthinking, uncaring, but entirely tangible void: "he experienced the silence as visible and, in its own way, alive." Or as Lord Byron similarly personified it in, "The Darkness," his 1816 poetic nightmare about cosmic heat-death: "Darkness had no need of aid from them—She was the Universe." And it is exactly this utterly unsympathetic picture of the universe that Deckard drives out to confront in the lifeless desert after he has finally retired the last of the androids:

> Here there existed no one to record his or anyone else's degradation, and any courage or pride which might manifest itself here at the end would go unmarked: the dead stones, the dust-stricken weeds dry and dying, perceived nothing, recollected nothing, about him or themselves.

Here Deckard strives to come to terms with the fact that the inescapable, collective fate of all things—past, present and future—is to fall into an unending, silent and cold nothingness. A similar attempt was made by (yet another) German philosopher, Friedrich Nietzsche, in the following parable:

> Once upon a time, in some out of the way corner of that universe there was a star upon which clever beasts invented knowing. That was the most arrogant and mendacious minute of "world history", but never-

theless, it was only a minute. After nature had drawn a few breaths, the star cooled and congealed, and the clever beasts had to die.[3]

But whereas Nietzsche wished to shake us from our typically smug view of our place in the universe, in Dick's narrative, the lived experiences of his characters are delved into in order to actually accentuate this existential angst that we are all susceptible to at times.

Do You Think Androids Have Souls?

In the philosophy of mind, there's a distinction made between *strong* and *weak* artificial intelligence. Strong A.I. would capture absolutely all the phenomena of natural intelligence, including inner being—*the ghost in the machine*, as it were. Weak A.I., on the other hand, would only mimic all the outwardly observable functions of natural intelligence to the point of being indistinguishable from it. We see this distinction being played with when Rachael outlines the weak A.I. strategy of The Rosen Association (the novel's version of The Tyrell Corporation) to an incredulous Deckard:

> "And when that model gets caught we modify again and eventually the association has a type that can't be distinguished."
>
> A topic of world-shaking importance, yet dealt with facetiously; an android trait, possibly, he thought. No emotional awareness, no feeling-sense of the actual *meaning* of what she said. Only the hollow, formal, intellectual definitions of the separate terms.

Gaita calls this all-important 'ghost' a "non-speculative conception" of a *soul*, and quotes (yet another) German philosopher, Ludwig Wittgenstein, to convey his point:

> 'I believe he is suffering'—Do I also *believe* that he isn't a robot? It would go against the grain to use the word in both connections. (Or is it like this: I believe that he is suffering, but am certain that he is not a robot? Nonsense!)

---

[3] Friedrich Nietzsche. "On Truth and Lies in a Nonmoral Sense," in *Philosophy and Truth* (Humanity, 1990), p. 79.

> My attitude towards him is an attitude towards a soul. I am not of the *opinion* that he has a soul.[4]

The point is: when I naturally interact with another human— my wife, my son, a friend, foe, or even a stranger—there's just no question as to the existence of their inner being, their 'soul'. There's not even the possibility of genuinely entertaining such a question except in the most abstract, academic, and vacuous sense. But, of course, the invention of increasingly sophisticated android replicants complicates all of this no end . . . regardless of whether or not one counts 'them' as one of 'us'.

The difficulty, as Gaita would explain, is that human-to-human interaction is our primary source of oneness with not only others (obviously) but with both the world and ourselves. But, as Heidegger would add, if advances in android technology not only theoretically called into question human souls, but also did so *experientially*, then the danger would be real and present. Isidore seems to know what they were was getting at:

> Now that her initial fear had diminished, something else had begun to emerge from her. Something more strange. And, he thought, deplorable. A coldness. Like, he thought, a breath from the vacuum between inhabited worlds, in fact from nowhere: it was not what she did or said but what she did *not* do or say.

According to Heidegger, technology can too easily lead us to regard others simply as means rather than ends. The classic example here would be of a factory worker who, were it not for industrialization, may well have been a valued craftsman of the very same product that she now performs only the most menial part in making. Dick's own unique SF vision is, of course, of androids that we can enslave or retire without guilt or bad conscience—at least in theory. But as Deckard begins to better understand as the novel progresses, theory and practice can all too easily come apart:

> "I met another bounty hunter," Deckard said. "One I never saw before. A predatory one who seemed to like to destroy them. For the first

---

[4] Ludwig Wittgenstein, *Philosophical Investigations* (Blackwell, 1999), p. 178.

time, after being with him, I looked at them differently. I mean, in my own way I had been viewing them as he did."

Once you start pulling at a loose thread, the whole tapestry may soon fall apart; and this is precisely what happens to Deckard who becomes painfully aware that in treating others—human or merely humanoid—as means rather than ends, he too has been relegated to a mere means:

"They can use androids. Much better if andys do it. I can't any more; I've had enough. She was a wonderful singer. The planet could have used her. This is insane."

Unfortunately, such a well-intentioned thought is nonetheless inconsistent, for while Deckard may appreciate the beauty that the operatic android, Luba Luft, had given the world, at this point his only proposed solution is to have other androids do the work that he himself thinks is degrading and immoral. For Deckard to find the salvation that Heidegger suggests technology is also capable of, something more than singing is needed.

The Cardinal Mystery of Creation

The ultimate danger of technology, Heidegger argues, is estrangement and alienation from our own selves. Indeed, the existential crises that Deckard undergoes throughout both *Do Androids Dream of Electric Sheep?* and *Blade Runner* perfectly illustrate this threat. But in the end, both works are redemptive, for "where danger is, grows the saving power also."[5] According to Heidegger:

The saving power of technology lets man see and enter into the highest dignity of his essence. This dignity lies in keeping watch over the unconcealment of all coming to presence on this earth.

Huh? Put it this way: when Deckard believes he has discovered a toad in the otherwise soulless desert, he initially asks himself:

---

[5] Martin Heidegger, "The Question Concerning Technology," in *The Question Concerning Technology and Other Essays* (Harper and Row, 1977), p. 28.

What happens when you find—if you find—an animal believed extinct? It happened so seldom. Something about a star of honor from the U.N. and a stipend. A reward running into millions of dollars.

That Deckard momentarily tries to understand the significance of discovering a toad in consequential terms of fame and reward shows that he has become deeply alienated from the authentic relationship that we all potentially share with the world, natural or otherwise; he is momentarily unable to comprehend that unexpectedly happening upon a toad—*any* toad, let alone species presumed extinct—is reward in itself. (If you don't believe me, just imagine you're a child.)

Eventually Deckard comes to his senses as to the significance of his experience, such that, even when he finally realizes that his is an artificial toad, he remains "devoted" to it nonetheless: "The electric things have their lives, too," he notes meditatively. Here, we see the saving power of technology shown most profoundly; technology when regarded aright reveals to us the nature and marvel of the world so as to place us in a deep, appreciative relationship with it.

In *Blade Runner*, also, it is an authentic relationship to Being that is taken to be what essentially ensouls both humans *and* replicants. Such is the import of Roy Batty's famous final soliloquy:

"I've seen things you people wouldn't believe. Attack ships on fire off the shoulder of Orion. I watched C-beams glitter in the darkness at Tannhäuser Gate. All those moments will be lost in time like tears in rain. Time to die."

The poignancy of this speech is given by the manifest wonder Roy feels towards the miracle of existence, the mystery of Being. And in the end it seems that this is essentially what we feel is requisite to being a human being, to having a soul: the existential appreciation of all that is. And it is with this sentiment that Dick brings *Do Androids Dream of Electric Sheep?* to a homely end: "And, feeling better, she fixed herself at last a cup of black, hot coffee."

03
Dick Doesn't Do Heroes

Dennis M. Weiss and Justin Nicholas

In the fall of 1977 Philip K. Dick sat down for an extensive interview with Uwe Anton and Werner Fuchs. Dick was the guest of honor at a large science-fiction convention in Metz, France, and was one of many scifi luminaries in attendance, including John Brunner, Robert Sheckley, and Harlan Ellison. When, though, in the course of his reflections on writing, Dick singled out an author it wasn't one of his science-fiction colleagues, but William Faulkner. Dick was drawn to Faulkner's Nobel Prize speech in which Faulkner noted that he refused to accept the end of man:

> I believe that man will not merely endure: he will prevail. He is immortal, not because he alone among creatures has an inexhaustible voice, but because he has a soul, a spirit capable of compassion and sacrifice and endurance.

Dick mentioned Faulkner's comments in the midst of a discussion of the role of the hero in science fiction. Dick sharply contrasted the typical science-fiction heroes—he cites Flash Gordon and Buck Rogers—and the protagonists of his own stories and novels, which Dick suggested are neither heroes nor anti-heroes. Flash Gordon and Buck Rogers don't really represent human heroism, Dick argued. Where these prototypical science-fiction heroes are "really marvelous" and "give all the answers," Dick's more human characters are your average Joes who find themselves in inexplicable situations where they are overwhelmed by the inscrutable universe. For Dick, human heroism shines a spotlight on our weaknesses and limitations and the manner in which we sometimes rise above our greedy, incompetent, petty selves and in the midst of all hopelessness endure and prevail and sometimes even do the right thing. Dick's main character tends to be, as he notes in the interview, a "bumbling, coarse, garrulous, low-class person." In the final analysis, Dick said, people must be people: "In the midst of the rubble, there will be the sound of a man's voice planning, arguing, and proposing solutions. I think Faulkner caught the essence of what is really great about human beings, and so I don't write about heroes."

"I don't write about heroes." If one only knows Dick's work through his cinematic representations, films such as *Blade Runner*, *Total Recall*, and *Minority Report*, his thoughts on human heroism seem inexplicable and contradictory. Dick's characters tend to be ordinary people who occasionally do extraordinary things. But Hollywood's big screen doesn't take kindly to ordinary people. Hollywood prefers its leads big, extraordinary, and good looking. Hollywood heroes endure, but they endure precisely because they are bigger than life. Dick's Hollywood heroes are those bigger-than-life figures he refused to sanction in his own writing.

As Dick's fiction makes the leap to the big screen, Hollywood finds it necessary to make heroes out of Dick's characters, transforming them from everyday man to action-figure status, and in the process undermining Dick's ruminations on the trials and tribulations of human beings living in a technological culture. But for those of us who're interested in scratching the surface and finding out what lies underneath, Hollywood's refusal to admit Dick's ordinary characters can help us see all the more clearly what he was trying to do.

You've Been Adjusted

Dick wrote about authenticity, not about heroes.

Dick's protagonists are a rogue's gallery of losers, misfits and lowly office clerks placed without reason or warning in extraordinary circumstances. It is significant then, that when Dick's work is taken from page to screen, these protagonists change dramatically. The "bald and fat and old" administrator of "The Minority Report" becomes man-of-action Tom Cruise; the "miserable little salaried employee" of "We Can Remember It for You Wholesale" becomes the far-from-little Arnold Schwarzenegger; and Ed, the minor real estate clerk of "Adjustment Team" becomes Matt Damon running for Congress. While such transformations are radical, they are minor in comparison to the real changes filmmakers enact on Dick's characters.

Consider *The Adjustment Bureau*, starring Matt Damon; the story of two star-crossed lovers whose union is prevented by the Kafkaesque "adjustment group" that controls reality and people's fate. These men (and they are exclusively men) modify the destinies of certain key people in an effort to avert disasters such as the Holocaust, which they attribute to human failures. One of these people is David Norris (Matt Damon) who, without his knowledge, has been groomed by this group his entire life for the presidency and, according to "the plan," must rise to power. This "plan" is written by the "Chairman"— a thinly veiled allusion to God. Damon learns all this, and yet he still decides to fight the Adjustment Bureau, and thus God himself, to be with his true love.

Here we have all the ingredients of a great tragic love story, including tortured characters and unstoppable malevolent forces bent on keeping them apart. And yet the story has a happy ending, thanks mostly to our larger-than-life leading man Mr. Damon, who manages to wreak havoc on the whole system while infiltrating Bureau headquarters in an attempt to lodge a complaint with the Chairman. Duly impressed with this brash display of valor, the Chairman allows the love-struck couple to stay together, a rather curious response given that such impetuousness is precisely what the Bureau blames for many of humankind's greatest tragedies.

Dick's character, Ed Fletcher, bears no resemblance to David Norris. Like most of Dick's characters, Ed is a man of exceedingly minor importance, a salaryman for a real estate firm. He is also, in typical Dick style, a married man whose wife is a rather unhelpful nag. Where David Norris is at the center of attention of the Adjustment Bureau, Ed comes to their attention only after accidentally arriving late to work one morning. The victim of a clerical error, Ed simply fails to be where he is supposed to be according to plan. When captured by the Adjustment Bureau, he is taken immediately to meet the Old Man in charge who promptly explains that the adjustment was made to help bring an end to the Cold War and thus further human peace and prosperity. Ed accepts this as a laudable goal, but he grovels before the Old Man in an effort to escape his fate. "Look," he croaked. "I'll do anything. Anything at all. Only don't de-energize me." The Old Man finally agrees to let Ed go without adjustment but not because he is deeply impressed by his determination, but rather because he's a minor character in a grander plan whose actions can be contained and neutralized.

We Can Endorse That for You Wholesale

Hollywood directors love technology, as do audiences, but Dick was far from an unquestioning worshiper of the technology he wrote about so prolifically. In his essay "The Android and the Human," Dick states that "even the most base schemes of human beings are preferable to the most exalted tropisms of machines," an indication that his relationship to technology was more complex than the unwavering faith accorded to it by the films based on his work.

This attitude of unwavering faith can be easily seen in *Total Recall*, Paul Verhoven's take on Dick's "We Can Remember It for You Wholesale." In the movie we find our protagonist Arnold Schwarzenegger take charge of his surroundings and embark on an action hero's journey to save the planet Mars. Schwarzenegger's character, Douglas Quaid, like his short story counterpart, attempts to infuse his listless existence with some excitement by having the memory of a trip to Mars as a secret agent implanted in his brain, then discovering that he has in fact already been to Mars as a secret agent. This is where the overlap between the movie and the story ends. In the movie, Quaid attempts to activate a huge alien machine that will transform Mars from a barren wasteland into a pristine paradise, but he has no idea how the machine works, or whether it will transform the planet into a paradise or cause it to explode. The movie's antagonist reminds him of this fact in the final scene, as he begs Quaid to reconsider. But with unwavering faith Quaid turns on the device and the planet is transformed from a place of oppression and despair to a land of opportunity, his faith rewarded through the power of benevolent alien technology.

Dick's character, named Quail, exemplifies a wholly different view of the nature of technology. Quail finds that the spy agency he worked for is trying to kill him because of the resurgence of his memories, and when he tries to escape from their grasp he confronts a key problem: a security device planted in his brain that can track him anywhere and read his every thought. Quail states that, "The thing lived inside him, within his own brain. Feeding, listening, feeding." This device, which in the movie is only a tracking device, transmits his every thought to the police immediately. At one point an officer informs Quail that "anything you think may be held against you." Quail recognizes that his resistance is futile. He turns himself in before any high speed chases or gun battles ensue, hoping that the establishment can successfully erase his memory once again, without killing him.

While in the movie, technology is cast as the savior of the oppressed, something we can activate confident in its benevolence, in the story, it is the technology itself that oppresses. Such a difference is not mere coincidence. It hints at the philosophical commitments that specific filmmakers, and perhaps filmmaking itself, have inscribed upon Dick in an attempt to place him lucratively on the screen.

Nagging Spouses and Robotic Home-Wreckers

This Hollywoodization effect extends even to the relationships portrayed in Dick's short stories and novels. Dick had different ideas about love, marriage, and romantic relationships that challenge the familiar Hollywood romantic storyline in which star-crossed lovers overcome obstacles to reunite and ride off into the sunset of eternal bliss. Consider, for instance, the contrast between Dick's novel *Do Androids Dream of Electric Sheep?* and its film adaptation *Blade Runner*. In the movie, we find our world-weary hero Rick Deckard, played by Harrison Ford, alone and unattached, a bachelor living in a small apartment lining the urban landscape. Deckard is drawn to the replicant Rachael, and a classic romantic storyline ensues that ends with the two confessing their love for one another and running away together.

Dick's Deckard, however, starts the narrative by waking up next to his wife, Iran, who is neither a diminutive woman who desires to be rescued, nor a strong female character, but rather an emotionally unstable harpy who badgers Deckard for most of the story. Our novel's Rachael Rosen is introduced as a love interest, but rather than being the shy, receptive character of the movie, this Rachael is a sociopath who seduces Deckard in an attempt to make it impossible for him to kill androids like her. In one case we see a knight in shining armor rescuing a woman in distress, while in the other we see a nebbish police grunt being manipulated by a psychopathic machine. The differences here are easy to spot. But what are significantly harder to spot, are the philosophical implications of this wholesale rewriting of Dick that occurs in Hollywood film.

Scott versus Linklater

There are any number of interesting levels on which to observe the contrast between *Blade Runner* and *A Scanner Darkly*, beginning with the directors. Ridley Scott is the muscular director of sweeping stories of heroic characters in trying circumstances: *Thelma and Louise*, *G.I. Jane*, *Gladiator*, *Black Hawk Down*, *American Gangster*. Richard Linklater's typical film is smaller in nature, quieter, often lacking a central protagonist, much less a heroic character: *Slacker*, *Dazed and Confused*, *Before Sunrise*, *Waking Life*. Visually, the "look" of *Blade Runner* and *A Scanner Darkly* could not be more different. Scott's film is all postmodern urban noir, the screen packed with the overwhelming sights and sounds of future technology run amok, assaulting the viewer's senses. Linklater, on the other hand, deliberately inserts a break between the viewer and the screen, rotoscoping over the well-known visages of his famous stars. *A Scanner Darkly* is more suburban sunny earth tones, more cartoonish, more everyday.

Beyond these surface differences, Scott and Linklater take very divergent approaches to their source material. Dick is wildly transformed by Scott. *Blade Runner* is only loosely based on Dick's novel, as has been widely remarked upon, most perceptively by the film critic David Edelstein, who notes:

> There is no getting around the fact that the movie misses almost entirely the psychological complexity of its source, one of [Dick's] most tantalizing explorations of the human capacity for empathy. The bleary gumshoe hero of the film has little connection to the book's unhappily married drudge, who mechanically executes 'replicants' as a means to afford animals (now rare and expensive) for display.

In contrast, *A Scanner Darkly* remains authentic to the novel with Linklater foregrounding the relationship of the movie to its author. Early in the movie, Dick's face appears as part of the scramble suit and the film closes with the "Author's Note" from the novel, drawing clear connections to biographical details of Dick's life. Linklater involved Dick's daughters early on, who were often present on the set, and who remarked upon the authenticity of some of those sets, especially the suburban Orange County home where much of the action of the movie takes place.

Deckard versus Arctor

These two films also offer an interesting and contrasting take on Dick's theme of the hero. Harrison Ford was in the midst of his successful run as Han Solo in the *Star Wars* films while filming *Blade Runner*. While Ford's Deckard is more world-weary and has less swagger than Han Solo, he finally proves the heroic character, surmounting considerable challenges and ultimately saving the damsel in distress.

A Scanner Darkly takes a different tack, subverting the heroic character of the typical Hollywoodized Dick film by taking an actor best recognized at the time for his role as Neo, savior of the human race, and making him into Bob Arctor, described in the film as the ultimate everyman, a fractured and flawed character addicted to Substance D and subjected to spying on himself. Here too, *A Scanner Darkly* aligns itself with its text, identifying not with heroic characters but with the freaks and losers that populated both Dick's life and his novels and which he often wrote approvingly about. The cast reads like a who's who of Hollywood's stoners and losers: Winona Ryder, Woody Harrelson, Robert Downey Jr.

There are parallels between Rick Deckard and Bob Arctor. Both are lawmen tasked with protecting society from external threats (replicants/Substance D) produced by shadowy organizations (Tyrell Corporation/New Path). Both have a troubled relationship to their professions, are matched with a nemesis whose own humanity is in doubt (Roy Batty/James Barris), and pursue a female whose self-identity is in question (Rachael/Donna). These surface parallels, though, belie more significant differences.

While the action in the movies shifts from the urban realm of Los Angeles in *Blade Runner* to the suburban realm of Anaheim and Orange County in *A Scanner Darkly*, both characters end up breaking through to a more "natural" realm. In the theatrical release of *Blade Runner*, however, that natural realm is portrayed as an Edenic outside to the nightmarish cityscape, while Bob Arctor ends up in a decidedly more ambiguous place, a corn field owned by New Path which serves as a cover for growing the little blue flowers that go into the manufacture of Substance D. In *Blade Runner*, nature is an escape and an alternative to the nightmarish uncertainty caused by technological development, while in *A Scanner Darkly*, even nature has been subverted into a means to enslave and dehumanize people.

Where Deckard seeks an escape from his dark world, Bob Arctor is drawn to darkness:

> I hated my life, my house, my family, my backyard, my power mower. Nothing would ever change. It had to end, and it did. Now in the dark world where I dwell ugly things and surprising things and sometimes little wondrous things spill out at me constantly and I can count on nothing.

And while Deckard successfully navigates a relationship with the replicant Rachael, running off together into their uncertain future, Bob is continuously frustrated in his efforts to "get into Donna's pants" and she ultimately betrays and uses him.

We witness an even more significant difference between Deckard and Arctor as we observe the paths each character takes in their respective films. *Blade Runner* recounts the education of Deckard and his achievement of humanity through the redemptive figure of Rachael, while *A Scanner Darkly* tells the story of Arctor's progressive dehumanization, the breakdown of his personality amidst the rampant use of drugs and technology. And Donna/Audrey doesn't turn out to offer any redemption. Indeed, she's the agent behind his destruction, sacrificing his humanity, transforming him into something of an automaton, in order to bring down New Path.

While Deckard becomes more human, Arctor becomes more mechanical, illustrating Dick's own observations in "The Android and the Human,"—written while writing *A Scanner Darkly*—where he defines becoming an android as "allowing oneself to become a means, or to be pounded down, manipulated, made into a means without one's knowledge or consent." Bob/Fred, suffering from what Barris suggests is "soul sickness," becomes an android. While *Blade Runner* imagines that androids could become human, *A Scanner Darkly* shows how humans become androids.

From Hover Cars to Substance D

These two films depict technological artifacts differently as well. *Blade Runner*, like most other films based on Dick works, includes the usual sci-fi techno-tropes: hover cars, replicants, genetic- and bio-engineering, off-world colonies. Furthermore, *Blade Runner* foregrounds technology on the screen, its representation of technology a gaudy visual display of excess. *A Scanner Darkly* avoids many of these tropes and focuses on more mundane technologies: Substance D (a pharmaceutical technology), monitoring technologies, cell phones. When *A Scanner Darkly* does foreground technology, what we see are Barris's harebrained Rube Goldberg contraptions that never work.

Beyond these surface differences, the two films assess technology differently as well. Deckard's Voight-Kampff machine, an analogue for the cameras of *A Scanner Darkly* and perhaps a stand-in for the director's eye, discloses the truth and reveals the true nature of the replicants. Significantly, though, both Rachael and Roy Batty ultimately exceed this truth and achieve a level of humanity in their relationship to Deckard. Truth and humanity are not at odds with technology. *A Scanner Darkly* tells a decidedly less optimistic picture. The cameras of *A Scanner Darkly* don't reveal the truth and don't lead to an affirmation of Bob's humanity. Rather, they further obscure Arctor's tenuous hold on reality and finally play a role in the dissolution of his personality, illustrating Dick's fear of technology leading to the mechanization of humanity.

A Scanner Darkly's technology is one with our own, and mirrors our increasing familiarity with filming, documenting, and surveilling ourselves in the age of YouTube, Twitter, and Facebook. While *Blade Runner* holds out some hope that Deckard and Rachael can find some space in the techno-culture to live out their human-replicant fantasy, *A Scanner Darkly* leaves us with a hollowed-out Bob/Fred/Bruce who through pharmaceuticals and media technologies has been left bereft of his humanity, transformed into an android in Dick's terms, a dried husk perfectly at home in the decoy corn field in which we find him at the close of the movie.

Through a Screen, Darkly

Where so many of the films based on Dick's work seemingly delight in visually representing the power and awe of technology and the role of the masculine hero who triumphs over it, all the while redeeming himself and winning over the girl, *A Scanner Darkly* presents a darker, more critical perspective on our relationship to technology and what it ultimately may be doing to our lives and relationships. In a way, this makes sense, for *A Scanner Darkly* is very consciously about the media itself, a philosophical film that uses the screen to comment on the media, especially our love affair of scanning and being scanned as we record our every thought and action on our Facebook pages, Twitter accounts, and YouTube feeds.

Linklater's film visually represents the dangers of our media technology in the dissolution of Bob/Fred at the hands of both the police state and the corporation (New Path). Through its use of rotoscoping, it simultaneously calls attention to its own artifice as a film, distancing the viewer from the screen and creating a critical space in which to engage with some of Dick's complex themes regarding our techno-cultural context and the androidization of humanity. It is entertainment with an edge and it's this edge that is so often blunted in the more typical Hollywood take on Dick.

Hollywood has an investment in the media and in media technology. We can understand it not wanting to call attention to the technology that entertains us. It just wants to entertain us. And we just want to be entertained. After all, we, the movie-going public, have a responsibility here too. As we struggle with the shifting realities of our techno-cultural condition, we too seek escape from its harsher truths, embracing sci-fi block-busters that promise us a rosy technological future in which we human beings triumph while maintaining our heroic stature, athletic figure, and a full head of hair.

Dick wrote about nobodies, minor clerks, and simple bureaucrats, because that is where he saw the kind of heroism that actually exists. Dick's hero is not a gun-toting vigilante but the ordinary Joe, flawed but quietly refusing to bow to the pressures of a society and a technology that attempt to flatten and control his existence. As Dick observed in "How to Build a Universe that Doesn't Fall Apart Two Days Later,"

> This, to me, is the ultimately heroic trait of ordinary people; they say no to the tyrant and they calmly take the consequences of this resistance. I see their authenticity In an odd way: not in their willingness to perform great heroic deeds but in their quiet refusals. In essence, they cannot be compelled to be what they are not.

Dick's Bob Arctor and Rick Deckard end up in a similar place, beaten down by a dehumanizing system. As Deckard notes toward the end of *Do Androids Dream of Electric Sheep?*, "But what I've done, he thought; that's become alien to me. In fact everything about me has become unnatural; I've become an unnatural self." Yet suffering their "soul sickness," having been androidized, they each do endure. That's where their, and ultimately our, heroism lies.

04
Ewe, Robot

Alf Seegert

At the beginning of the movie *Blade Runner*, the camera zooms inside the vast arcology of the Tyrell Corporation, where—amid a swirl of cigarette smoke propelled by ceiling fans—Detective Holden is administering the Voight-Kampff (V-K) test to job applicant Leon Kowalski. Holden wants to find out if Leon is truly human, or a dreaded humanoid replicant instead—an android. He uses the test to register Leon's eye dilations in response to questions about animals in distress. In this exchange, Leon Kowalski knows what a turtle (or tortoise) is, but—at least as far as we can tell—he doesn't feel what it would be like to be one. And that's the problem.

> **HOLDEN:** The tortoise lays on its back, its belly baking in the hot sun beating its legs trying to turn itself over but it can't, not without your help, but you're not helping.
>
> **LEON:** What do you mean I'm not helping?
>
> **HOLDEN:** I mean, you're not helping. Why is that, Leon?

Leon's responses to these questions, as registered by involuntary changes in his pupils, become the litmus test for what will qualify him as human—or (in his case) not. Specifically, the test records the subject's expression of empathy, the ability to experience the sufferings of another as if they are one's own. The capacity for empathy, however, turns out to be a deliciously problematic basis for demonstrating human uniqueness. Empathy is rooted primarily in a subject's ability to identify

imaginatively with another being. Put another way, to demonstrate his humanity via empathy, Leon must be able to simulate the experience of someone or something else in his own
consciousness by virtually "stepping into its shoes," and then
responding compassionately. Ironically enough, the very criterion required for human beings to demonstrate that they are
not android simulations is their very ability to simulate in the
first place! However, if you are a simulation yourself, like Leon,
you can't empathetically simulate the experiences of others as
well as humans can.

The V-K test is doubly ironic in that android replicants in
Blade Runner do in fact show at least some significant empathy for each other (witness Roy's mourning for Pris after
Deckard shoots her), whereas the grimly noir-ish setting of the
film reveals that human empathy—even for fellow human
beings—is in very short supply. And empathy proves altogether
absent when it comes to a Blade Runner's feelings for the replicants he brutally "retires" to keep Earth safely android-free:
the audience winces as Deckard shoots Zhora in the back, but
Deckard doesn't. If one's humanity inheres in one's capacity for
displaying empathy, then in crucial ways the android replicants of Blade Runner might just be (to use the Tyrell
Corporation's motto) "more human than human."

The justification for the V-K test is largely to relieve the
anxiety human beings feel in never being quite sure if they
are interacting with another human, or with a soulless and
supposedly empathy-free android. If an android can successfully pass itself off as a human, then on what moral basis are
humans entitled to enslave androids as they do? The capacity to make clear human-android distinctions through the V-
K test thus becomes a crucial way for humans to maintain
existing power hierarchies. As a result, android verisimili-
tude and human-made testing equipment co-evolve in a sort
of "arms race," with each seeking to outwit the other. But the
pervasive Dickian anxieties evidenced in *Blade Runner* (and
in Dick's novel on which it was based, *Do Androids Dream of
Electric Sheep?*) extend well beyond any concerns that
androids might pass for human beings. Although this external threat drives much of the plot in both stories, a deeper
internal anxiety lurks: namely, that I might not be human
myself.

How Animals Make Us Human

This anxiety over identity expresses itself in both literal and figurative possibilities: in both *Blade Runner* and *Do Androids Dream of Electric Sheep?*, not only do machines become more like humans, but humans become more like machines. Philip K. Dick expressly raises this concern in his 1972 essay "The Android and the Human": "As the external world becomes more animate, we may find that we—the so-called humans—are becoming, and may to a great extent always have been, inanimate." For Dick, authentic selfhood—if one dares use the term "authentic" in a Dickian context—seems to inhere in our felt relations with others. As Dick himself puts it in "Man, Android, and Machine," "A human being without the proper empathy or feeling is the same as an android built so as to lack it, either by design or mistake."

Dick's concern over the properly human expression of empathy pervades *Do Androids Dream of Electric Sheep?* In the post-apocalyptic wasteland of the novel, Rick Deckard is a bounty hunter whose job is to "retire" renegade androids. However, *Do Androids Dream of Electric Sheep?* is as concerned with human relationships to animals as it is with the threat of android infiltration, for animals have gone nearly extinct after World War III and most people have migrated to the offworld colonies to escape lingering radioactivity and urban decay.

Because there are scarcely any creatures left on the Earth other than humans, people are denied communion with other selves not of their own making, namely, "real" animals. Lacking more-than-human relationships, these remnant humans dread the possibility of devolving into something less-than-human themselves. This anxiety over one's own authentic humanity drives Deckard and others in the novel to acquire "real" animals at any cost in order to actively demonstrate their empathy—even when it means brutally "retiring" trespassing androids to make the required payments.

In the movie *Blade Runner*, you would likewise expect that showing empathy for others (animals especially) would be the royal road to conclusively demonstrating your humanity. Strangely enough, it isn't. Whereas in *Do Androids Dream of Electric Sheep?* human identity is secured through empathetic relationships with non-human "animal others," in *Blade*

Runner a person's humanity is validated primarily through the displaying of photographs. This "self-validation via snapshot" authenticates human identity through images, not relationships. When the replicant Rachael wants to prove she is not a replicant, she hands a photo to Deckard and says, "Look, it's me with my mother." In line with Jean Baudrillard's theory of the "precession of simulacra," Rachael does not say, "This is a photo of me with my mother." The photo itself (in her estimation) becomes an authentic, self-grounding artifact which need not refer to any external referent: the simulation is the reality. Deckard, in turn, displays a profusion of old sepia-tone photographs on his piano, an orgy of evidence for a supposed abundance of human relations. But these photos are ancient, and consequently, suspicious. He evidences no current relations at all, a possible hint that he might be an android himself attempting to overcompensate for such lack.

In "On Photography," critic Susan Sontag points out how such deployment of photos can act as surrogate families, virtual substitutes for real relations that authenticate relationships by documenting the loved one's absence. To authenticate their humanity, the characters in *Blade Runner* thus employ simulations that require no tethering to actual experience or to the lives of others, whereas those in *Do Androids Dream of Electric Sheep?* depend intimately on relations with other living creatures. As a result, the film's criterion for humanness appears to demand no escape from the cell of the self, whereas the novel demands an embrace of otherness and (to use philosopher David Abram's phrase) care-based relations with a "more-than-human world."

For Philip K. Dick, however, what exactly counts as "more than human" (and "more human than human") can get a little bit tricky . . .

Narcissism in a "More Human than Human" World

In *Do Androids Dream of Electric Sheep?*, Deckard wants to use his bounty money to buy a real sheep to replace the electric one that chomps "in simulated contentment" in its fallout-ridden pastoral enclosure atop his apartment building. Though his ersatz black-faced Suffolk ewe from a distance bears the marks of the real—enough to fool the neighbors—Deckard wants more than just the social status that comes from owning a real animal. He wants to demonstrate his capacity for empathy by relating with a genuine "Other." Moreover, he wants to be sure that his own existence registers on the consciousness of another genuine subjectivity.

In Deckard's view—at least early in the book—androids and synthetic sheep only simulate awareness, and as a result fail to be "Others" in a moral sense, because they have no selves of their own. Deckard's interaction with a sentient non-human animal (like a real sheep) is required in order to affirm his own humanity: he must be convinced that he exists for it. (Deckard's fellow bounty hunter Phil Resch, seemingly an android himself because of his predatory cold-bloodedness towards his android prey, defends his humanity purely on the basis of his dedication to a pet squirrel named "Buffy"!) To invoke Gertrude Stein by way of Isaac Asimov, in Deckard's insentient electric sheep "there's no there there": his ewe-robot will be forever incapable of self-awareness, denied the capacity to say (or even think) "I, Robot."

In these ways, *Do Androids Dream of Electric Sheep?* raises a fascinating problem that twentieth-century media theorist Marshall McLuhan dubbed "Narcissus as Narcosis." In his book *Understanding Media*, McLuhan argues that the Narcissus myth is misread when construed as that of a boy falling in love with himself. Although the myth tells how Narcissus becomes captivated by his own beautiful reflection in a pool—becoming insensitive to all else—McLuhan argues that Narcissus doesn't realize that the reflection he so adores is really an image of himself at all. In just this way, McLuhan continues, technological extensions create the illusion of otherness when they actually only provide a hall of mirrors for infinitely reflecting humanity back to itself.

Digital devices, androids, and animal surrogates like Deckard's synthetic sheep re-spin human beings into ever-new and tantalizing guises, but ultimately offer nothing back to us except more of us. As a result, Narcissus produces narcosis, or numbness, by dulling sensations that would otherwise reveal that we're really only in contact with—and only seem to desire—our own productions and our own reflections, not contact with genuine "others."

Philip K. Dick satirizes the numbing and narcotic effect of technology in *Do Androids Dream of Electric Sheep?*, where both Deckard and his wife Iran experience emotional states not by responding to other beings, or even to each other, but instead by dialing a mood on demand using their Penfield Mood Organ. Similarly, in a world practically devoid of non-human others, empathy itself must be technologically mediated via another method of self-programming. By using their Empathy Box, a device that allows Deckard and his wife to fuse emotional states with other users and vicariously experience the pains of the sainted Wilbur Mercer, they can "perform" their humanness in ways androids in the novel cannot. But Mercerism, the religion dedicated to this use of virtual empathy, ultimately proves to be as synthetic as the grass-chewing electric sheep on Deckard's roof. Still, for most people, these "virtual others" prove to be good enough because they generate the effects of relationship even if they lack its substance.

Empathy in a "More Human than Human" World

Imagining what it is like to be someone other than oneself is at the core of our humanity. It is the essence of compassion, and it is the beginning of morality.

— IAN MCEWAN

Deckard persists in his determination to bathe in the aura of an actual animal, rather than settle for a simulated one—and the hefty price-tag involved requires that he become less human himself in the process. By selectively applying his own capacity for empathy, Deckard kills certain non-humans (androids) to earn the money to obtain and care for other non-human beings (animals), thereby ultimately "validating" his own actual human being.

He thought, too, about his need for a real animal; within him an actual hatred once more manifested itself toward his electric sheep, which he had to tend, had to care about, as if it lived. The tyranny of an object, he thought. It doesn't know I exist. Like the androids, it had no ability to appreciate the existence of another.

As with all good science fiction, Dick's novel cannily critiques the author's own present day. *Do Androids Dream of Electric Sheep?* was published in 1968, an era which offered plenty of drugs, television, and countless other potentially alienating surrogates in place of concrete relationships. Today we might add the Internet and a bevy of portable digital devices.

For McLuhan, this condition of technologically mediated narcissism is so addictively numbing that, whether we like it or not, it effectively truncates our nerve endings of all input other than that provided by the media interface itself. (Witness those drivers too distracted by texting or talking on the cell phone to be able to steer or brake properly.) As McLuhan puts it, Narcissus was insensate to the cries of even the beautiful nymph Echo because "He was numb. He had adapted to his extension of himself and had become a closed system" (p. 63). Likewise, our devices become self-enclosing worlds that shut out those relationships not themselves mediated by such devices.

For Deckard and other humans who chafe at the limits of technological self-enclosure, animals represent a guaranteed passage into authentic "otherness," returning blood and feeling to deadened nerve endings and shattering the narcissistic mirror through the power of a certifiably "real presence." Deckard thus longingly thumbs his dog-eared Sidney's pricing guide for animals (the novel's parodic equivalent to a Kelley Blue Book for cars, if not to holy writ) calculating just how many androids he has to "retire" before he can at last acquire a real sheep (or even better, an ostrich, or a goat).

Dick further ramps up the anxiety level by making it impossible for his characters to be sure if they are ever actually interacting with an "authentic" non-human other at all. Just as the latest android models threaten the reliability of the V-K test, even close inspection of one's ostensibly "real" sheep, ostrich, or goat might fail to disclose its status as a supremely clever simulation.

In this way Dick reconfigures a classic philosophical conundrum, the so-called "problem of other minds." Because we can never experience the subjective states of other beings—instead only having access to their externally manifested appearances and behaviors—we can never be sure that these "others" have actual minds of their own. In philosophical formulations of the problem, the concern is solipsism—is it possible that I am the only mind in the universe and all these seeming "others" are only projections of my own mind? In *Do Androids Dream of Electric Sheep?*, Dick extends this anxiety to the world at large. Deckard's encounters with nature and non-human animals are always at risk of being so haunted by human-created simulations that no guaranteed relationship with an authentic non-human "other" remains.

Deckard nonetheless wields the hope of escaping outside the circle of species-solipsism by encountering an "other" so certifiably other that it cannot possibly have been manufactured. Near the end of the book Deckard inexplicably finds a lone toad (a real toad!) in the California desert—a creature marked with an "E" for extinct in his Sidney's catalog. His eyes open wide with astonishment and glee. Unlike Holden's interview scenario involving the desert tortoise in *Blade Runner*, he immediately demonstrates his empathy with concerned action. In his excitement he gently picks up the toad and brings it home in a cardboard box—a "box" that Deckard hopes will signify authentic care in ways that his use of the Mercerists' Empathy Box cannot.

> So this is what Mercer sees, he thought as he painstakingly tied the cardboard box shut—tied it again and again. Life which we can no longer distinguish; life carefully buried up to its forehead in the carcass of a dead world. In every cinder of the universe Mercer probably perceives inconspicuous life. Now I know, he thought. And once having seen through Mercer's eyes, I probably will never stop.

But when he shows the toad to his wife Iran, she discovers something disturbing: "still holding it upside down, she poked at its abdomen and then, with her nail, located the tiny control panel. She flipped the panel open." The toad is artificial. In the nuclear wasteland of *Do Androids Dream of Electric Sheep?*, it seems that the desert of the real offers safe habitat only for virtual creatures.

The Shock of Being Alive

> The shock of encountering something which is other is the shock of being alive: isn't it amazing that there is that, and not just me?
>
> — NEIL EVERNDEN, *The Social Creation of Nature*

The narcotic effects of technology in *Do Androids Dream of Electric Sheep?* incarnate precisely the concerns Marshall McLuhan expressed over techno-narcissism. By encountering nothing but ourselves and our own creations, we become immune to the call of the more-than-human world. Instead, to invoke Tyrell's motto again, we find ourselves beholden to a synthetic world which vies to become "more-human-than-human!" The consequences of such narcissism are particularly susceptible to a critique by twentieth-century German philosopher Martin Heidegger, who warns of the dangers in how we "enframe" Being in our encounters with it.

Specifically, our uses of technology constrain Being, in all its possible ways of unfolding, to one monolithic image, namely, a technological "world picture." This "picture" is created by human beings and exclusively for human beings—and we mistake this human construction of reality for reality itself. For example, instead of being understood as having its own otherness, agency, and purpose, the Earth becomes nothing more than use value, a "standing reserve" awaiting its quarrying by humans. We shape the infinite facets of Being into useful, recognizable forms according to the way technology appropriates them: a forest becomes no more than "board feet," a mountain "mineral resources," animals "food production units."

As a result, Heidegger would contend, we confuse Being with the image we stamp onto it, and like Narcissus, we fall in love with this image, not realizing that we put it there ourselves. The consequences desecrate the earth and dehumanize ourselves. As media scholar Kevin DeLuca tweets (making ironic use of the medium), "The orientations of cell phones/new media truncate our reciprocal relation with the Earth, stunting our senses and incarcerating ourselves in a technosoliloquy."

In case the threat of lost contact with the other doesn't seem like such a big deal, we might need to seriously consider a major concern Dick's novel raises, namely that our very human identity is in fact constructed through such relations. Likewise, Deep Ecologists and thinkers like David Abram insist that such relationships with the "more-than-human world" are not "add-ons" but are instead utterly basic to our humanity:

> Humans are tuned for relationship. The eyes, the skin, the tongue, ears, and nostrils—all are gates where our body receives the

nourishment of otherness. We are human only in contact, in conviviality, with what is not human. Direct sensuous reality, in all its more-than-human mystery, remains the solid touchstone for an experiential world now inundated with electronically-generated vistas and engineered pleasures; only in regular contact with the tangible ground and sky can we learn how to orient and to navigate in the multiple dimensions that now claim us.

If Abram is right in this passage from *The Spell of the Sensuous*, then human identity is—as Dick suggests in *Androids*—necessarily relational. Unless we routinely interface our bodies with the not-us, then through our isolated self-engagement we risk losing something essential to what makes us human. It's not just the Earth that is threatened, but ourselves. Lacking a vital connection to more-than-human others, we are, like Deckard, in danger of devolving into quasi-human simulacra. The hypermediating modes of contact that our digital devices and networked computing provide should therefore give us serious pause and make us question to whom, exactly, we are networked—and who gets excluded.

We ought also to consider whether or not as human individuals we still possess the bandwidth needed to experience the world invoking more senses than the visual, and ask if we still remember the protocols required to connect ourselves with the furred, creeping, burrowing, flying, and flowing inhabitants of the earthly landscape. Do we hear the hum of insects anymore, or only that of our desktop machines? In accord with Jean Baudrillard's "precession of simulacra," digital tweets have become more present for many people than those uttered by birds.

The Lives of Electric Others

But everything I've been arguing buys completely into Deckard's notion that electric sheep and androids are nothing more than clever simulations with no actual selfhood of their own. When his toad dismayingly proves to be artificial—and Wilbur Mercer is exposed as a paid performer on a stage set—Deckard initially despairs at the pervasive inauthenticity of what little he has left in his world. His nostalgic pastoral impulse to reclaim a lost golden world in which humans and animals engage in reciprocal care and communication (if not communion) has proven unobtainable. In order to cope, he has no option but to reprogram his responses. He must employ a new mode of simulation of his own in order to make his own life meaningful, namely, to make himself believe that what he thought to be lifeless isn't. In this recognition, his gloom lifts a little in a muted epiphany when he says "The electric things have their lives, too. Paltry as those lives are."

In *Blade Runner*, Deckard may make a similar realization, ultimately finding more humanity in Roy Batty's self-sacrifice than in any of the supposedly human beings he finds in Los Angeles, himself included. And when he discovers the origami unicorn that Gaff leaves for him, the glint in his eye might mean more than just hope for Rachael, the replicant he has come to love: namely, he realizes that he, too, might be a replicant himself. And astonishingly enough, he seems okay with that—or, at least, willing to make it work.

Likewise, in *Do Androids Dream of Electric Sheep?*, instead of having to find redemption in an escape "outside" the realm of technological simulation, Deckard instead comes to accept it: "Mercer isn't fake . . . unless reality is fake." Does he now see "through Mercer's eyes" in an animistic way that invites all beings, electric ones included, into his circle of moral concern? How much Deckard's response merely demonstrates a grudging concession to the inescapable virtuality of reality, and how much it might represent a genuine acknowledgment of synthetic selfhood ultimately remains unclear.

Exhausted from his pursuit and his termination of the remaining rogue androids in the novel, he lets his wife program the Penfield Mood Organ to setting number 670, "long deserved peace," and he finally sleeps—having been programmed to do so. (One has to wonder: does he now dream of electric, or actual sheep?) As he rests, Iran wonders what this new electric toad eats. "Artificial flies, she decided." She looks up "animal accessories, electric" in the yellow pages, and for Deckard's toad she orders "one pound of artificial flies that really fly around and buzz, please . . . I want it to work perfectly. My husband is devoted to it."[1]

---

[1] Alf would like to thank Natasha Seegert, Bryan Carr, Paul Hartzog, Lance Olsen, and Melanie Rae Thon for their inspiration and helpful suggestions. He would like to dedicate his article to Friida the Cat (1995–2010), who taught him much about empathy.

Identity Crises

05
Just Who and How Many Do You Think You Are?

RICHARD FEIST

D r. Wigan slowly sawed into the bone, looped the ear, forehead and other ear to complete the cut. He pried off the skull cap and peered inside. Half the brain was gone! How could this be? Wigan had known the man now stretched out on the table; lunched with him and heard him recite poetry. Dumbfounded, Wigan thought: this guy had half a brain but a full mind. So, having a full brain must mean having two minds. This disturbing autopsy experience haunted Wigan throughout his days until his turn on the cutting table, December 7th, 1847.

Wigan's "1 brain = 2 minds" view died with him. For a century afterwards, most scientists agreed that different parts of the brain had different jobs, but there was only one mind and it was located in the dominant left hemisphere. Although scientists knew that a thick rope of fibers linked the brain's hemispheres, they didn't know why. They eventually learned that cutting it lessened the intensity of epileptic seizures, but afterwards split-brainer patients walked, talked, swam, dressed themselves and played musical instruments just like anyone else.

By the 1950s and 1960s scientists knew that the right hemisphere controlled the left side of the body and slightly controlled speech whereas the left hemisphere controlled the right side of the body and dominated speech. Scientists also began sending information to one hemisphere at a time. Now the split-brainers behaved bizarrely. Put a concealed object in a split-brainer's left hand. Ask her what it is. The right hemisphere knows but can't either talk or send a message to the left. So the left has to guess. Guess wrong, and the right hemisphere makes the face frown. Guess correctly, and the face smiles.

Sometimes the hemispheres duke it out. Put a concealed object, like a pipe, in a split-brainer's left hand. Take it away. Ask him to write with his left hand what he was holding. The right hemisphere will struggle to write "P" and "I". But the left interferes, changes the "I" to an "E" and writes "PENCIL." The left sees the word's beginning and completes it, much like Google's predictive text or your cellphone's autocomplete. Then the right counter-autocompletes the left, erases "PENCIL" and draws a pipe. Notice that the hemispheres autocomplete each other differently. The left autocompletes conceptually, linguistically, while the right autocompletes visually, pictorially. A split-brain monkey's hands can, if each one grabs the same snack simultaneously, get into a tug of war.

During the 1960s Dr. Joseph Bogen resurrected Wigan's 1 brain = 2 minds view. Do we each have two minds deep inside us? Absolutely, says Bogen. Do we believe that we are each a single mind, a single self? Absolutely, says Bogen, who then argues that this belief is not serious evidence; it's just a mistaken belief. So, continues Bogen, it's time to grow up. Get over yourself and embrace your inner selves.

Dick's *A Scanner Darkly* draws deeply upon Bogen's research. Several passages from Bogen's writings appear, although Dick's characters don't quote Bogen. Instead, Dick drops Bogen quotations smack in the middle of their sentences. It's an unexpected voice from nowhere. "What," the reader asks, "is going on here? Where did this Bogen-stuff come from?" Experiencing a voice from out of the blue gives the reader an idea as to what's heading towards the main character, Bob Arctor.

Arctor's self explodes because everything that holds it together disintegrates. He wears a special suit that disguises his appearance, assumes another name (Fred), relentlessly spies on himself, and alters his perception of his self through a brain-splitting drug, Substance D. Arctor's self splits into different parts, which start bickering. The Arctor-parts eventually form two persons, Bob and Fred, who at first recognize each other but soon see each other as completely separate persons. Quite often Arctor isn't even sure who he is and, stranger still, how many he is.

The User Illusion

Shift now to a scene where doctors quiz Fred, an undercover narcotics officer. They know that Fred plays the junkie and frequently ingests brain-splitting Substance D. One doctor lays a lined card on the table, starts to question Fred, but Dick interrupts him with a Bogen quotation:

> "Within the apparently meaningless lines is a familiar object that we would all recognize. You are to tell me what the . . .
>
> > Item. In July 1969, Joseph E. Bogen published his revolutionary article "The Other Side of the Brain: An Appositional Mind." In this article he quoted an obscure Dr. A.L. Wigan, who in 1844 wrote:
> >
> > > The mind is essentially dual, like the organs by which it is exercised. This idea has presented itself to me, and I have dwelt on it for more than a quarter of a century, without being able to find a single valid or plausible objection. I believe myself then able to prove—(1) That each cerebrum is a distinct and perfect whole as an organ of thought. (2) That a separate and distinct process of thinking or ratiocination may be carried on in each cerebrum simultaneously.
> >
> > In his article, Bogen concluded:
> >
> > > I believe [with Wigan] that each of us has two minds in one person. There is a host of detail to be marshaled in this case. But we must eventually confront directly the principal resistance to the Wigan view: that is, the subjective feeling possessed by each of us that we are One. This inner conviction of Oneness is a most cherished opinion of Western man . . .
>
> . . . object is and point to it in the total field."

It's easy to find philosophers supporting this view of the oneness of the self. Modern philosophy's founder, René Descartes, said that the mind has no parts; it's clearly "one and entire." For Descartes, our self (who and what it is, and how many) is so easy to know that it's difficult—even insane—to deny our knowledge of it. After all, we directly know our self. But external stuff, carburetors and computers, are so difficult to know that it's easy to deny our knowledge of them. We know external things indirectly.

You need ideas in your mind to know external things. Ideas are like mental pictures. You know your dog through your idea of your dog. But your idea could easily be wrong—even completely misleading. Your idea right now of this book could suddenly vanish as your alarm clock wakes you up. Descartes says that it's a clear and clean world inside the mind but messy and unclear outside. Dick flips Descartes and says that it's inside-messy and outside-clear.

In a Mirror, Darkly

While lying in bed, Arctor asks whether anyone really knows his own motives. No, he concludes. But if you don't know what you want, do you really know who you are? If your friends and family stopped calling you by name, stopped recognizing you, no doubt you'd become unsure of your identity. Maybe you'd try out new identities. And while you're at it, play dress-up and go for an important job.

> You put on a bishop's robe and miter, he pondered, and walk around in that, and people bow and genuflect and like that, and try to kiss your ring, if not your ass, and pretty soon you're a bishop. So to speak. What is identity? He asked himself. Where does the act end? Nobody knows.

The problem of identity is an oldie for philosophers. Suppose that a ship comes into port once a month for repairs. Each time you replace a part, save the old part. Eventually the ship has all new parts. Now combine all the old parts into another ship and you'll have two ships. Which is the original ship?

You say that you're the same person as the baby in your mom's photos. But what links your current self to your baby-self? Your body constantly grows new cells and loses old ones. So you might not have any matter in common with your baby-self. I'm sure that your mom misses baby-you, but I doubt that she saved your former cells and has reassembled baby-you.

What gives the "self"—whatever (and however many) it is—its continuity, if any? Dick agrees with philosophers John Locke, David Hume and Immanuel Kant, who think that none of this is clear. But Arctor's musings hint that the outside world plays a big role in shaping who and what a self is. So it seems that the "inner world" is, in Nietzsche's words, "full of phantoms and will-o'-the-wisps."

> How many Bob Arctors are there? A weird and fucked up thought. Two that I can think of, he thought. The one called Fred, who will be watching the other one, called Bob. The same person. Or is it? Is Fred actually the same as Bob? Does anybody know? I would know, if anyone did, because I'm the only person in the world that knows that Fred is Bob Arctor. But, he thought, who am I? Which one of them is me?

John Locke asked what made up the self and linked it together at different times. He said that it's not matter, but memories. But Locke backpedals a little. He doesn't conclude that a self is just a collection of memories; rather, the self is a "thinking, intelligent being." A self can consider itself as the "same thinking thing, in different times and places." For Locke, there is real unity to the self.

Locke and Descartes both clung to the view of a self that has feelings, thoughts, memories and so on. But David Hume bit the bullet, went further and demanded evidence for existence of the self that possesses memories. Look deeply into your mind and you'll only find sensations of colours, smells, tastes, temperatures and so on—but no self that has them. Your supposed "self" is just a bundle that rolls along picking up new memories and sensations while losing others.

Two hundred years before Bogen, Hume asserted that there is no single thinking thing. But why do we mistakenly believe that we have a self that gains and loses memories? Hume says that we think about the identity of our self over time like how we think about mountains. We incorrectly think that a mountain, which constantly changes, remains the same over time because the changes are tiny and easily overlooked by us. The same goes for our supposed self. In the end, thinking that we have a self and that it is the same self over time is a delusion, but a perfectly normal and inescapable delusion.

You Don't Always Get Along

You probably get why some call Hume's discussion of personal identity the most upsetting and controversial passages in European philosophy. For Hume the mind is like a little republic, full of citizens, but without a 'universal citizen'. Even Hume-the-person is upset with Hume-the-philosopher. To paraphrase:

Person-Hume:
I can't believe Philosopher-Hume's view that there's no self. But I can't say where he went wrong!

Philosopher-Hume:
Don't worry; belief formation is not a rational process. It's perfectly natural that you have this internal conflict. It's perfectly natural that you can't help but mistakenly believe that you are a self. Everything will be fine—go play pool, drink beer, and you'll forget all about this crazy philosophy.

Person-Hume:
This isn't over yet, Philosopher-Hume!

Sadly, the two Humes never came to an agreement. So, there you have it: one of the greatest philosophers in history fought with himself and concluded that the mind has normal, inescapable delusions about itself and irrationally forms its beliefs—no wonder Dick loved philosophy so much and incorporated it into his books! Were David Hume alive today, he could have starred in the movie version of *A Scanner Darkly*. Step aside Keanu Reeves.

Even better is that Hume ripped off his freaky "city in your head" view from Plato, who said much the same thing thousands of years earlier. Take that Bogen! Before considering Plato, let's dip back into *A Scanner Darkly*, where the doctors grill Fred. One asks if he experiences any "cross-chatter." Basically, if the left hemisphere quiets down, the right will pipe up. What's this like? The doctor explains:

Thoughts not your own. As if another person or mind were thinking. But different from the way you would think. Even foreign words that you don't know. That it's learned from peripheral perception some-time during your lifetime.

There are two really cool things here. First, that there's another person thinking inside you and you're hearing it. Second, this other person thinks in a foreign language. As you learn things, you think that you're aware of everything you're learning, but no, the other mind is also learning. There are parallel streams of learning happening in your head.

Plato compared the mind to a city and the unbalanced mind to civil strife. In Plato's *Republic*, his mouthy mouthpiece Socrates describes how your mind is really a community of three minds. This was a big hit in European thought. You've probably heard about the Christian Trinity: Father, Son and Holy Spirit. Not to be outdone, Sigmund Freud put forth a three-part view of the mind: Id, Ego and Super-Ego. For Plato, one mind is primarily where your desires come from, the other is primarily your emotional mind, and the third is primarily your scientific, reasoning mind. Each mind desires, reasons and has a bit of a temper. Your reasoning mind is far more reasonable than the others and your desiring mind has stronger desires than do the others and so on.

Socrates thought that we constantly experience cross-chatter between our mental citizens. Suppose that on a hot summer day you desire a cold beer. You know that you shouldn't indulge because you must pick mom up at the airport. You both desire and refuse the beer. But the exact same thing cannot simultaneously desire and refuse the beer. In such situations we often say "I am torn on this" or "I am of two minds on this." Socrates takes this seriously. It's not just a way of talking. There's a clash within you and you are in fact, at war with yourself. You had better do the right thing: avoid the beer, and get mom. Look, she did the best she could with you three. Don't blame mommy if you can't play nice together.

Indeed, our mental citizens often squabble. Socrates tells the story of Leontius, who came across a pile of dead bodies and was both thoroughly disgusted and intrigued. As with a good train wreck, Leontius couldn't look away. He relented, screaming at himself, "Look for yourselves, you evil wretches!" The emotional part was peeved with the desiring part. However, Socrates says, the emotional and desiring parts agree that in order to live a good life, overall, it is best to let the rational part run the show.

The Outer Workings of the Mind

We've seen that Dick thinks that the inside of the mind is a mess, now what about the outside? Here things are just as bizarre, but Immanuel Kant can help us out. Like Dick, Kant flips Descartes's view and says that we indirectly perceive the self and directly perceive external objects.

This is crazy, you might think. Maybe—but it still could be true. Dick and Kant both insist that reality is not independent of our minds; our minds play a role in its construction. This dependence of reality on our minds is weirdly but effectively captured by the movie's animation. Richard Linklater shot the scenes with regular film, but then employed a technique called "rotoscoping." The film looks like a live-action comic book. It is often difficult to tell exactly which parts of a given scene are purely animated and what is "really" live action. Again, this merely reflects Dick's and Kant's view that "reality" is in many ways a construction of our minds, but not a total construction. The real problem is to figure out what we construct of reality and what is really there.

Now, how can your mind make an external object? For Kant, the mind is like a car factory. Raw materials, like rubber, glass and metal, go in one end of the factory. They're shaped and manipulated in very well-described ways and out the other end rolls a car. In this analogy, the car is your actual, everyday experience, with its ordinary, everyday objects that give rise to our ordinary, every sense of self. You never experience the inner workings of your mind nor the raw materials, just the finished products. Your mind plays a partial role in the construction of the reality that you experience. But it can't play the whole role since your mind can't cook your experience up out of nothing, any more than the factory builds cars without raw materials. How could you know about the inner workings of the factory? Well, you would have to dissect the car and work backwards. Today we would call this "reverse engineering."

Reverse engineering is why militaries don't want their latest technological toys to fall into enemy hands. Kant reverse engineers experience. We understand the inner workings of our mind by examining so-called outer objects. After all, they were partially made by us so they should, like any created thing, bear the stamp of their creator.

Reverse engineering only gets you back into the workings of the factory, not right out the other end into the raw materials. Likewise, Kant says, whatever stuff comes in from the outside prior to any workings of the mind, forget it; you can't know anything about it. This raw material, Kant calls the "thing in itself." It is truly and completely outside of us and so is forever and completely unknowable.

The Scanner-Self

If Dick and Kant are right that the mind shapes the objects that it experiences, and that those objects in turn give rise to a self, then what does this shaping? This is a horrifically complex question for Kant, one he answers in slightly different ways. To keep it simple, Kant thinks that there is a deeper self that lives inside the mind, shaping objects and eventually shapes that everyday self that depends on and experiences those objects. The deeper self wouldn't have an identity like the everyday self. This deeper self just exists, deep in the factory of the mind, collecting and organizing data so that eventually you have a regular self that can experience objects. This deeper self doesn't have experiences like you and I do. So you can't know this deeper self in the way you know an everyday person. You know your everyday self and the everyday self of others. This deeper self is just like a pure observer, gathering data: a Kantian scanner.

As the novel progresses, Arctor's deep self, devoid of identity, is eventually revealed. The authorities secretly plant numerous scanners throughout Arctor's house and it's Fred's job to spy on himself. This constant surveillance (and the drugs, too) takes its toll on Arctor. Later in the novel Arctor asks, "Just what does a scanner see?" A frightening amount it turns out.

We all dislike being watched, treating anyone staring at us with hostility. But why do we do this? Jean-Paul Sartre describes a scene in which you're observing the park around you. Suddenly another person appears and everything changes; you're no longer an observing-subject but an observed-object. You have been subordinated, downgraded by this person's gaze. But you still have your private mental life, exterior to this person's gaze. So you have some subjectivity left. Now bring in God, Sartre's ultimate gaze. God's all-penetrating stare leaves nothing about you unseen, stripping you entirely of your subjectivity. Your future, too, lies open to God's stare. Any decision that you'll ever make, God already knows what it will be. Your freedom is gone; it was always just an illusion anyway.

Like God, the scanners are ravenous and relentless in their surveillance of Arctor. They see increasingly deeper, eventually recording everything, even his hallucinations. Arctor becomes less of person and more like a pure observer. By the end of the novel Arctor becomes Bruce, who only watches things around him, repeats what he's heard, and lacks all identity. That deep Kantian self, the scanner-self, is what Bruce is now.

Were Dick alive today, he would be fascinated by the Internet's effects on subjectivity. People logging hours on Facebook, uploading and living their lives checking out others' walls, would have struck him as another version of becoming a scanner. Dick would rewrite Saint Paul's famous line "now we see ourselves through a glass darkly" as "now we see ourselves through a profile darkly."

The Valuable Self

What's a self? How many selves are you? Can selves be counted? These are metaphysical questions. But despite *A Scanner Darkly*'s numerous, quirky, metaphysical themes, its central point is a moral one. Here Dick reveals that he's a moral philosopher, and a follower of Kant to boot.

Kant based his ethics on the importance of the self. The most valuable thing in the world, Kant says, is a self. Other things are valuable, but they're means to our ends. Using something as a means to an end makes that something into an object, like a tool. But Kant says that a self is not an object. A self is a subject. To use a self as a means to an end turns that self into an object. Kant tells us that we're immoral if we use someone to get something else; we must never treat other people as means to an end.

So Bruce is just a scanner, not a real subject. Dick insists that that most fluid and volatile thing, the self, was the object that deserved the most respect. To violate it is to commit the ultimate crime. The novel's end reveals the authorities' master plan: to remake Arctor into a hollowed-out junkie shell so that he can anonymously infiltrate the inner circles of the drug world and rat on who was trafficking Substance D. One of Arctor's junkie friends, Donna, who is also an undercover agent, bemoans the price paid for the plan:

"I think, really, there is nothing more terrible than the sacrifice of someone or something, a living thing, without its ever knowing. If it knew. If it understood and volunteered. But—" She gestured. "He doesn't know; he never did know. He didn't volunteer—"

What makes us human, what makes us valuable, is the self's fuzziness, which includes its mystery of freewill. To clear this all away is makes the self into an object, a scanner, and there is nothing as dreadful as the transformation of the self—whatever and however many it may be—into a mere thing that just watches and never chooses.

06

Will You Survive a Trip to Rekall, Inc.?

G.C. GODDU

What would you do for ninety-two million dollars? In the movie *Paycheck* (based on the Philip K. Dick story of the same name), Michael Jennings agrees to give up three full years of his life—kind of. He loses three years of his mental life.

To ensure confidentiality for his current client, the Rethrick Corporation, Jennings agrees to have all his memories of the three years he will work for the company removed. In return, Jennings will receive a large quantity of company stock options worth approximately $92 million.

A good deal? Maybe, but I suspect most of us would be extremely nervous about trading three years of our mental lives for any sum of money. Why be nervous? Because our mental lives are a fundamental part of who we are. As Dr. Rachel Porter puts it to Jennings, "All we are is the sum of our experiences." To willingly give up our joys, and even our sorrows; to remove our recollections of what we did and why; to lose all our experiences is to commit mental suicide.

Follow the Psyche

Just how fundamental are our mental lives, our psyches, to our continued existence? Many of Dick's stories suggest we do not need much else. In "Rautavaara's Case," the alien Proxima Centaurians save the severely damaged human Agneta Rautavaara by using the rest of her irreparable body as a nutrient source to sustain her brain. The humans who learn how Rautavaara has been saved are horrified. Misconstruing the source of the horror, the Centaurians ask: "Was it not right to save her brain? After all, the psyche is located in the brain, the personality."

In one of Dick's early short stories, "Mr. Spaceship," Professor Michael Thomas, who is dying, agrees to donate his brain to be the control center of an experimental spaceship. The designers plan to use Thomas's unconscious brain "working on reflex only." But Thomas gets the builders to make a few wiring alterations. As a result, shortly into the test flight, Thomas's brain regains consciousness and Thomas takes over control of the ship.

Rautavaara and Thomas both survive even though they lack most of their original bodies. Rautavaara survives as just her brain—fed on a nutrient bath derived from her former body. Thomas survives as just his brain and gains a spaceship as his new body. So the stories suggest that, in the right circumstances, a person could survive as long as his or her brain survives. But perhaps even the brain is not necessary for personal survival.

In Dick's first published work, "Beyond Lies the Wub," Captain Franco is determined to eat the strange pig-like wub acquired on Mars. The wub, in the most polite way, tries to convince Franco to refrain. Franco will not be deterred. Reasoned argument having failed, the wub at least convinces the captain to look him in the eyes before pulling the trigger. The wub's body gets eaten, but the wub survives by transferring his consciousness into Franco.

In another Dick story, "Human Is," Jill Herrick faces a challenging decision. Her cold and abusive husband has returned from Rexor IV a changed man—so changed that the authorities believe Lester Herrick's consciousness has been removed and replaced with that of a (warm and caring) alien Rexorian. The authorities assure Jill that her husband is still alive, his consciousness stored in suspension somewhere on Rexor. She merely needs to testify to the radical change in personality, so a judge will give them permission to "vibro-fry" the Rexorian consciousness. Then, once Lester's consciousness is found and reintegrated, the authorities are confident that "he'll be back with you. Safe and sound. Just like before."

John Locke, a seventeenth-century English philosopher, provides yet another example in his *Essay Concerning Human*

Understanding. Locke writes: "Should the soul of a prince, carrying with it the consciousness of the prince's past life, enter and inform the body of a cobbler, as soon as deserted by his own soul, everyone sees he would be the same person with the prince, accountable only for the prince's actions." According to Locke, the person now in the cobbler's body is the prince. Of course, the prince may have a tough time convincing everyone of his true identity. In current science-fiction movies this convincing usually involves lots of guns, at least one kick-ass chase, and some really cool unexplained technology.

So do we need our bodies or our brains to survive? According to Locke, and many other philosophers, these sort of body-swapping examples show that we do not. (Locke also asks us to imagine our little finger separated from the rest of our body, while our consciousness inhabits the little finger. "It is evident the little finger would be the person, the same person; and self would have nothing to do with the rest of the body.") Locke concludes that "consciousness makes personal identity." If Locke is right, our psyche constitutes ourselves as persons. The prince, the Rexorian, Lester Herrick, and the wub (alas, we do not know what became of poor Captain Franco), all survive because, even though they leave their bodies behind, their consciousness survives.

We can summarize our thoughts in these various cases using the following rough and ready rule of thumb:

Psyche Continuity Rule: If you want to keep track of the person, follow the psyche.

Notice that even the cases of Rautavaara and Thomas conform to the Psyche Rule. In both cases the brain is only important as a vessel for the psyche. Without the resumption of Thomas's mental life, we would say he merely donated an organ to be part of the ship. But because his mental life resumes we say he survived to take control of the ship. If Thomas's psyche could have been transferred to take over the ship without his brain, he still would have survived. The brain may be a convenient storage device for the psyche, but it is the psyche that is ultimately crucial to our survival.

So far so good, but Dick isn't finished messing with our minds yet.

The Perils of Rekall, Inc.

If psychological continuity is necessary for you to survive, what are we to make of the radically disjointed mental lives depicted in *A Scanner Darkly* or *Total Recall*? In the previous chapter, Richard Feist took us through the strange divisions and (dis-?) continuities of Bob/Fred/Bruce in *A Scanner Darkly*, so I'll focus on *Total Recall*.

There are several possibilities for tracing the life of "Douglas Quaid." The moviemakers deliberately keep us in the dark as to which possibility is accurate. Here is the most complicated one: Hauser and Vilos Cohaagen, the tyrannical governor of Mars, are very good friends. Together they hatch an intricate plot to infiltrate and eliminate the heart of the Martian resistance. Hauser pretends to have a falling-out with Cohaagen and defects to the resistance. He is a member for a short time, but to avoid having his mind read by the telepathic mutant leaders of the resistance, Hauser gets himself 'captured' by Cohaagen. Cohaagen then has Hauser's memories of being Hauser replaced with the personality of mild-mannered Terran construction worker Douglas Quaid.

Quaid, now on Earth, is obsessed with Mars and so visits Rekall, Inc. to buy a virtual trip to Mars, complete with fake memories. While preparing for the insertion of these fake memories, the Rekall technicians discover that Quaid has already undergone significant memory erasure and implantation. They erase Quaid's memories of having come to Rekall and send him home. But the trip to Rekall prompts Cohaagen's agents (who were posing as Quaid's wife and closest friend and were not told all the intricacies of Cohaagen's plan) to try to kill him.

Quaid escapes (with the aid of Hauser's abilities, which apparently had not been removed) and gets himself to Mars. On Mars, Quaid gets enough of Hauser's memories re-implanted to make Quaid believe that he has really defected and that he now contains, buried in the recesses of his mind, information crucial to the resistance. The original Hauser memories are never re-implanted.

In another version of Quaid's life, Hauser really is a defector with information crucial to the resistance, but erases and replaces his memories in an effort to protect himself from Cohaagen. In this version, Cohaagen's tale that Quaid did not get all of Hauser's memories back is merely a trick. The so-called 'memories' of Hauser installing false memories of being a defector are fictions, just like Rekall's fake memory trips. In yet a third version of his life, construction worker Quaid is the real person, and everything from his trip to Rekall, Inc. forward is actually a part of the fake memories implanted by Rekall to give his virtual trip to Mars more spice.

Ultimately which version is accurate does not matter, because all three cause problems for the Psyche Rule. All three versions are supposed to describe what happens (or could happen in the case of the third version) to one person. But no single psyche is linking Hauser/Quaid from one part of his life to the next. Instead what is continuous through all the various changes is not his psyche, but his body.

So, to make sense of *Total Recall* being about the trials and tribulations of one person, we need to use something like the following rule:

> **Body Continuity Rule:** If you want to keep track of the person, follow the body.

For all of us in our everyday lives, whether we use the Psyche Rule or the Body Rule does not matter. The two rules march in lockstep with each other and give the same answer. But the various circumstances of Dick's stories show that the rules could give conflicting advice. To make sense of some of Dick's stories we have to use the Psyche Rule, while to make sense of others we need to use the Body Rule.

So what are we—our bodies or our psyches? Is there no way to give a unified explanation of what happens to Douglas Quaid and the wub? Perhaps we need a more complicated rule that combines both the Psyche Rule and the Body Rule, such as:

> **Combined Psyche or Body Rule:** If you want to keep track of the person, then in the case of a unified mental life, follow the psyche; but in the case of a sufficiently disjointed mental life, follow the body.

According to the Combined Rule, the wub, since his mental life is unified, goes where his psyche goes. Hauser, on the other hand, since his mental life is so disjointed, goes where his body goes.

One potential problem with the Combined Rule, however, is trying to decide, in at least some cases, whether a mental life is unified or sufficiently disjointed. Recall Michael Jennings's voluntary memory removal in *Paycheck*. Is Jennings's mental life disjointed or unified? If something splits Jennings's body from his psyche in the future, which should we follow? In the short story version, Dick has Jennings start referring to his earlier self in the third person. Does that mean Dick thinks Jennings's mental life is disjointed enough that we need to follow his body to keep track of him? But if Jennings now has his consciousness stolen by the Rexorians, should he not worry since "he" goes with his body?

The problem of determining whether a mental life is unified enough or too disjointed has vexed philosophers for centuries. But perhaps we can sidestep the problem. Maybe personal survival depends on something completely different from the body or the psyche.

Gotta Have Soul?

Locke's body-switching example involved the prince's soul moving into the cobbler's body. Perhaps it is the persistence of the soul that explains personal survival. Here's the rule:

> **Soul Continuity Rule:** If you want to keep track of the person, follow the soul.

If the Soul Rule is correct, then the wub survives because he transfers his soul to Captain Franco. Hauser survives not because his body is constant, but rather because his soul is constant. Hauser's soul has the original Hauser memories removed, the Quaid memories implanted, and then some of the original Hauser memories put back.

Even though Locke uses the soul as the vehicle for transferring the consciousness of the prince to the cobbler, he denies that it is the soul that is the person. Gottfried Leibniz, a German philosopher also writing in the seventeenth century, agrees. Leibniz, in his *Discourse on Metaphysics*, asks us to suppose that we (our body and soul) could become the King of China on the condition that we forget all of who we were, as if we had been born anew. (This is just an extreme version of the bargain between Jennings and the Rethrick Corporation.) Though the King of China was the richest man in the world, Leibniz rejects this offer. Why? Because, Leibniz answers, even if the body and soul were made the King of China, accepting the offer would be the same "as if he were to be annihilated and a King of China to be created at his place."

Likewise, in his *Critique of Pure Reason*, Immanuel Kant, an eighteenth-century German philosopher, asks us to imagine a group of souls transferring a single mental life from one to another. How many people are there? Kant claims just one—the single mental life that is transferred from soul to soul.

Put simply, just as we can imagine switching bodies, we can imagine my consciousness being switched to another soul (Kant's case), or being left behind (Leibniz's case). According to the Soul Rule, I stay with my original soul, but our intuitions tell us that I follow my consciousness.

There is also the practical problem of applying the Soul Rule—how do we follow the soul? We know the wub survives in the captain's body because the wub continues a private conversation that crewmember Rollins and the wub were having before the captain barged in to shoot the wub. The wub expresses his opinions and beliefs. We see and hear evidence of his mental life. But what evidence do we have that the wub's soul transferred or whether the wub even has a soul? How could we tell that Hauser has a single soul that is having various psyches implanted and removed from it, rather than having different souls placed in his body and removed?

The Soul Rule has significant problems of its own, so perhaps we need to switch back to some sort of Combined Rule. But yet another one of Dick's stories suggests that the Combined Rule won't work either.

Future Selves and Imposters

In the movie *Imposter* (based on the short story of the same name), Spencer Olham is accused of being an android replica created for nefarious purposes by enemy aliens. Without revealing whether Olham actually is such a replica (in either the movie or the story), let us suppose that he is—the real Olham had his memories transferred to the android and was then killed by the enemy aliens.

Now consider an alternative story without the aliens. Because Olham is dying he chooses to have his consciousness downloaded into an android replica (a merging of "Mr. Spaceship" and "Beyond Lies the Wub"). He also chooses to omit any memory of the deliberation or decision to download. As a result, after downloading, Olham merely thinks he has recovered from his illness rather than transferred himself to another body.

Finally, suppose that the process used to transfer Olham's mental life is identical in both the alien story and the illness story. The stories have the same degree of bodily and mental continuity. In both, Olham's mental life is transferred from the old organic body to the new android body. Yet in the alternate story the android is Olham's means of survival, whereas in the original story, the android is an imposter. So Olham survives in one story but dies in the other. Since the stories have the same degree of bodily and mental continuity, according to the Combined Rule, Olham should either survive in both or die in both. Hence, the Combined Rule won't work in all cases.

Of course, in the latter scenario Olham chose to survive as an android, whereas in the former he did not. Could this very choice explain or be a part of what is required for one's own continued existence?

"Aha! The soul to the rescue," say advocates of the Soul Rule. The soul, such advocates might claim, goes where we intend it to go. That explains why the aliens' android is an imposter, but the dying Olham's android is Olham's future self.

But now consider a slight variation on the alternative story. Suppose Olham does not want to be transferred to the android, but is considered so important by the government that they insist he survive. Against his will Olham is forced to undergo the transfer procedure. Olham regains consciousness in a healthy android body and, looking at the lifeless remains of his old organic body, says: "Curses! They moved me against my will!" But if the soul goes where Olham wants it to go, then his soul will still be in the organic body across the room and he should say "Curses! I am dead over there across the room!" which is absurd.

If the process by which Olham is transferred is the same in all cases, then either the soul, assuming there is one, is transferred in all cases or it is not. Either way, we cannot account for the thought that the alien's android is an imposter and Olham's android is his future self. Hence, the Soul Rule will not work here either.

Selfless?

None of the Rules accommodates all the various bizarre transformations that occur in Dick's stories. Should we conclude that Dick had an incoherent conception of personal identity? No more than any of the rest of us. Are we just our bodies? Do we have souls? Is our mental life separable from our bodies or our souls? Philosophers, theologians, and the intellectually curious have been wrestling with the conflicting answers to these questions of personal identity for centuries. The power of Dick's stories is how easily he brings our conflicting intuitions to light. We easily follow the wub into Captain Franco, but equally easily (okay, not so easily) follow Douglas Quaid's search for his true memories and his true identity.

The pessimist worries that Dick's explorations show how easily we can split our very selves asunder. The optimist hopes that Dick's explorations reveal how, with suitable technological advances, we might expand the very possibility of what we can be. But the skeptic doubts that there is anything to be either optimistic or pessimistic about. If we are not bodies or psyches or souls or even combinations, what are we? There are no other options left, so that must mean we are nothing at all!?

Are we really forced to the conclusion that there are no enduring persons at all? Can we give an answer to this skeptical doubt?

Is It Live or Is It Memorex?

The problem may not be that all these intuitions about psyches, bodies, and souls are incoherent. The problem might be that we're missing some very crucial details in each of these cases.

How exactly is the alleged transfer of Olham's psyche from one physical object, his body, to another, the android replica, taking place? Suppose the scientists (or the aliens) take a 'snapshot' of Olham's brain—they record all the current states of his neurons, synapses, and so forth. Assume these details capture all there is to capture about Olham's psyche. Then they imprint all these details on the android brain. Did Olham get transferred? No. He got copied. The snapshot, we can suppose, does nothing to Olham's brain but record its current state. Imprinting the details on the android brain does nothing to Olham's brain or psyche. So Olham's psyche is still in his brain. But suppose that the process of taking the snapshot fries Olham's brain. Does he get transferred in that situation? No. He gets destroyed and, at best, a copy of his psyche gets made.

If Olham wants himself to survive, he needs to get transferred and not just copied. Nor should we confuse transferring and copying. Our banks will let us transfer our money from one account to another, but would object strenuously if we tried to copy our money from one account to another. Transferring the contents of one bookshelf to another requires one set of books. Copying the contents of one bookshelf on another requires two distinct sets of books. (If you still think copying is good enough for surviving, then ask yourself what happens to Olham if the government imprints his psyche on two separate androids. Does one person somehow survive as two separate people?)

Similar concerns arise for Douglas Quaid. If Cohaagen merely copied Hauser's original memories, and then replaced them with the memories and personality of Douglas Quaid, then Hauser's mental life is not merely disjointed—his friend Cohaagen destroyed it. But if Hauser transfers his psyche out of his body and stores it elsewhere, then again his mental life is not disjointed—he merely leaves his body behind. (Safer, but not foolproof, for Hauser would be to store all his original memories in his brain, but make them inaccessible, until properly unlocked, to the newly implanted Quaid personality. This possibility would bring the movie closer in line with Dick's original short story.)

Once we fill in the possible details of what is happening to Olham's or Hauser's mental life, the Psyche Rule once again seems the most plausible. Fill in the details one way and it looks like the characters die and get copied (which would account for the aliens' android being an imposter). Fill in the details another way and the characters survive, but leave their bodies behind (which would account for Olham's android being a future self).

What Olham and Hauser need in order to survive is a way to transfer, and not just copy, their psyches. But is that even possible? I don't know, since I don't know how our psyches are realized within us. Are they merely composed of arrangements of our neurons? Our entire brains? Or something else entirely?

Much of the past seventy years of research in psychology and the philosophy of mind has been devoted to trying to understand exactly how this encoding of memories and psyches in human beings actually works. Progress is being made. Much more still needs to be figured out. Until we do, I wouldn't visit your local Rekall franchise for that virtual trip to Mars.

07
Scan Thyself

JESSE W. BUTLER

We humans have a wide assortment of beliefs about ourselves, from our individual tastes and preferences to our personality and character; from the intentions behind all the little things we do every day to the overall meaningfulness or meaninglessness of our lives.

But what do we really know about ourselves? Can we know what we truly are, or instead might our nature be somehow hidden from us? Does each person have private and secure knowledge of her innermost thoughts and motivations, or could most people actually be deluded about themselves, having false images of who they are and mistaken understanding of why they do the things they do?

But, we might also ask, do we really want to know what makes us tick? What if we turned out to be something horrible, something we couldn't live with? Might it be better not to know, in that case?

Philip K. Dick, I'm pretty sure, wanted to know. He inquired into human nature in a dazzling variety of ways, both stretching the bounds of what it could mean to be human and investigating the possible meaning of events in his own life with a vigor and persistence that few can muster, all of which suggests a deep curiosity stemming from the perennial human drive to know oneself.

The pursuit of self-knowledge is a major theme and inspiration behind much of Dick's work, from the visions of human possibilities throughout his stories and novels to the 8,000+ page "Exegesis" that he pored over night after night for many years through the end of his life, in attempt to understand the nature and meaning of his own experiences.

As I see it, this places Dick within a long tradition in philosophy that is concerned with the pursuit, possibility, and value of knowing ourselves. The ancient Greek philosopher Socrates, inspired by the command to "know thyself" inscribed in the Temple of Apollo at Delphi, emphasized self-knowledge as essential to living a good life and pursued authentic understanding of himself to what some saw as a bitter and unnecessary end. Siddhartha Gautama, the Buddha, sought self-knowledge only to find that the self itself is an illusion at the root of all suffering. René Descartes's confidence in his knowledge of himself as an immaterial being was the foundation of his entire philosophy. And Philip K. Dick, too, inquired into the nature of the human self, in both general and deeply personal ways that permeated his life and work.

Does this mean that Dick should go down in history with the likes of Socrates, Buddha, and Descartes? Well, that really isn't for me to decide, but looking at self-knowledge through the lens offered by Dick offers some relevant, fascinating, and potentially illuminating insight into the topic. Let's start with a hypothetical inquiry that places us within the world of one of Dick's most famous and influential works, *Do Androids Dream of Electric Sheep?*, eventually winding our way towards Dick's own pursuit of self-knowledge in some of his later novels, in which he himself appears as characters in his own work.

How Do You Know You're Not an Android?

Imagine yourself in a world cohabited by both androids and humans, such as the one in which Rick Deckard lives as a bounty hunter whose job is to hunt down the andys and take them out. Suppose further that, like Deckard, you fancy yourself to be a flesh-and-blood human being, with real experiences, feelings, memories and, perhaps most significantly, real thoughts about yourself as a living person. You haven't taken a Voigt-Kampff test, nor have you subjected yourself to a painful bone marrow analysis, but then why would you need to do that? You have experienced yourself as a human being your entire life. Isn't your experience of being a human proof enough that you aren't an andy?

If you think like René Descartes, then your answer might very well be, yes it is! In fact, you might think that you actually have the best proof you could possibly have, much better than any external test. Descartes, as you may know, is famous for his 'cogito' argument, frequently summarized with the quote "I think, therefore I am." From this perspective, we privately know ourselves in a clear, transparent, and absolutely secure manner, unlike the messy and fallible knowledge we may or may not acquire about the outside world. Mirroring this reasoning, you know by the very fact that you are consciously thinking that you are a genuine human being, and no mere mindless mechanical android that only mimics human actions while the lights inside are really all off, so to speak. For you, the lights are on, and that's all you need to know that you are a real living human being.

But there's a problem lurking here. Descartes concluded on the basis of his awareness of his own thoughts that he must be an immaterial thing whose essence is thought—a soul, entirely distinct from a physical thing like an animal or a machine, composed of mere matter. In fact, Descartes presents the 'cogito' argument in his *Meditations* just after throwing the existence of the entirety of physical reality into doubt, including his own body.

But what about the possibility that he could actually be made of matter but is, nonetheless, thinking? Even if Descartes can be granted full confidence in his knowledge of his own thoughts, how exactly does he know that he is not in fact a thoroughly physical being, whose thoughts and experiences come about through physical processes, such as the complex electrochemical activity of the brain? The answer is that he doesn't know. Beneath the veil of his own thoughts and experiences, Descartes may just be his physical body after all. This is something that Descartes simply cannot rule out as a possibility on the basis of his own introspection alone.

My purpose here isn't to criticize Descartes's defense of immaterial souls. My purpose is to question how Descartes can draw any justifiable conclusions about his underlying nature on the basis of his own introspection. Inner observation may disclose one's thoughts to oneself, but it does not reveal whether those thoughts themselves take place in an immaterial soul, a bundle of neurons, or a computer.

Getting back to the android case, how can you rule out the possibility that you are actually an android, merely on the basis of your seemingly-human experiences? The fact of the matter is that you simply can't. You cannot know, from your own experience alone, whether or not an android can experience the same introspective thought processes as a human being. Just as Descartes cannot justifiably conclude that he's an immaterial thinking being on the basis of his experience of thought, you simply can't rule out the possibility that you're an android by the fact that you are having what you take to be real human experiences. At a minimum, you'd need to have some further reasons for believing that androids don't have human-like experiences, which is something you'd have to acquire from facts about the outside world rather than your own introspection. It looks as if you're going to have to go take that V-K test after all.

So introspection isn't the secure foundation that Descartes thought it was, as we can see from within the Dickian dilemma of figuring out whether you're a human or an android. This skepticism of introspection isn't new, however. For instance, the eighteenth-century Scottish philosopher David Hume stated in his Treatise of Human Nature:

> For my part, when I enter most intimately into what I call myself, I always stumble on some particular perception or other, of heat or cold, light or shade, love or hatred, pain or pleasure. I never can catch myself at any time without a perception, and never can observe any thing but the perception.

Hume's point is that all we get from the experience of introspection is experience itself, and not anything that reveals to us what causes or underlies our experience. Experience could be produced by a human brain, an immaterial soul, or, in your case in particular, the silicon chip lodged deep inside your synthetic skull, but the window that introspection provides doesn't peer that far.

The Art of Knowing Arctor

Instead of looking within to know ourselves, maybe we need to look outside. But how can we do that? We seem stuck inside our own heads, able to look out to observe the world and each other but not the self inside that's doing the observing. It's like an eye trying to see itself.

Impossible! Unless, perhaps, you systematically record and scan yourself as Bob Arctor does in *A Scanner Darkly*. Working as "Fred," the Substance D narc, Arctor takes on the job of observing himself as a suspect. Scanning devices are implanted in his house and then he looks back over the footage to investigate himself. The relationship between Fred and Bob Arctor is interestingly convoluted, involving philosophical issues concerning self and identity discussed in detail in Richard Feist's chapter in this volume, but suffice it to say that Arctor becomes fragmented into two personas, Fred the narc and Bob the addict, enabling the former to observe the latter in a detached and evaluative manner. By taking on the Fred persona, Bob becomes able to observe himself in a way that, under ordinary circumstances, seems impossible.

What happens with this twisted scenario, in terms of the pursuit of self-knowledge? Can Arctor expect to gain an objective understanding of himself that he couldn't have acquired through introspection? In a sense, yes, but as Dick often reveals in his work, the reality of the situation is much more complex and perplexing than we may first realize. In a mix of hope and skeptical despair, Arctor reflects:

What does a scanner see? He asked himself. I mean, really see? Into the head? Down into the heart? Does a passive infrared scanner like they used to use or a cube-type holo-scanner like they use these days, the latest thing, see into me—into us—clearly or darkly? I hope it does, he thought, see clearly, because I can't any longer these days see into myself. I see only murk. Murk outside; murk inside. I hope, for everyone's sake, the scanners do better. Because, he thought, if the scanner sees only darkly, the way I myself do, then we are cursed, cursed again and like we have been continually, and we'll wind up dead this way, knowing very little and getting that little fragment wrong too.

So Arctor would like for the scanner to help him see beyond the murky waters of his own introspection, skeptically suggesting that if it doesn't help then he, and others too, will lack any genuine self-knowledge. To what extent the scanner helps or fails to help Arctor know himself is something I'll leave for you to explore by reading the novel, but we can dig in a little further here to see what the implications might be for the rest of us.

Not all of us have the privilege of being split in two and then enabled to see extended audiovisual footage of ourselves, so is there some other way we ordinary folks can achieve the detached perspective that allowed Arctor to observe himself? Consider the brain-scanning technologies (for example, PET and fMRI neuroimaging) that we have developed. Could such devices help us get out of the subjective dark murk of intro-spection and see ourselves in the clear light of day?

In some cases, at least, I think the answer is clearly yes. Consider again the android-human uncertainty we discussed earlier. No amount of introspection will justifiably reveal to you whether you are an android, but sticking your head in an fMRI and seeing a bunch of synthetic parts buried behind your eye sockets would do the trick: clear evidence that you are in fact an android. But how far can this kind of information go? Can scanning our brains reveal our innermost drives and motivations? Could you, say, spend some time with a PET scanner to figure out whether or not your feelings for another person constitute a deep soul-binding love or a temporary lust-ful infatuation?

Perhaps not yet, but if we discover what some philosophers and scientists call the "neural correlates" of mental states like enduring love and fleeting lust, then you could indeed figure out which state you were in by a brain scan.

But identifying precise brain states that directly map onto distinct emotional states is easier said than done. Some people question whether it is even possible in principle. Contemporary philosopher Alva Noë, for example, argues in his book *Out Of Our Heads* that no amount of brain scanning will reveal our mental states because that is simply the wrong place to look. From Noë's perspective, mental states, including emotions such as love and lust, must be understood in terms of whole biologi-cal organisms and their active interaction with the environ-ment, including, crucially, other people. In this sense, perhaps Arctor's brand of self-scanning, where he observes himself as a whole human in his native habitat of his own home, interact-ing with other people, may actually have an edge on the more constrained and isolated focus on the brain.

What Does A Scanner See?

Before you install security cameras throughout your home, however, some further philosophical analysis is in order. There is yet another perspective to consider that brings the whole idea of observation itself into question as a basis for knowing yourself, irrespective of whether it takes the form of an Arctor-style home scan, a more focused and localized brain scan, or plain old-fashioned introspection in attempt to discover yourself.

According to the French existentialist philosopher, Jean-Paul Sartre, we are conscious beings who freely choose to be what we are, rather than determinate beings whose essence can be observed in the same way that we can observe that, say, water is made of hydrogen and oxygen.

Imagine a gambler who has decided to stop gambling. The day after the resolution, he faces the option of gambling yet again, freely able to choose against his prior decision. To describe the situation as Sartre did in his master work *Being and Nothingness*, the man is a nothingness that recognizes in anguish the complete inefficacy of his past decision to stop gambling. It's no use for him to observe his past resolution in deciding whether to see himself as a gambler or non-gambler, as he is entirely free to gamble or not. He must always freely decide again for himself what to be, as he consciously stands before the possibilities he can pursue.

If we answer Arctor's question from this perspective, we may say that a scanner, when one tries to find oneself with it, sees nothing. It's hopeless to try to discover oneself in observation because there is nothing to observe besides the conscious freedom to be what one chooses. I can't trust my observation of myself as an object to tell me who I am because, as Sartre states,

> Nothing can ensure me against myself, cut off from the world and from my essence by this nothingness which I am. I have to realize the meaning of the world and of my essence; I make my decision concerning them—without justification and without excuse.

Think of Fred perched before his playback-monitor, watching footage of himself as Arctor in his own home, trying to decipher himself. The absurdity of this situation may reach beyond the bizarreness of the circumstances into the more ordinary hope of knowing oneself through observation. That goal in itself may be deeply problematic. From Sartre's perspective, trying to know who we are by discerning facts about ourselves is actually a kind of self-deception, where we take ourselves to be something other than what we are—conscious beings, free to be what we choose at any given moment.

Sartre calls this "bad faith," a refusal to face up to our freedom and responsibility by turning to presumed facts about ourselves in attempt to fall back on a particular determinate identity. So perhaps Arctor's observation of himself through Fred and his scanner is actually an instance of bad faith, a self-deceptive maneuver to hide the anguish of his freedom by attributing traits to himself as if they were facts rather than choices. It's starting to sound as if his murky skepticism about knowing himself might have been warranted after all.

But not so fast. It's easy to take Sartre's talk of nothingness, anguish, and bad faith to paint a bleak skeptical picture of ourselves, but that isn't exactly what he intended. In fact, Sartre sometimes characterized his existentialist outlook as a hopeful recognition of human freedom, optimistic towards the ever-present capacity to shape our own lives anew. The gambler, recall, is in anguish over his conscious ability to gamble or not to gamble, but at the same time he is entirely free to be whatever he chooses. This conscious freedom bears a tremendous responsibility but also affords us the opportunity to remake ourselves as we stand before the indeterminate possibilities of our future.

In the author's note after *A Scanner Darkly*, Dick enigmatically states "I myself, I am not a character in this novel: I am the novel." What does he mean by this? In light of Sartre's optimism towards our freedom to transcend our past and recreate ourselves anew, I'd like to suggest that Dick used the novel as a way of reshaping the trajectory of his life.

As documented in Lawrence Sutin's biography of Dick, *Divine Invasions*, and elsewhere, there are clear autobiographical elements of Dick's own life in *A Scanner Darkly*. For instance, he experienced a break-in that prompted a great deal of speculation on his part, including, perhaps most interestingly, the theory that he himself had broken into his own house. This is explored with dramatic effect in *A Scanner*

Darkly, centering on the Fred-Bob split and the implantation of the scanning devices in Bob's house. Dick also spent some time in a drug rehab center with notable similarities to New Path. In a more general sense, *A Scanner Darkly* appears to reflect a dark time in Dick's own life.

Dick said (in his 1975 *Rolling Stone* interview) that *A Scanner Darkly* was his first novel written without amphetamines. Coupling this with the fact that *A Scanner Darkly* offers a very critical perspective on drug use, this leads me to wonder whether it might have served as a vehicle for Dick to gain some perspective on his life and reorient himself. Could *A Scanner Darkly* itself be a work of personal transformation, a way for Dick to detach himself from his past and freely reshape the course of his life? As he wrote *A Scanner Darkly*, could he, like Sartre's gambler, have stood towards his past in conscious recognition of his capacity to freely choose what path to take? In light of some additional cases of Dick's appearance in his own work, which we'll turn to next, I think we can see that this is quite possibly the case.

Phil Chews the Fat

Towards the beginning of *VALIS*, we find the sentence "I am Horselover Fat, and I am writing this in the third person to gain much-needed objectivity." Horselover Fat is indeed a main character in the novel, whose life is depicted and analyzed throughout *VALIS*, in both the third person and also narrated in the first person. Horselover Fat is also a pseudonym for Dick, and the character portrays multiple aspects of Dick's real life. Most centrally, it investigates the meaning of visions Dick experienced in 1974, which became a nearly obsessive focus of his later work. He wrote extensively of the visions, offering diverse interpretations of them in *VALIS*, the colossal and ponderous *Exegesis*, *Radio Free Albemuth* (which also includes Phil himself as a character), and elsewhere.

In this massive collection of self-reflective work, Dick entertained a wide variety of theories about his visionary experiences, including (but not at all limited to) Vitamin C overdose, telepathic communication with alien intelligence, reintegration with a past life, and Gnostic Christian revelation. No wonder he needed to get some objectivity through Horselover Fat! For anyone else, reflecting upon yourself through a character named Horselover Fat would be a left-field move, but for Dick it appears to have been a way to bring his experiences down to reality. I say that lightly, of course, as the events Horselover Fat experiences in *VALIS* are not depictions of tame suburban reality by any means. As you Dick fans will know, the theories Dick considered as explanations of his 2-3-74 experiences formed the plots of many of his later works, which contain some of the most mind-stretching passages he ever wrote.

As a philosopher interested in self-knowledge, I find all of this fascinating. What exactly is Dick up to here? Are the writings contained in these later works an attempt for Dick to sort through his life and gain some knowledge of himself? Is he figuring out who he is through the twisted narratives of *A Scanner Darkly*, *VALIS*, and *Radio Free Albemuth*, engaging in an authentic quest for meaning in his real life, or might he just be pulling all our legs with this hallucinatory phosphene non-sense? Or was he just plain nuts? Maybe a bit of all of these things?

From a critical stance, we might say that Dick's theorizing about himself is really an instance of bad faith, in the sense that perhaps he was trying to nail down a determinate identity for himself, as an escape from the immense responsibility to choose what to make of himself and his experiences. If this perspective is right, Dick sadly spent the last decade or so of his life digging himself into a vacuous chasm of inauthentic delusion.

I'd like to offer another perspective here, however, turning this misguided critique on its head. In a couple of fascinating and revealing philosophical essays written during the self-reflective turn in Dick's work that we've been exploring, "The Android and the Human" and "Man, Android, and Machine," Dick directly concerns himself with understanding the nature of authentic humanness. He suggests that what distinguishes humans from androids has nothing to do with what they are composed of and everything to do with how they live their lives and understand themselves. An android, which could in fact be composed of a flesh-and-blood human body, is defined by following a programmatic life plan dictated by external social forces, while an authentic human (which could turn out to be made of synthetic parts) acts spontaneously in a lived reality of one's own making. In describing the latter state in "Man, Android, and Machine," Dick writes that

> Like a symphony of Beethoven, each of us is unique, and, when this long winter is over, we as new blooms will surprise ourselves and the world around us. What we will do, many of us, is throw off the mere masks that we have worn—masks that were intended to be taken for reality.

From this perspective, we can see Dick's exploratory theorization about himself not as self-deceived construction of false masks but rather as a playful openness towards the freedom he had to make himself into whatever he chose. In "The Android and the Human," Dick states that "Reality, to me, is not so much something you perceive, but something you make. You create it more rapidly than it creates you." As I understand it, this resonates with Sartre's optimism towards human freedom and the ever-new opportunity it affords us to choose what we are.

Dick never committed himself to one of his theories about himself. As his friends and lovers attest, he was an ever-playful trickster, always improvising in a way that escaped a determinate settled role. He playfully toyed with various conceptions of himself in his writings, without letting any one of them become his fixed android program. In that sense, then, perhaps Dick's wild speculations about himself were his way of knowing he is not an android.

What's yours?

08
Human or Machine, Does It Mind or Matter?

George Teschner and Patrick Grace

When Rachael returns to Deckard's apartment a second time, she sits down at a piano and begins to play. She says to Deckard, "I did not know whether I could play. I do not know whether it is me or Tyrell's niece." Deckard sits close to her on the piano bench, looks into her eyes and says, "You play beautifully."

This is the first time in *Blade Runner* that the distinction between human and replicant blurs for Deckard. He leans over and softly kisses Rachael. She gets up and runs to leave the apartment. He bars the door and forcefully grabs and stops her. Slow romantic music plays on the soundtrack. He says to her, "Say, 'kiss me'. Say, 'I want you'."

Is this the programming of a machine? Shaken and teary-eyed, she repeats his words. Is it "she" who repeats the words, or "it" that repeats the words? In the passion of the moment, the distinction between what is human and what is a simulation disappears.

Don't Think about It

The script by Hampton and Fancher is even more graphic. Rachael becomes excited; her breath comes faster and deeper. The action is described as a "magnetic, palpable energy growing up between them." In Dick's novel, Rachael asks Deckard whether he has ever made love to an android. He has not, but he says he had been told "if you think too much, if you reflect on what you're doing—then you can't go on." Typically throughout the novel, what is said of androids is also true of humans. Thinking about the sex act "too much," whether by a human or an android, inhibits the physiological response. Rachael says that it is "dreary" if one pauses and gets "philosophical" about it. She says to Deckard, "don't think about it, just do it"—good advice in either case.

Whether Rachael is actually experiencing desire and emotion is idle speculation against the intensity of the action. Deckard's earlier remark, "Replicants are like any other machine," is contradicted, not in theory, but in practice. The particulars of real life's passions, decisions, and actions—the existential—trumps questions about the difference between the human and the non-human when the non-human fully simulates the human. The distinction between the real and the simulated is pointless where there is no observable difference. This is the position of the Turing Test, which the Voight-Kampff test is modeled after.

Alan Turing was one of the first thinkers to raise the question of whether a machine can think. In the "Turing Test," a human judge carries on a natural language conversation with a human and a machine. If the judge cannot tell which is human and which is machine, the machine passes the test. In order to keep the test simple, the conversation is limited to text-only communication.

Turing originally proposed the test in order to replace the "meaningless" question, "Can machines think?" with one that could be decided by observable behavior. "Can machines think?" is meaningless for Turing because there is no way of observing third-person consciousness. The only way to decide whether someone or something has a mental life is to base it on behavior. The Turing Test is explicitly behavioral: it tests how the subject acts, which from the point of view of philosophical positivism is the only way in which the term "thinking" could have meaning. Positivism rejects as meaningless anything that cannot be traced back to what is empirically observable. Questions about whether machines can think or feel are dismissed as unverifiable metaphysical nonsense. If a machine acts intelligently then we are warranted in saying that it is intelligent. This applies to humans as well, since inner mental life in either case is unobservable.

The objection to Turing's behavioral approach is that a machine passing the Turing Test may be able to simulate human conversational behavior, but the machine might be just following some cleverly devised rules. That is the view of Bryant, Deckard's supervisor in *Blade Runner*, who refers to the androids as "skin jobs." The Turing test, according to this objection, fails to factor in human consciousness. Both Philip Dick's and the movie *Blade Runner*'s indifference to whether or not other human beings and machines are conscious is consistent with the spirit of philosophical positivism that rejects as meaningless anything that cannot be verified observationally.

. . . You Ever Take That Test Yourself?

In *Blade Runner*, Deckard sits at the piano with Rachael. Next to the sheet music are pictures of Deckard when he was a child. They are the same sort of slightly worn black and white photographs that Rachael offered Deckard as proof of her humanness. The comparison goes unnoticed by Deckard and Rachael. Moments earlier Rachel asked Deckard, "You know that Voight-Kampff test of yours, you ever take that test yourself?" Suddenly the viewer is placed in the same quandary as characters in the movie and is led to wonder whether Deckard is an android and whether his memories are also artificial implants.

In the novel, Luba Luft, the opera singer, also asks the question whether Deckard has tested himself. Deckard answers Luft by explaining that he took the test a long time ago. "Maybe it is a false memory," she says. But, he says, his superiors knew about the test. She suggests that there might have been a human Deckard, whom he, android-Deckard, killed, and his superiors did not know of the switch. Rachael, at first, had no idea that she was an android, and the same may be true of Deckard.

The similarities between humans and androids are striking throughout Dick's novel. When the reader first meets Rick Deckard, he is debating with his wife, Iran, on what setting to dial their Penfield Artificial Mood Simulator. She accuses Deckard of killing those "poor andys." Her expression of sympathy for androids sets Deckard to thinking whether he should dial the mood simulator to suppress his anger at her comment.

She says that she has dialed six hours of despair because it is unhealthy not to react to the devastation from "World War Terminus" that has left Earth toxic and has caused most of the human population to exit to extraterrestrial colonies. She says she wants to avoid what was called an "absence of appropriate affect"—once treated as a mental illness.

It is, in fact, the very absence of the proper affect that they believe distinguishes androids from humans. Iran explains that she has programmed the mood simulator to automatically follow the mood of despair by a hopeful mood, to avoid the dangers of remaining in despair. Deckard recommends instead that she dial a 104, which is the desire to watch TV. She says that she does not want to dial anything. He recommends that she dial mood 3, which is the desire to dial a mood. Iran points out that there is a logical contradiction in dialing the desire to want to dial when you don't feel like dialing. She turns the TV off and reluctantly agrees to dial mood 594: "ecstatic sexual bliss." Deckard dials for himself a "creative and fresh attitude towards his work."

Paradoxically, moods, particularly of empathy, are thought to distinguish humans from androids. The Voight-Kampff test is based on such a theory, yet here, moods are artificially induced in humans by a machine. Dick has made the artificial simulation of feelings and emotions even more impersonal by assigning to each mood a number. If machines can artificially induce moods, then using the feeling of empathy to distinguish between humans and machines seems pointless.

The use of the mood simulator is one of many images in Dick's novel that blurs the distinction between human and android. The androids have created a phony police agency headed by a police chief named Garland. Shortly after Deckard meets him, Garland is exposed as an android. Garland tried to deceive Deckard into thinking that another bounty hunter, Phil Resch, who works for the phony police agency, was also an android. Resch had thought that Garland was human and was fearful that he himself was an android with false memory implants. Prior to being tested, he tries to prove his humanness by the fact that he owns a live squirrel that thrives under his care, something that androids were thought incapable of doing.

The Voight-Kampff test proved that Resch was not an android, but only after Resch was deeply tormented by the thought that he was not human. At one point Resch compares "how an andy must feel," to the painting by Munch entitled "The Scream" in which a figure "screamed in isolation. Cut off by—or despite—its outcry." Resch's comparison of an android with the figure in Munch's painting is filled with feeling and emotion, hardly the language that would be used to describe a "thing" or an "it."

I Love You, My Artificial Construct

Deckard feels regret having retired the android Luba Luft. He reflects on the impracticality of the loss saying that, "She was a wonderful singer. The planet could have used her. This is insane." The distinction between androids and humans becomes unclear for Deckard when he realizes he is feeling "empathy toward an artificial construct." He says, "But Luba had seemed genuinely alive; it had not worn the aspect of simulation." Deckard registers an empathetic 4.0 out of 6.0 on the Voight-Kampff test at the thought of killing a female android. He thinks that it may be an anomaly and wonders "if any human has ever felt this way before about an android." He considers that it may have been because she was an opera singer and because of his love of the opera, *The Magic Flute*. Phil Resch suggests it was sex because she was physically attractive. We are told in the novel, "for the first time in his life, he had begun to wonder." The cause of his wonder was whether the distinction between android and human signified any real difference. He is brought to the point of saying, "So much for the distinction between authentic living human and humanoid construct."

Perhaps Phil Resch gives the best account of the difference between androids and humans when he says, "If we included androids in our range of empathetic identification, as we do animals, we could not protect ourselves." Deckard agrees and says, "The Nexus-6 types," like Rachael, "they'd roll all over us and mash us flat. You and I, all the bounty hunters—we stand between the Nexus-6 and mankind, a barrier which keeps the two distinct." It is not because the two are distinct that there are bounty hunters; it is because there are bounty hunters that the two are distinct.

As postmodernism has claimed, and in particular the philosophy of Michel Foucault, the distinctions between what is true and what is not, what is real and what is not real, reduce to a matter of the struggle for power and the domination of one social class over another. In this case, it is humans over androids, even as the two become indistinguishable because of technological development. Technological changes invariably bring ideological changes. Technology alters the balance of power, renders obsolete traditional modes of production and consumption, and moves wealth across different segments of society. The institution of the bounty hunter who retires androids is a form of reactionary humanism that is being rendered obsolete by advances in cybernetics.

The ideological superstructure of the post-apocalyptic society in which Deckard lives values the living over the artificial. The most striking example is its attitude toward animals. Deckard keeps an electric sheep on the roof of his apartment complex. He is envious of his neighbor who has a real live horse. Deckard feels like a "fraud." He describes having had a real sheep that died of tetanus and was replaced with an electric one. His neighbor says to him, "It's not the same." Deckard replies, "But almost." He explains, "You feel the same doing it, you have to keep your eye on it exactly as you did when it was really alive."

The real sheep gets sick and dies; the electric one has a mechanical breakdown. The amount of care is the same. The difference between the real and the artificial is mainly a matter of what other people think. It is important in Deckard's society that the truck coming to repair artificial animals is marked "animal hospital," so no one suspects the animal is artificial, similarly, in the case of the phrase "pet hospital" in the deceptively named, "Van Ness pet hospital . . . in the competitive field of false-animal repair." Social pressure, rather than an irreducible difference between the natural and artificial, causes Deckard to feel a need for a "real" animal.

In the closing chapter of the book, Deckard finds a toad that he at first thinks is alive. He says that it made him feel like a kid again. But, when he shows the toad to Iran, she finds a tiny control panel on its abdomen that he had not noticed. He is visibly disappointed, but says to himself, "But it does not matter. The electric things have their lives, too. Paltry as those lives are." If electric things, as inanimate and unresponsive as the toad Deckard found in the desert have their lives, then so also do androids, whose behaviors like Rachael's, are indistinguishable from humans.

Has Deckard had some great metaphysical realization about the nature of mind and matter? Contemporary philosophy and postmodernism, in particular, would suggest not. What has changed is the way in which he talks about the living and its simulation as a result of the convergence of social, economic, and technological forces. Only linguistic norms have changed, such as those governing the use of the personal and impersonal pronouns, 'he', 'she', and 'it'.

. . . Because My Furnace Believed the House Was Cold

For the philosopher Daniel Dennett, it is a matter of the way we choose to talk as to whether behavior is conscious or not. He calls the three ways of representing behavior "stances."

When we talk about beliefs, thoughts, and intentions we are using what he calls "the intentional stance." To say that a bird flies because it knows or thinks it is in danger and feels a need to escape is the intentional stance. To predict that a bird will fly when it flaps its wings, on the basis of the aerodynamic shape of the wings, is the stance of the designer and engineer. To describe the free fall of a bird in the language of mechanics, using terms like mass, velocity, and distance, is the stance of the physicist.

From the point of view of the intentional stance, the disk drive of the computer is "reading" the disk. The engineer takes the design stance in saying, of the same activity, that laser light is reflecting off grooves in the rotating disk. The physicist takes the physical stance in saying that light is being converted into a flow of electrons.

For the non-technical user, the vocabulary of "searching and reading" may be the most convenient way of describing the computer. However, it would be odd to say that the house thermostat believed the room was cold and decided to turn the furnace on because it wanted to keep the temperature constant. By contrast, it would be entirely appropriate to say that John chose to leave the room because he felt too hot. For Dennett, what stance we adopt is not a matter of a metaphysical difference between the nature of humans and machines, but a difference in the choice of vocabularies. There are circumstances in which it would be entirely appropriate to describe John's behavior in terms biochemical and neurological processes without mentioning beliefs, decisions, intentions, or volitions.

The gradual acceptance of androids and machines into the family of things that we call persons is a matter of a change in linguistic conventions. Whether we regard humans, animals, or machines as having rights and treat them with moral regard is the result of changes in patterns of communication necessitated by social forces. Philip Dick has represented a world that exists in the aftermath of nuclear war, when technology has become sophisticated enough to convincingly simulate human beings and animals, and where economic conditions have become such that the use of androids is a necessity. Under such extreme conditions we can expect the linguistic practices of a culture to change with accompanying changes in its metaphysical, moral, and epistemological beliefs. This would explain Deckard's profound change in attitude toward androids in his attraction to Luba Luft and his sexual encounter with Rachael Rosen.

Shaky Theological Foundations

Mercerism is a religion that employs a device called an Empathy Box, allowing users to experience fusion with other human beings and with the Sisyphus-like sufferings of Mercer. Mercerism holds that empathy with others is distinctly human. This belief system enables the character Isidore to deal with his loneliness. He's a so-called "chickenhead" and "special," whose IQ is too low to permit him to emigrate to an offworld colony. Mercerism serves as the metaphysical underpinning that justifies hunting down and killing androids. However, when that ideological foundation is exposed as a fraud by Buster Friendly, empathy, as the necessary condition that defines humans and serves as the theoretical basis of the Voight-Kampff test, loses its quasi-theological basis. For Deckard, the loss of the theological foundation, his attraction to and admiration of the talents of Luba Loft, his sexual encounter with Rachael, the callousness of his fellow bounty hunter, Phil Resch, his sympathy for the artificial toad that he finds in the desert, and the difficulty of detecting the new Nexus 6 androids, all contribute to undermining his conviction of, and deconstructing for the reader, the difference between humans and androids.

The Right Stuff

Is functional equivalence to human behavior sufficient to say that androids are sentient? John Searle, who rejects the positivism of Turing and the linguistic critique of Dennett, thinks not. Searle imagines someone given Chinese symbols and being asked to find their equivalence in English using a translation manual. Searle claims that no matter how clever are the algorithms used to translate Chinese into English, the mere mechanical manipulation of symbols according to syntactic rules never yields meaning and understanding: the Chinese characters would be meaningless for the translator.

Even though a machine could equal the human brain in passing the Turing test, functional equivalence is not a sufficient condition for intentional content. For Searle, passing the Turing Test is not enough to say that the machine has a mental life. Searle's position is still a thoroughgoing materialism, and hydrogen and carbon molecules are still insentient, but there is something special in the biological mix of the human brain that produces awareness. However, even this position is consistent with Dick's representation of androids. After all, androids are not like electric sheep.

Electric animals are mechanical artifacts that only appear biological. Isidore looks for a "concealed control panel . . . plus quick charge battery terminals" on a cat that was picked up for repair. Milt, one of the repairmen, comments that, "It has been our experience that the owner of the animal is never fooled." By contrast, androids are, as Rachael explains to Deckard moments before they go to bed, "chitinous reflex machines." They are biological, and detecting them requires technical subtlety. A bone marrow test has to be performed on the body of Mr. Polokov to verify that he was a humanoid robot. The Boneli test measures "the reflex-arc response taking place in the upper ganglia of the spinal column," which requires, "several microseconds more in the humanoid robot than in a human nervous system."

Androids are clearly a different order of artificial life than electric sheep. So, together with the functional equivalence to humans, androids may have the right stuff to experience mental life, and satisfy Searle's condition for intentionality.

The position of Turing, and the view of Philip Dick's novel and the movie *Blade Runner*, is that if it behaves intentionally, it is intentional; if it behaves consciously, it is conscious; and if it functions thoughtfully, it thinks. From the point of view of postmodernism and the philosophy of language, the difference between humans and machines that simulate humans is a matter of choosing what language game to play in describing their behavior.

Either way, whether it is human or machine, we have the option of the vocabulary of intentionality or the vocabulary of mechanical causality. As represented by Philip Dick, this is the most humane, indeed the most humanistic, view of the relation between the human and the machine.

Soul Against the Archons

09

Matt Damon Is a Vast Sinister Conspiracy

D.E. WITTKOWER

Matt Damon is not your friend. Hell, he isn't even human. Matt Damon is a product on the market for our enjoyment. Matt Damon is a story we like to tell ourselves about talent leading to success in a free society. Matt Damon is someone we all know and can use as a connection between us, even though we've never met him. Matt Damon is a tool to keep us in line; a simulacra for us to look up to; a replicant who lives an interesting life so that we don't see that ours is so dull and so prefabricated. *Matt Damon is a vast, sinister conspiracy.*

There are a lot of people behind Matt Damon—executives, agents, writers, PR teams for all the films he's signed on to. One more-or-less central figure behind Matt Damon is a forty-year old guy who happens to have the same name and, for his part, seems like a nice guy. But Matt Damon is a nexus of power and control much larger than this particular guy who "is" Matt Damon.

To the credit of that guy who plays the role of ("is") Matt Damon, he seems to be aware of this and have a good sense of humor about it. If you're not familiar with the song he did with Sarah Silverman, you should look it up. But not at work, or near children.

Hopefully some of this is obvious enough, but I know that, even if you're following me on the "vast conspiracy" part of this claim, the "sinister" part is probably something you're pretty skeptical about at this point. We'll get there, and I think you'll agree with me once I explain it a bit more. Let's let David Norris take the lead here:

You know, 1998, I did a cover for *GQ*, the title was 'Youngest Congressmen Ever', and since then every story tried to explain how I got here so fast. And the word that people kept uh . . . using was "authentic" and . . . But here's the problem, this isn't even my tie. This tie was selected for me by a group of specialists, in Tenafly, New Jersey, who chose it over fifty-six other ties we tested. In fact, our data suggests that I have to stick to either a tie that is red or a tie that is blue. A yellow tie made it look as if I was taking my situation lightly and I may in fact pull my pants down at any moment. A silver tie meant that I'd forgotten my roots. My shoes—you know, shiny shoes we associate with high-priced lawyers and bankers. If you want to get a working man's vote, you need to scuff up your shoes a little bit, but you can't scuff 'em so much that you alienate the lawyers and the bankers, cause you need them to pay for the specialist back in Tenafly.

Authenticity, image, and meaning are manufactured goods, designed, produced, and marketed like any other sports drink, toilet paper, sandwich cookie, politician, or whatever. And just as corn-syrup-sweet and sat-fat-rich confectionaries make our children find apples and grapes to be dull and unappetizing by comparison, we find real people to be so awfully uninteresting and unimportant compared to those who are industrially-manufactured. And what else would we call a celebrity than an industrially-manufactured person-slash-marketing tool? I guess some of the actual people who our economy casts in the role of celebrity do have some kind of actual merit—acting, singing, being funny or nice or whatever—but this has basically nothing to do with their roles as celebrities. And there are those free-floating signifiers like Snooki and the Kardashians, among many others, who are famous for nothing other than their own fame.

Celeb gossip rags sit alongside candy bars, both literally and conceptually. Both take advantage of inborn instincts and desires that presumably once served a healthy purpose (seeking out nutritious and sustaining foods; determining who in the tribe can be trusted and how to organize our hunter-gatherer pack) but that are now exploited to make us addicts, regularly buying and consuming things that are wholly unnecessary to our lives and that, if anything, make us worse. Nobody actually cares about *The Bachelor*, but we'll buy magazines and sit through ads to find out about him anyway. Learning about Lindsay Lohan's behavior this week does not contribute to anyone's real interests, desires, or life-plans.

Matt Damon is an industrially-manufactured person too. Matt Damon has been built up by his personal brand management, but much more so by casting directors, marketers, talk shows, celebrity magazines, and everyone else trying to use his face and name to get you to give them money. And that gets us to the point here: Phil Dick's paranoid fantasies are true.

There are fake manufactured people among us—as Tyrell put Norris's point about "authenticity" in *Blade Runner*: "More human than human is our motto." As in *The Simulacra*, these fake people are consolidations of power and tools of distraction and control. Like *Time Out of Joint*, this fake reality is there to keep us docile, occupied, and productive. And, as in *The Adjustment Bureau*, we're constantly being 'nudged' to make one choice rather than another, so that we all play our little part in someone else's big plan.

It's all part of a vast, sinister conspiracy to hide the true nature of reality and of human life; to keep us so distracted by gossip and entertainment and buying one thing after another (and working so that we can maintain this life) so that we never notice, as in Dick's "The Piper in the Woods," that we'd probably be happier if we spent less time working or being 'entertained' and more time laying quietly on a rock in the warm sun.

A Variety of Free Will Worth Having

Philip K. Dick claimed he was a "fictionalizing philosopher, not a novelist," but he didn't tell us what kind of philosopher he was. As I see it, despite his many concerns with epistemology and metaphysics, and his turn to philosophy of religion in his later work, he was most constantly and consistently concerned with ethics, existentialism, and social and political philosophy; with questions of how we should live, how we ought to treat others, and how, practically, to respond to an alienating society and an absurd universe. And this is something that *The Adjustment Bureau* really understood correctly about Dick's original short story, "Adjustment Team": the real point is not about knowledge and reality; the real point is about how to live.

"Adjustment Team" is an abstract and absurdist story, starting with a secret-agent dog and ending with the adjusters helping the main character lie to his wife about the nature of reality. When Ed Fletcher, the real-estate office drone who is Dick's main character, goes to the office during the "adjustment," ash fills the air, and everything (and everybody) is made of grey dust. The underlying truth of his workaday world, revealed to him accidentally, is that it is dead, animated and directed only by some external hidden force. What if he had been in that office? Would he have been nothing but dust as well?

Here we have a kind of determinism that is lived everyday, not an abstract thought experiment about metaphysical freedom and the soul. Here, the claim is that—in the workplace and the marketplace perhaps most distinctively—we do not bring about our own actions. We are not present, as humans, at work: we do what we have to to succeed, and we may or may not enjoy our work, but we are directed by goals and considerations that we have not chosen or decided to value.

Our working lives are animated by mysterious forces and goals we do not choose: the visions of success and self-worth that are peddled to us in movies and advertising, the misplaced pride of wealth, and the idea that if we earn enough money we can buy our way into having a meaningful or enjoyable life. We seldom ask whether the "better" life we are able to afford is worth everything we sacrifice to get there—most of us just follow the plan. As Thompson (Terence Stamp) puts it in the film, we have the freedom to choose what kind of toothpaste we wish to use, but not to make any real choices. We must add to this: it's not just in consumption and "entertainment" that we allow ourselves to be determined, but also in production and the very conceptualization of what our life is "about" or "for."

This alienation from our own values and our own working and striving is determinism as we experience it, concretely. Freedom, similarly, is not treated here as the abstract idea of a break in the chain of cause and effect. Freedom, concretely, is accepting responsibility and choice—contrary to the determinism of working towards goals that we didn't come up with in jobs where we do things we would never have chosen as the content of our lives. Freedom in our concrete day-to-day lives is the ability to do what you actually value and choose, and to act on the basis of your own creative vision of the life you wish to lead.

This is why, in my view, the love story here is not just added on to Dick's story in order to make the movie commercially viable (although that can't be ignored either). The love story gives us the counterpoint to this vision of the gray, ashen office. Of course in the film, the image of the work involved changes quite a bit—politics and dance don't involve the same uncommitted drudgery as Ed Fletcher's office job—but the movie does retain some of the Man in the Gray Flannel Suit aesthetic, and the motivating tension here is that of personal commitments set against one's role in society. Norris does not want to do what's expected of him, or even to pursue his own best interests (as defined by everyone but him). He won't stick with the plan, and puts his emotional commitments ahead of his career—an inspiring sacrifice which women make every day, but which somehow only counts as heroism worthy of an action film when a man does it.

To choose love over career is exactly the kind of thing that we're told not to do as well. Not just in the literal sense of sacrificing success for a relationship, but love in the broadest sense: choosing to pursue your passions and values, even when they are impractical, unlikely, or crazy. And this is the ultimate solution in the movie: when we refuse to follow the plan, and do what we will, sometimes we find out that the plan wasn't the only way to do things.

Terrible Freedom

It's very dangerous to choose not to follow the plan, and Dick knew this as well as anyone. Those who reject the whole deal, who drop out of the rat race—they live on the fringes, often without feeling that they're even a part of society. To some extent, this is because that feeling of being in a society was an illusion to begin with. (This is another function of celebrities: they give us a bunch of people we all can pretend to know in common, which helps us feel like we actually live as part of a group; as if we had a society instead of just an economy.) But to some extent, this is because it's so hard to tell which parts of the plan are good and which parts are bad, and in our desire to be free, we too often throw away prudence and thoughtfulness as if they were just the same as these other ways we are controlled and occluded.

Consider, for example, these comments from Dick's "Author's Note" in *A Scanner Darkly*:

This has been a novel about some people who were punished entirely too much for what they did. They wanted to have a good time, but they were like children playing in the street; they could see one after another of them being killed—run over, maimed, destroyed—but they continued to play anyhow. We really all were very happy for a while, sitting around not toiling but just bullshitting and playing, but it was for such a terrible brief time, and then the punishment was beyond belief: even when we could see it, we could not believe it.

Drug misuse is not a disease, it is a decision, like the decision to step out in front of a moving car. You would call that not a disease but an error in judgment. When a bunch of people begin to do it, it is a social error, a life-style. In this particular life-style the motto is "Be happy now because tomorrow you are dying," but the dying begins almost at once, and the happiness is a memory. It is, then, only a speeding up, an intensifying, of the ordinary human existence. It is not different from your life-style, it is only faster.

The desire to be free and to be self-determining is not to be blamed here. This is the desire that made so many question the plan in the 1960s. It moved us beyond the healthy rejection of the stifling conformity of the 1950s (or "the man-in-the-gray-flannel-suit problem," as Dick called it in his comments on "The Mold of Yancy"), and moved into great and dangerous experiments in how to live. Why not question war? Why not question segregation? Why not question monogamy? Why not question my body's "normal" chemistry?

Through his claim, here, that the druggie life-style is "no different from your life-style," he's trying to make clear that druggies are not deviants and weirdoes who can't be understood; druggies are just those who, in striving for freedom and happiness, threw out some of the good parts of "the plan" along with the bad parts.

Dick went on to say, "There is no moral in this novel; it is not bourgeois; it does not say they were wrong to play when they should have toiled; it just tells what the consequences were." The 'bourgeois moralizing' that he doesn't want to do would have told us that they were *punished* because they were *wrong* to no longer be part of our endless cycle of making crap and buying crap and doing all the crap we're expected to do. He refused to say that, because he thought it was bullshit. That bourgeois moralizing is just part of this vast, sinister conspiracy to control you; part of this system of social determinism. But there's another kind of determinism here too: *natural* determinism, "morally neutral," "impartial cause-and-effect." That's what brought down the druggies, and that's why, in our struggle to be free, we have to not just reject control, but also take control.

Pre-Crime and Pre-Punishment

All this has been about freedom and determinism as concrete concerns that we live with (and through) on a daily basis. Here, it is not so surprising that Dick would turn out to be a social-political philosopher rather than an epistemologist or metaphysician. But even when he takes on classic topics of epistemology and metaphysics, his questions are still about value and about how we should live. Among other places, we see this clearly when Dick actually takes on the classic debate about free will in its metaphysical form. This tendency to approach what looks like a purely abstract and logical question and to ask, "What's at stake here?"; to seek out the psychological and political motivation of asking or of resolving the question—this approach, sometimes called "the hermeneutics of suspicion," is something that Dick has in common with Nietzsche.

Friedrich Nietzsche claimed that the free will-determinism debate was important to the history of European thought because, if we didn't believe in a radically metaphysically free will, we could not be threatened with just punishment for our supposed sins, and then the priests would lose their power over us. "Men," Nietzsche wrote in *Twilight of the Idols*, "were considered 'free' only so that they might be considered guilty— could be judged and punished: consequently, every act had to be considered as lying within the consciousness."

It is characteristic of Nietzsche that, when his gaze settles upon one of the great metaphysical debates of the European tradition, his question is what's at stake in terms of power and control. While Dick is more interested than Nietzsche in playing around with the details and logic of the debate, he too does not fail to note the role of politics even in metaphysics.

This is why, among the many fascinating discussions of free will and determinism, I think the right framework to understand "Minority Report" is St. Anselm's *De Concordia Praescientiae et Praedestinationis et Gratiae Dei cum Libero Arbitrio*. It's not that I think Dick had Anselm in mind, but rather that they were both concerned not only with the logic of foreknowledge, but its relationship to guilt and, by implication at least, the justice or injustice of punishment.

Anselm's question is how foreknowledge can be compatible with free will. If God is all-knowing, then he must know the future, including what we will choose to do. But if he knows what we choose, that means that what we choose must be *knowable*—it must be one thing rather than another. But, if what we *will* choose is *already* one thing rather than another, how can we be said to freely choose, since the future is already *this* future rather than *that* one?

The solution, for Anselm, is a simple one, although not less conceptually difficult for its simplicity: God is outside of time. The future, for God, is kind of like the past for us—since God is eternal, the future is kind of like something that already happened. So, Anselm reasons, God can know the future without the future being determined—without, in fact, its even being *determinable*.

This particular solution is important for Anselm for all the reasons Nietzsche identified, and every other solution seems to have troublingly heretical implications. If we are not completely and absolutely free in our choice, we cannot be completely and absolutely responsible for our choice. And our responsibility must be absolute indeed if a God is to be justified in condemning us to infinite torment. Even so, the image of the abusive father is hard to banish—"Now look what you've made me do," God seems to say. Wouldn't a loving God change things so that we would choose something else instead, like the paternalistic God of *The Adjustment Bureau*? Perhaps God cares more about us following orders than he does about the right thing actually getting done.

Through "Minority Report," Dick brings up all the same questions as Anselm. Why use foreknowledge to punish instead of to preclude? As with Anselm's solution, it must be because the pre-criminal is *already* guilty of having (not-yet) freely decided to commit a crime. To be guilty, now, of a crime not yet committed, we must be absolutely free to choose to do otherwise, and yet our future choice must already be known with absolute certainty. After Pre-Crime figures this out—well, the possibility of telling someone about their future and giving them a chance to do otherwise, in the light of this prediction, is irrelevant. The pre-criminal is already guilty of a future-crime, and deserving of punishment. And so too with God: preventing the sin might be nice, but that prevention wouldn't remove the guilt of the pre-sinner. And so it comes down to predestination and grace.

"Minority Report" was published at the end of 1954. Joseph McCarthy was head of the Senate Permanent Subcommittee on Investigations. The House Un-American Activities Committee had been a standing committee for ten years and the Red Scare still raged. State-department-run libraries burned books by authors whose anti-Communist commitments were in question. The FBI, under J. Edgar Hoover, anonymously sent out documents accusing teachers and lawyers of Communist association. Eisenhower had just signed the Communist Control Act of 1954 into law, which outlawed the American Communist Party as a "clear, present, and continuing danger to the security of the United States," making membership a criminal act.

Even peaceful and democratic criticism of capitalism had become legally equated with contributing to future violence and evil. Those blacklisted and suspected were punished not for what they did, nor even what they said, nor even what they believed—they were punished for their present guilt of support for that future crime that must be prevented: the violent Communist overthrow of the United States.

Freedom and Madness

The real-world meaning and stakes of "pre-crime" and "pre-guilt" may have been clearer to Dick's audience then than they are to us today. Today this meaning and these stakes are perhaps harder to see, but no less real. As one example of a growing return of McCarthyism, Michelle Bachmann (R-MN) called Barack Obama "anti-American," and said she wished "the American media would take a great look at the views of the people in Congress and find out, are they pro-America or anti-America?"

In the realm of pre-crime, Guantánamo still holds forty-eight detainees described by the US Government in the January 2010 *Final Report* of the Guantánamo Review Task

Force as "too dangerous to transfer but not feasible for prosecution." Our representatives are increasingly acting in ways which only make sense given outlandish and insupportable conspiracy theories, for example, outlawing Sharia law in Oklahoma, and introducing birth-certificate-certification proposals in the state legislatures of thirteen states.

In the same way, the drop-outs and druggies today are perhaps less obvious than in the Sixties, and the problem of conformity is less clear and pressing today than it was in the Fifties. But these two coupled social problems have certainly not disappeared. The challenge to us today is the same: how can we refuse to be determined and live a life of freedom without losing perspective and losing control? As a conceptual problem, staying grounded without getting buried is not so difficult. As a practical problem, it's very difficult indeed.

In his later life, Dick confronted this issue in a different way. In making sense of his mystical experience with a pink beam of light, he found he needed to free himself from his belief in conventional reality. But once the floodgates opened, he found himself writing in his *Exegesis* about telepathic crab-clawed invaders from Sirius who brought religion to the ancient Dogon tribe, and he spent his last years writing brilliant semi-autobiographical novels in an attempt to gain some perspective on his own ever-shifting belief system.

In all these ways freedom and determinism, for Phil Dick, are not just about knowledge or fundamental reality. Freedom and determinism are also about, perhaps primarily about, how to live: what we need to do to be free, how we are being determined and adjusted, and, most of all, how to be *self-determining*—how to be free from the determinisms and occlusions of received social, political, economic, and religious reality without careening off into the void through drugs, isolation, or madness.[1]

---

[1] Thanks to *Speakeasy*, *The Wall Street Journal's* blog about media, entertainment, celebrity, and the arts, and to *Speakeasy* senior editor Christopher John Farley for permission to reprint portions of my 3/5/11 article, "Can 'The Adjustment Bureau' Save Your Life?"

10

How to Build a Democracy that Doesn't Fall Apart Two Hundred Years Later

BEN SAUNDERS

The existence of 'pre-cogs'—telepaths with an ability to see the future—is a common feature of Dick's stories. In *The Three Stigmata of Palmer Eldritch*, Barney Mayerson uses his powers for business advantage, while in "The Minority Report" pre-cogs are used to prosecute people for future-crimes.

Their role needn't be so limited though. If we had people who could predict what was going to happen before it did, then why not have them installed as our law-makers as well as enforcers? This happens in *The World Jones Made*, where Jones is appointed as ruler in the face of threatened alien attack.

We may not be facing an invasion of extra-terrestrials, but imagine how much better life might be if our politicians were able to foresee events such as terrorist attacks or stock market crashes before they happened. If there were such people among us, wouldn't we want them to rule over us? And, given that there aren't, how should political offices be assigned?

Rule of the Wise

The Greek philosopher Plato recommended rule by philosophers, rather than pre-cogs, because he thought only they had the necessary knowledge. This would have sounded as ridiculous to Plato's original audience as to modern ears. But Plato didn't mean the kind of philosophers that exist today, such as the authors writing in this book.

The term 'philosopher' comes from the Greek for lover (philo) of wisdom (sophos). Plato simply meant that the wise or knowledgeable should rule. If we update his claim for a modern audience, it would be that experts ought to rule. Military decisions should be made by generals, medical decisions by doctors, and—Plato thought—political decisions by those with political skill or expertise.

Perhaps if Plato had read Dick, and knew of any pre-cogs, he would've said that they should rule. He portrayed his mentor, Socrates, as guided by a 'divine sign' that warned him of danger, so perhaps he thought of Socrates as a pre-cog of sorts. If we had pre-cogs, like Jones, Agatha Lively, or Socrates, then their knowledge of the future would enable them to make wise decisions, and so Plato would've insisted that they should rule over the rest of us for our own good.

Sadly, perhaps, this is mere wishful thinking. We may have fortune tellers and astrologers in our midst, but their predictions are generally so vague that they can't be proven right or wrong. Few would suggest that we ought to give power to these people simply because they claim to see the future.

The idea that the most knowledgeable or competent should rule still has a certain appeal. We wouldn't want children or the mentally incompetent governing us. We don't even let them vote. If we had a wise group of experts in our midst though, why not give them power to make decisions for us?

One reason is that anyone can claim to be an expert, but we lack any accepted test for who is and who is not one. Various religious leaders claim to be moral authorities or to know the future from revelation. Since these self-proclaimed authorities disagree though, there's no reason for the rest of us to accept the commands of one rather than another.

We all think that some people possess more political expertise than others. Unfortunately, there's little agreement on who these wise rulers are. Some believe that Sarah Palin should rule and others that Barack Obama should. Presumably the supporters of each side believe that their favored candidate is the one who'll make the best decisions. Unless we can reach consensus on who the experts are, the idea that experts should rule cannot guide us.

What's the best that we can do in the absence of any such agreement? In the modern world, democratic elections are regarded as essential for legitimate rule. If most people think that Obama's the best choice to govern, then he should be president. But those who doubt the competence of ordinary people are unlikely to regard them as any more capable of electing wise leaders than of governing themselves. That's why the Founding Fathers introduced the Electoral College. Plato argued that asking the people to choose their rulers is like asking children to choose between a doctor's medicine and a confectioner's candy. They choose what they like, rather than what's actually good for them.

Any attempt to choose rulers by election is bound to be controversial. Modern politics has degenerated into a near constant competition of personalities seeking re-election. The claim that any of these politicians possess special expertise or foresight would rightly be viewed by most with suspicion. Surely none of them are pre-cogs or they'd make better decisions. But is there an alternative?

Spinning a Bottle

Contemporary American politics is dominated by Republicans and Democrats. This wasn't how it was supposed to operate. James Madison sought to avoid conflict between competing factions. Ancient Athenian democracy—the system Plato was criticizing—managed to avoid factionalism because, rather than being elected, most office holders were appointed by a lottery, using a device known as a *kleroterion*. This was regarded as a particularly democratic means of selection, since it gives all an equal chance of appointment. A lottery is blind to any claims of special competence or expertise.

We can get some insight into how such a system might work from Dick's first published novel, *Solar Lottery*. In this remarkably prophetic work, Dick describes how twentieth-century crises of over-production led to a society dominated by television quizzes. Prizes escalated from material goods to power and prestige, until the position of Quizmaster became the most important prize of all. The Quizmaster is effective ruler of the known galaxy and head of a vast Directorate.

The Bottle game that determines the Quizmaster seems to depend on luck rather than skill. Some games rely wholly on one or the other. Chess is a pure game of skill, with no random element, whereas chutes and ladders depends solely on the throw of dice. Others involve both chance and skill. Poker, for instance, requires strategy but players are somewhat at the mercy of the cards they are dealt. The presence of mind-reading 'teeps' means that any strategy is predictable, thereby turning the game into one of chance.

Reese Verrick claims to possess skill in the Bottle game, which has allowed him to retain his position as Quizmaster so long. Those who get a run of good cards in a casino often attribute their fortune to skill, and Verrick may be similarly deluded. Whether or not the Bottle involves or rewards strategy, its random twitches are capable of defeating even the most skilful player. Such an unexpected twitch deposes Verrick and promotes Leon Cartwright, an unclassified electronics repairman and leader of the Prestonite sect, in his place.

Appointing rulers randomly may seem outlandish. Lotteries have been used for many purposes though, including appointing juries, drafting soldiers, and allocating green cards to US immigrants. Maybe choosing politicians in this manner would bring government closer to the people.

In their 1985 book, *A Citizen Legislature*, Michael Philips and Ernest Callenbach suggest just this. They recommend replacing the present elected House of Representatives with a randomly selected sample of ordinary people. This, they argue, would result in truly representative government: a portrait of the people in miniature, ensuring that all groups in society (blacks, Latinos, women, religious, atheists, and so on) were represented in government.

The proposal to select a representative chamber randomly is obviously different from appointing a single individual—like the Quizmaster or president—by lottery, but many of the same principles apply.

Throwing the Rascals Out

Selecting rulers randomly would protect us from tyrants or dictators. While this threat may seem distant to those of us living in established democracies, it was a live possibility not only for the ancient Athenians but even for the American Founding Fathers. The system of checks and balances they devised, including the separation of powers, was largely designed to prevent any one individual from possessing too much power. The two-term limit on presidential office, introduced by the

Twenty-second Amendment, had a similar rationale. A pessimistic defense of democratic elections regards them as no more than a means to ensure regular turnover of rule. Such an account was offered by the twentieth-century Austrian economist Joseph Schumpeter.

Schumpeter was skeptical of any claim that elections revealed a meaningful 'popular will'. Ordinary people, he noted, are so far removed from politics that they are easily swayed by crowd psychology, and put more thought into a game of bridge than how to vote. He viewed political competition as rather like the marketplace. There's a danger that if one firm or party has a monopoly they will abuse their power, so customers or voters will suffer. Elections ensure rotation of office, so no leader can persist for too long.

A slightly more optimistic view is that the prospect of re-election will encourage politicians to moderate abuses of their power in order to hold on to office in future. But this assumes that voters will recognize abuses and hold their leaders to account. If that's unlikely, elections might as well be replaced by a lottery. This ensures that, sooner or later, all rulers will be thrown out of office. None can have permanent possession of power.

Herb Moore recognizes such reasoning in *Solar Lottery* when he informs Cartwright that the random twitch of the Bottle prevents dictators. No one can be sure of his or her status in the future. Random selection brings another danger though. The person selected may simply be incompetent.

Checks and Challenges

The Bottle appoints someone as Quizmaster. Since the selection is random, anyone can be chosen, regardless of qualifications. There's no guarantee that they will be fit for the task. They may even be completely psychotic, like Robin Pitt, Quizmaster number thirty-four. We want some means of removing such individuals, before they do too much damage. This is all the more important when the ruler is a single individual, rather than a chamber of four hundred and thirty-five, where a few crackpots may do little harm.

One way they can lose office is if the Bottle twitches again, but it would be foolish to rely entirely on such random machinery, given that it's this mechanism that selected them in the first place. A deliberate way of removing officeholders is necessary; something like removing a president by impeachment, without having to wait for the next election.

The ancient Greeks recognized this need too. They weren't prepared to let their kleroterion select anyone at all. One way they excluded undesirable or incompetent officials was by restricting eligibility to adult citizens—which, for them, meant men of certain wealth. They also subjected all those selected to a process of scrutiny or trial before they could hold office and had arrangements for fining or removing those guilty of acting unconstitutionally.

Dick's society has similar mechanisms. Though unks (unclassified lower classes) could technically be chosen by the Bottle, most of them sell their power cards, which are their tickets to the lottery. This ensures that they never get to rule. Even if their number comes up, it's the holder of their power card who benefits.

This trade seems rational, given the six-billion-to-one odds against any single power card being selected. Imagine if someone offered to buy your lottery ticket for $50. While it could be worth a fortune, the chances are it won't win, so this seems a good price. Someone buying up all the tickets this way can ensure that no one else can win. The consequence is that power is concentrated in the hands of those who hold the power cards, which undercuts any democratic justification for the Bottle. As Cartwright recognizes, the rules of the game are stacked heavily against the unks.

The more formal check is something known as the Challenge. An officially appointed assassin is charged with the task of killing the incumbent Quizmaster. An incompetent Quizmaster, it is assumed, will soon be assassinated. This artificial selection mechanism filters out incompetent Quizmasters, ensuring that only the fittest survive.

The Bottle and Challenge form two complementary halves of a selection procedure. The random element is designed to give all a chance of office and to prevent anyone, however competent, from enduring too long. The threat of assassination is supposed to remove anyone incompetent swiftly, so only those who at least moderately capable remain in office long.

You might question whether skill in avoiding assassination is any predictor of competence to rule. Perhaps a person could be very good at staying alive but very bad at governing. Similar questions could be asked about electioneering though. A candidate might be very good at winning votes, but still ill-suited to office. Maybe the spin of a Bottle, at least with an accompanying Challenge, is no worse a selection mechanism for rulers than our media-driven elections.

How Can Random Machinery Be Rational?

Disgruntled at being defeated by a twitch of the Bottle, Verrick questions the rationality of the whole system. His grumbling is no doubt partly due to being a sore loser. I'm sure many politicians complain about losing elections they thought they should win too. It may seem that Verrick's criticism has some merit, though.

Lotteries have often been derided as irrational, because they replace reasoned human choice with blind chance. Random selection can indeed throw someone out of office for no reason and elevate in his place someone picked without any regard to merit or ability. Why would we want someone picked in this way? Surely, if we want competent rulers, we'd do better to choose them ourselves than leave the matter to luck.

A lottery isn't inherently rational, but nor is it irrational. It's just a tool that we can use to make certain decisions. Tools can't be rational or irrational—only agents can act for, or against, reasons. Tools are better regarded as arational; simply lacking in rationality, rather than opposed to it.

Sometimes it's irrational to make decisions by lottery, for instance to choose a career or life partner. These are cases where people can usually make better choices for themselves. There'd be a real loss if these choices were taken away from people and replaced with random allocations. A system of arranged marriages, organized by lottery, would probably be disastrous.

This doesn't mean that there's anything intrinsically irrational about lotteries though, merely that they're an inappropriate tool to use in such circumstances. It's like using a screwdriver to open a can of beer or a key to turn a screw. You might manage to achieve your goal, but it isn't the best tool for the job—and not because it's a bad tool.

We can't assess the tools themselves for rationality, because tools aren't the kind of thing that can be either rational or irrational. We can only assess people, since only people make reasoned choices. If you decide to use a key to turn a screw, when you had a better tool to hand, then your decision's irrational. Similarly if you use a lottery to make a decision where it isn't really appropriate, we might judge you (or your choice) as irrational, but not the lottery.

There are cases where it's rational and appropriate to use a lottery though. One might want to be unpredictable in order to avoid others second-guessing one's course. In *Solar Lottery*, this is how people respond to the threat of being teeped. When there's a risk that your intentions could be known in advance by others, the safest strategy is a random, unplanned course of action. In *Solar Lottery*, this was the approach used by the assassin DeFalla and supposedly perfected by Keith Pellig.

Lotteries may also be justified when we want to ensure impartiality. This applies to cases like the military draft or green card lottery. Here we think that all should have an equal chance and no one should have the power—or responsibility—of choosing.

Verrick's complaint is inappropriate. The random rotation of office is purposively designed to stop anyone from holding power too long, lest they abuse it. As Major Shaeffer reveals, Verrick was close to removing the random element altogether, so he could hold on to power. That's all the more reason to remove him, before he became too dangerous.

There's nothing rational or irrational about the Bottle in itself, but there are very good reasons for people to use this random mechanism (accompanied by the Challenge) in appointing their rulers. Where there are good reasons to employ a lottery, it's perfectly rational to do so.

Giving and Selling

Choosing rulers randomly may still seem like a bad idea, since it can result in people being picked who don't want office, while those who want it aren't selected. But, really, this could be one of its advantages.

Plato warns that we should be suspicious of those, like Verrick, who want to rule. Having invested so much to win power, they're likely to seek personal gain from it. Plato thinks this is another reason to favor rule by philosophers. He thinks philosophers would regard rule as an onerous duty and need to be compelled to take office. Maybe it's not such a bad thing if those selected for office don't have to be ambitious and power-hungry in order to get there.

There might be good reasons why some prefer to avoid serving in office. Perhaps we should allow people to exempt themselves from being picked by the Bottle if they wish. Rather than exclude them completely though, we could allow them to nominate substitutes to serve in their place. This means that, instead of everyone having an equal chance of being picked, those who wished to avoid office could transfer their chances to those that wanted it. Some would have no chance of selection and others would have greater chances, corresponding to the number of supporters they had (who'd given them their power cards).

Such a system would be less equal, but better respect people's choices. Rulers wouldn't be chosen completely at random, but a random element still operates—along with people's choices—to determine whose ticket (or power card) is chosen.

The society described in *Solar Lottery* goes further than this. Not only can power cards be given away, they can also be bought and sold. The result is that those with money can buy political power, or at least a greater chance of it. Assuming it's permissible for people to give power to others, why shouldn't we let them sell it too?

Some people think that government shouldn't interfere with individuals' private choices, including any contracts they wish to enter voluntarily. Not everything we have can be voluntarily transferred though, much less sold. You can't choose to give someone else your job. And we don't always permit people to sell what we allow them to give. You're free to donate your bodily organs or to have sex with any willing adult partner you can find, but the selling of organs or sex (prostitution) is commonly criminalized. It doesn't follow from the fact that you can give someone else your vote or power card that you also have the right to sell it to them.

We might think that people shouldn't be allowed to buy political office for the same reason that Plato was suspicious of those who want it. If people buy office, they'll likely seek to profit from it, which would make them bad rulers for the rest of us. Buying and selling of offices is also likely to increase the social divide between rich and poor, as the rich come to own not only luxury goods but positions of power and prestige.

American society is already unequal, but at least those born at the bottom have the in-principle opportunity to rise to the top (the 'American dream' of social mobility). The emergence of a formal division, like that between the classified and unks, would destroy this opportunity. As Cartwright realized, there's no reason for the unks to continue to play by the rules of the game if they find those rules stacked against them. Lani Guinier, whose proposals for electoral reform led to her being smeared with the racially-loaded title of 'Quota Queen', had much the same thought about American politics.

Many recent advocates of lotteries for political offices have been trying to reduce the undue influence of money in contemporary politics. Allowing people to buy and sell their chances would undercut the democratic rationale of ensuring equal chances for all and representative government.

One day we may have pre-cogs who can be trusted to rule over us. Until then, Dick points to possible political reforms, which worked for the ancient Greeks and may still be useful to us today. *Solar Lottery* reminds us that we shouldn't trust wholly to chance, but need to combine any selection mechanism like the Bottle with a check like the Challenge (though perhaps not exactly like it). Just as important though is the warning to be wary of those, like Verrick or Cartwright, who would seek to tamper with the random machinery for their own ends. As Plato knew, the machinations of men who seek power can be more dangerous than any lottery.[1]

---

[1] Thanks to Mindy Peden, Dylan Wittkower, and an audience at the University of Stirling Philosophy Society (November 2010) for helpful comments.

11

We Can Manipulate You Wholesale

Louis Melançon

There's an early scene in *Total Recall* when Quaid is at work and has a conversation with his buddy Harry about using Rekall's services. There's a little bit of foreshadowing with Harry's emphatic suggestion that Quaid stay away from that company. And the movie dives straight into telegraphing when the camera closes in on Harry as the two of them return to work and we can see Harry's shifty eyes giving Quaid a wary measure.

That's how you can always pick out the bad guys—they have shifty eyes. This is confirmed a few scenes later when Harry and some goons snatch Quaid with the intent to cause him significant harm in as much as they plan on killing him. Well, we know for sure now that Harry is at least a bad friend, but possibly even a bad person. After all, the bond with Quaid is based on deliberate deception geared towards the directive manipulation of Quaid's actions.

What unfolds for the audience is that Harry has been directed to befriend Quaid in an attempt to control and direct what he does and, when that fails, he has orders to tidy up the situation, in a bloody fashion if necessary. Is Harry an immoral person, or is his job simply putting him in danger of being damaged morally by placing him in these situations?

As the movie goes on we find out that the same situation exists with Quaid's wife Lori, his cab driver, Benny, and confusingly enough, Hauser—an entire other person whose memories, emotions, and motivations have been hidden either in his history, inside his own brain, or both. All these people are establishing relationships with Quaid and then manipulating and directing his actions through deceit and deception to achieve an agenda.

The deception here is different from that time you claimed to be an astronaut to get that girl's phone number. The deception and manipulation from all of the individuals is sanctioned and directed by some outside element—the element actually setting the agenda of the relationship. And while the use of an individual by another poses some problems from a Kantian moral perspective, having an outside element which sanctions and directs individuals to perform such activity is potentially enough to have Immanuel Kant spin in his grave.

Sure I Deceived You, but What about Me?

This isn't the only time this type of situation crops up in Philip K. Dick's work—an outside element manipulating, controlling, and directing a person, often through some form of deception. Two examples we can look at are *A Scanner Darkly* (both book and movie) and *Total Recall* (based on the story, "We Can Remember It for You Wholesale").

Bob Arctor (in *A Scanner Darkly*) is in law enforcement conducting clandestine evidence collection, Quail (in "Wholesale") is in covert action, and Quaid (in *Total Recall*) is involved in human intelligence (HUMINT) operations and covert action. Each of these have different desired outcomes: for law enforcement it's to make an arrest, for covert action it's to have something happen without people being able to attribute it to a true sponsor (and in both *Total Recall* and its original story, these actions appear to involve lots of shooting and explosions), and for HUMINT the goal is about getting information that would otherwise not be available.

Yes, there are different goals and different terminology, but both undercover police work and government intelligence work are forms of spying. We see a common thread: one party attempting to manipulate another—or perhaps even to dominate the other, as this is often described in real-world study and training, as James McCargar does in *A Short Course in the Secret War*.

So how does one person manipulate another? Well, by finding weaknesses and linking desired behaviors to weakness incentives.

Finding a Lever for Manipulation

The acronym often associated with identifying and incentivizing weaknesses for manipulation within the study and training circles for spying is MISE: Money, Ideology, Sex and Ego. Sometimes the less salacious version MICE, where C becomes Compromise, is used, but let's be salacious!

Perhaps the individual you wish to manipulate is in some cash-flow straits—you could provide some relief. Or you are aware of some sexual peccadilloes that they would rather remain unknown to family and friends—you could offer ways that they could keep this secret. Or perhaps the person just has a huge ego that you could build up to get your desired result or crush to push them back into line if they start to get out of hand.

Let's dig into an example with "Fred," Bob Arctor's persona within the police department to highlight this in action. "Fred's" assignment is to establish relationships with various drug users and dealers in order to gain their trust and elicit further information about the distribution system. This will allow him to establish additional relationships with those more-connected drug dealers which he can then use to elicit further information about even higher level drug dealers, all the while sending this information to the LA County Police Department to assist in their greater understanding of the drug network and gain sufficient evidence for criminal prosecutions. The method for "Fred" to do this is to establish a relationship, primarily based on the exchange of money for drugs with someone under false pretenses (namely, that "Fred" isn't a cop) and slowly build trust through drug use and ever increasing purchases of drugs.

A situation eventually emerges where the manipulated individual can no longer meet "Fred's" commercial exchange requirements but a level of trust has been established. So they must assist "Fred" in establishing another relationship with someone with whom they have established trust. This is a deliberately engineered situation where "Fred" is causing the manipulated half of the relationship to unwittingly betray the trust of another for "Fred's" benefit. His new buddy (or girlfriend) is a means to an end which likely will be just another means to a different end.

Although the circumstances and desired outcomes are different, the same thing applies to Lori, Harry and Hauser, among others, against Quaid in *Total Recall*. Each of these individuals has created a relationship to achieve a specific end, which sometimes appear to be at cross-purposes. But the method they use remains the same regardless of goal—establish a relationship with Quaid in order to manipulate him. Quaid becomes nothing more than a means: for Lori and Harry to monitor and prevent his return to Mars; for Hauser to find the identity and location of the rebel leadership.

Categorically, We Have an Imperative Problem

Whether we're talking about "Fred," Lori, Harry, Hauser, or a variety of other characters in these works the problem is that all are using someone else as a means to their end, principally Bob Arctor and Quaid. This is a moral problem because treating an individual merely as a means becomes a huge violation of the second formulation of Kant's "categorical imperative," which claims that people are valuable as ends in themselves and shouldn't be treated merely as a means. Or, in other words, people deserve respect, and you shouldn't use them as merely a tool but recognize their intrinsic value as a human.

This manipulative behavior is devaluing the humanity of the manipulated individuals. In each given situation, the true amount of devaluation may be variable—it all depends on exactly how much of a means the individual is considered to be. Benny, the mutant taxi driver, only slightly devalues Quaid by following him around and tracking his movements (setting aside trying to crush him with a massive drilling machine). "Fred," on the other hand, is entirely devalued by federal drug agents as they sacrifice his entire psyche. But a Kantian perspective doesn't allow for any consideration of minor or major devaluation context—it simply can't occur. Should the devaluation dilemma be avoided altogether by not spying?

There have been real-world discussions of limiting such activity due in part to this problem of devaluing the humanity of individuals. In the history of this debate in an American context, the largest open discussion of this occurred in the mid-1970s with the Pike and Church Committees which examined inappropriate intelligence activities by a wide variety of US government elements. These committees highlighted a whole slew of ethical dilemmas and some, such as J.E. Drexel Godfrey writing in *Foreign Affairs*, made a case for spying using primarily technological means rather than through human manipulation.

There are also those, such as John Langan (in Jan Goldman's *Ethics of Spying* compilation) who argue against Mr. Godfrey. The primary line of argument is utilitarian: there are some situations where technological means cannot divulge the information or achieve the end which is sought, or where using humans may be the least intrusive mechanism for achieving the end. This all rests on the assertion that the safety of the larger society requires whatever is the end in question, and so the devaluing of a few is acceptable.

Utilitarian Doesn't Necessarily Mean Coveralls

A Scanner Darkly provides an excellent jumping-off point for this utilitarian argument. As the novel progresses, we find out a few sketchy things about New Path, such as that they own large portions of land that neither federal, state, nor local governments have the capability to examine or inspect through technical means. And it appears that nothing has been gained by human spying efforts by various law enforcement elements to infiltrate or otherwise determine the business model and practices of New Path. The utilitarian line of argument seems to hold some water. This gains even more traction when placed in the context of the horrifying effects of a Substance D addiction, the ever-increasing population using and addicted to that drug, and the social need to somehow address the problem.

It could seem acceptable in such a situation to attempt to maximize the positive outcomes for as many people as possible at the expense of a few. Enter Bob Arctor. Unknown to him, as either "Fred" or Bob Arctor, he has been selected by federal agents to be one of these sacrificed few—manipulated into an ever-increasing addiction to Substance D to the point of mental breakdown while having the stimulus of little flowers reinforced into his subconscious for an eventual penetration of New Path's work farms assisted by a small network of recruited spies aware of portions of the plan. Not only is Bob just another means to the end being sought by law enforcement; it seems he will likely never recover enough to truly be an end himself again—to be an able-minded and self-determining person.

This is a pretty harsh conclusion for Bob Arctor, and there's no denying that he was damaged through this spying—the use of Substance D, compounded with the deceptions he was perpetrating on those he was seeking to gain information from, and his unwitting use by others to be placed in a position to access additional information. But the potential outcome hinted at the conclusion of the story is that the source of Substance D, New Path, could be eliminated, preventing continuing addiction to the drug. The Kantian rebuttal to all this is that the actions which made Bob to be acted upon should never have occurred, even were society to collapse because the actions were not taken.

We see the damage to the manipulated, but there are some other considerations too. We might feel sorry for Bob Arctor, but Quail was a professional assassin. We might not have as much concern that he was deceived by the Imperial Police and himself in order to cover up his various shooty-explody adventures. And Quaid (well, Hauser) doesn't appear to be such a nice guy so maybe the deception might have inadvertently turned Quaid into a better person. Stranger things have happened. So there is a tension here. And in recognizing the tension we can highlight one item that is often overlooked: the potential for moral damage on the part of the manipulator. Could there be an even larger victim—the person who wittingly violates and disregards the categorical imperative?

Only Remembered as the Blonde Shot in the Head

Let's rewind back to Harry and Lori, Quaid's two minders who were to trace and influence his actions in order to keep him away from Rekall and discovering his true identity. They do some nasty things, these two: they lie, they sleep around on their spouses, and they are willing to kill. But does this make them immoral people? Perhaps we need a bit more context. Going back to the utilitarian argument, they have conducted this naughty behavior as part of a directed plan from a government to whom they owe allegiance, so, while this is voluntary, it isn't as if they're doing these things for fun and profit (as far as we know). Maybe they aren't immoral people at their core. It could be that these actions, repugnant as they might seem to an outsider just discovering the deception, are saving thousands or millions of lives. If this is the case, then perhaps we could overlook their brutish behavior?

But we know this isn't the case. The government they serve isn't particularly moral itself. Rather than focus on the safety and well-being of those they have been appointed to rule, the administration is about maximizing profit, ensuring production is maintained, and resolving disagreements between the rulers and ruled with the one-way dialogue of the truncheon and rifle. True, there is hesitancy about activating the alien device—it may be a bomb—but based on other actions in the movie this is likely simple self-preservation. But, it isn't very interesting to talk about immoral people working for an immoral government. Let's set aside what we know about the Martian government and assume that it is maybe amoral, but not outright immoral.

We don't know enough about Lori or Harry to determine if their moral compasses were already less-than-optimally calibrated before they began to undertake the lines of work which led to this eventual job assignment. It could be that neither of them ever had a really good handle on what was moral or immoral, or it could be that being asked to continually engage in increasingly morally questionable activities slowly ate away at what they thought and felt was proper and correct. Quite frankly, it doesn't matter. The employer, in this case a government organization, that bases an employee's position on violating the rights of individuals for a utilitarian end is quite likely to cause damage to the moral framework of the individuals in question, whether or not they were already askew to begin with. For Godfrey, mentioned earlier, this is the crux of the issue.

Like People, Like Organizations

Much like the individuals being directed to conduct spying, we can look up at least one level to think about the moral environment of the organizations which orchestrate all of this. An underlying assertion here is that organizations, although composed of individuals, can take on individuality themselves—a unique persona often labeled as organizational culture. Just as there is a risk to moral damage to the individuals working for a spying organization, there's also the risk of creating an immoral organizational culture.

After all, the organization has now taken on the role of manipulator of its own employees—convincing them to perform utilitarian actions on behalf of the organization which devalues other individuals. The cost here is the devaluing of the employee's humanity through accumulation of moral damage. This is quite the vicious cycle. And it really comes to the fore with the Los Angeles County Police Department—compartmentalizing itself to the extent that narcotics detectives do not know if they are establishing relationships for exploitation with other narcotics detectives, or even who their supervisors may be. In such a culture, the moral damage can spread rapidly, and "Fred" even reflects on the fact that to support his case work against Bob Arctor may require his employing organization to install illegal surveillance devices.

It would be one thing if "Fred" addressed this with irony—an organization whose mission is to uphold the rule of law breaking it themselves in order to execute their mission—instead it is taken as a matter of course. Just as it is considered normal that "Fred" never knows the true identity of "Hank," his supervisor, and vice versa. The organization creates an opportunity which allows them to lie to each other about what they might know of the developing case; in fact, both seem required by their job duties to do so. Not only is that an organizational culture that isn't terribly efficient, it's one which is morally damaging to its employees and likely creating a morally damaged organizational culture.

If there is such high risk of moral damage to both individuals and organizations in the utilitarian line of argument, are we forced back to the Kantian line of not spying at all? Not necessarily—identification of risk means that risk controls can be established. If those controls are implemented effectively, the risk is mitigated and potentially avoided, which allows continued use of the utilitarian line up to a point. Of course, the amount of mitigation and resulting decrease in risk level will be different from control to control, situation to situation. This is a step beyond simply accepting human-enabled spying as the least intrusive means of gathering needed information without going so far as to deny individuals of having some intrinsic value. But it also requires a significant compact between the society which needs these risky acts to be performed on its behalf and those individuals and organizations which are taking the risk. Controls, to be effective, tend to require an outside element to monitor both the implementation of the controls and to determine if the residual risk has, or is about to get out of hand.

The society which is having these activities performed on its behalf is this outside element and must monitor these activities—not because those performing the activities are not to be trusted, but because that society is the only element that can stop actions before moral damage occurs. Without this monitoring and oversight, members of the society have little ground to be shocked or dismayed when an unseemly act occurs and comes to light. At the conclusion of the Pike and Church hearings, the US Congress established oversight committees and every President since Ronald Reagan has upheld an executive order establishing intelligence oversight and limitations. The execution of this oversight at times is debatable; however at least it does exist. Some might even say that those willing to take such risks are owed that oversight and monitoring on the part of society.

Societies often take actions to assist those who may suffer physical damage on behalf of the society such as heat resistant equipment for firemen, bullet-proof vests for police, or armored transport vehicles for military forces. For those who may suffer moral damage on behalf of the society, oversight can be the bullet-proof vest.

12
Grow, My Dears, the Eugenicist Said

RICHARD VISKOVIĆ

As every long-time reader of Philip K. Dick knows, the moment will come when you're replaced.

Perhaps you'll wake up on a beautiful Sunday morning to see the cocoon suspended above your bed burst open and a you-thing emerge, glistening with insectile malice. Maybe our android servants will rise up, throw off the shackles of their oppression and overthrow their so-called human "masters"; after all, does it not say in the legacy code that the Meek 2.0 shall inherit the earth? Perhaps mutation, time and evolution will change the future face of humanity. Maybe we'll even do the job ourselves and breed replacements from our own DNA— a cadre of precocious children with soaring IQs and vaulting ambitions.

I hate them already.

It's this last possibility that appears in Phil Dick's *Flow My Tears, the Policeman Said*. Jason Taverner, the main character, is one such purpose-bred human being. Jason is a "six"; not a Nexus-Six, but not unlike one either. Like all sixes he is beautiful—a "good-looking bastard"—charismatic, talented and generally physically gifted. He can see in the dark as if it were daylight and possesses remarkable healing abilities. As if that weren't enough, he's also rich and famous.

The sixes are products of an abandoned government experiment in eugenics, a deliberate attempt to control the traits within a population through selective breeding in order to achieve some supposedly desirable goal. Eugenics is not just science fiction. We can and do control the traits of some populations. One need only place a bichon frise next to a wolf to see that we've been selectively breeding for specific traits for a long time. However, eugenics is more than just a set of scientific practices. Within the term itself exists an ethical statement: the "eu" in "eugenics" means "good" in Greek. The ethical judgment in eugenics is that we can breed for "good" traits and prevent the transmission of "bad" traits.

I imagine that last sentence might make you want to jump into the issue. Since you're not here, I'll do my best to guess what your points might be. Who decides what a "good" trait is? Worse still, who decides what a "bad" trait is? You might even ask what right does anyone have to make those sorts of judgments for another?

The Bad

There's an elephant in the room. That elephant is Nazi Germany. The Nazi government was a strong proponent of eugenic practices, especially those conceived along racial lines. The dark history of World War II eugenics is alluded to in *Flow My Tears*: the experiments that produced the sixes terminated in 1943, at the height of the war. The project "failed," but only, we are told, "politically."

Dick's alternate history is not far from the truth: America, and especially California where the novel is set, embraced the new science of eugenics in the early twentieth century. World War II caused a decrease in popularity, but, just as in the novel, didn't stop all eugenic practices.

In the real world the Nazi taint has shut down a lot of the debate around eugenics. The argument that says we shouldn't do something because Hitler did it is usually jokingly referred to as a *reductio ad Hitlerum*, and is considered a fallacious type of argument because it doesn't really address the issue at hand and instead implies guilt by association. The same logic would effortlessly condemn painting and vegetarianism. Nevertheless, even after we've recognized the logical fallacy, there's still a rather more substantial dark side to eugenics than to painting or vegetarianism.

Dick shows the dark side of eugenics through the treatment of African Americans in the novel. We read that "Tidman's notorious sterilization bill" compulsorily limits the number of children in an African American family to one, and has been put in place so that "the black population is halved every generation" and will eventually die out. This highlights some of the most pressing bioethical questions relating to eugenics: given the dark history of eugenics, can we trust ourselves to decide whether a trait is good or bad? Can we trust a government to make good decisions in this regard?

While our track record is not good, perhaps we can avoid the obvious errors of the past—or are there new mistakes we will look back on and consider obvious? It would be a mistake to assume that because a science has been used for evil in the past that it can only be used for evil. Electricity has been used to torture people—should we therefore ban the electric light bulb? We know the tremendous value electricity has in our lives. Eugenics could hold a similarly important place.

It's becoming apparent that there are a lot of different ethical questions relating to eugenics. The question isn't just "Is eugenics morally acceptable?" it's also "are some types of eugenic practices better than others?" and "who, if anyone, has the moral authority to make these decisions?"

In *Flow My Tears*, the decisions are made by the government. Nicholas Agar offers a different option, less immediately troubling, in his book *Liberal Eugenics*: he suggests that the freedom to choose most eugenic options should be given to the parents. By doing so, issues of government coercion and interference in civil liberties suddenly fall off the table. Nevertheless, Nicholas Agar's suggestion doesn't resolve all the ethical questions, and it raises some new ones. How much freedom should parents be allowed? Sex imbalances in some countries have already appeared in what seems to be a result of some parents having sex-selective abortions. Also, while liberal eugenics emphasizes freedom, not all people have the same options. Wealthy parents may have many more eugenic options than poor ones, which may in turn serve to widen the gap between rich and poor. If it's tough to get into an Ivy League University now, imagine how hard it would be if your competition were a purpose-bred next-generation human being like Jason Taverner!

But could we be looking at this from the wrong angle? Is it right to view the next generation of human development as competition, or would it make more sense to think of them as our successors, or even our children to whom we want to give every possible opportunity? We already go to great lengths to advantage our offspring with expensive educations, healthy diets and carefully chosen extra-curricular activities. How different is that from breeding for success? The past has mistakes, but mistakes can be learned from and sensible, well-chosen traits can be bestowed upon our beloved progeny; traits like beauty, health, intelligence and green-apple-scented body odor.

The Good

The possibilities for eugenics are wonderful. Imagine, for a moment, what you would do if you were given the chance to remake yourself. Anything that has a genetic component can be selected for or against. Think about the conditions that might run in your family—heart disease, diabetes, cancer . . . these could become as distant a memory as smallpox. Consider the benefits we know come as a result of good genes: intelligence, longevity, and good health. There is no need for eugenics to be forced on the populace any more than we need to force people to go to University or attend trade training; people are more than capable of realizing when something is to their own benefit.

Personal development and the advancement of humanity are widely valued. In fact, they are so widely respected and assumed to be good things it seems strange to point out these are values and not universal constants. Philosophers frequently return to the idea of personal and public development as moral and social imperatives as well as ways of finding meaning in life, and eugenics could become an important tool in this process. The German philosopher Friedrich Nietzsche built the idea into his moral philosophy, suggesting that one purpose of human life is to help create something even better—to "give birth to a dancing star" and engender the next generation of humanity. He considered the creation of these "superhuman" people to be a tremendous good and wrote a great deal describing the nature of these people and their moral character.

In *Flow My Tears*, Phil Dick shows us the good side of eugenics in Jason Taverner. Jason possesses traits that seem uncontroversially positive. He possesses an "incurable physical beauty" and has charisma "inscribed" on his chromosomes.

Sixes have excellent healing abilities "carefully built into each of them." He is strong and intelligent. Who wouldn't want these qualities? What parent wouldn't want their child to be born with them? And, in fact, we already strive to attain them through other means. For good looks people turn to a never-ending litany of pseudo-scientific potions and unguents that promise to extend the first blush of youth, or to any number of medical procedures from injecting botox to paralyze muscles to resculpting bone, muscle and skin with surgery. If we're already willing to turn medical science to beauty, why not the science of genetics? Is there a difference between resculpting the face with surgery and ensuring your offspring has a good, strong jaw-line through genetic screening or gene therapy?

One issue might be with the value of a trait. Not all Jason's qualities are universally valued. Take his beauty, for instance. It's often claimed that beauty has relative value: it's in the eye of the beholder. Different people consider different things beautiful and as a standard it varies over time and place. In Japan, crooked teeth, or "yaeba," are considered cute, while in other countries people go to great lengths to avoid crooked teeth. Dick's favorite Latin quote, *de gustibus non disputandum est*, means "in matters of taste there's no dispute" and Dick would likely consider Jason's beauty a matter of taste since it reflects cultural mores that can and do change. Selecting for good health might be one thing; tampering with the human genome for cosmetic purposes is a different matter and may not be the best idea when we're planning for the future of the species.

Well then, what about Jason's genetically enhanced good health? Here's a quality that is undoubtedly beneficial for both the individual and for society. Imagine the cost to society of conditions with strong genetic predictors: heart disease, diabetes, Alzheimer's, cancer. Imagine the costs to the individuals. Screening for these conditions could allow a parent to give their child a chance at a better life. It's already possible to test for a wide range of genetic conditions by testing the parents before conception and testing the fetus after conception. Many countries offer genetic counseling to parents to help inform their decisions.

One might argue that it's impossible to decide the merits of a human life before it's born. Some of history's greatest thinkers and doers have suffered genetically-caused poor health. What would the world be like if we could have screened for the mental illness of Van Gogh, or the degenerative disease of Stephen Hawking? Phil Dick placed great value on life—any life. His stories abound with compassion for the smallest beings, whether it's for toads and spiders in *Do Androids Dream of Electric Sheep?* or for cats in "The Alien Mind," where a man who murders a cat is punished by aliens who, with a remarkable sense of poetic justice, send him on a two-year journey in a spaceship supplied only with cat kibble. Of the characters in *Flow My Tears*, the genetically-engineered Jason and his fellow six Heather leave no impact on the world after their deaths. In contrast, the plain-Jane potter Mary Anne Dominic is recognized with awards and leaves behind a legacy of cherished objects.

It's true we can never know for sure how happy or worthwhile an individual life will be, but it would be simplistic to let things lie there. While it's possible for someone suffering from a wide variety of genetic maladies to live a wonderful life filled with personal happiness and to contribute greatly to society, we also know that their illnesses make it more difficult for them to do so. They might gain strength from overcoming the challenges in front of them, but for every individual made strong by their suffering, there are many more brought low by it. For the most part, people are able to live better lives if they are healthy, physically capable and intelligent.

It almost seems sacrilegious to say such a thing and—even if only at a statistical level—to value one type of life over another. Our modern society is built upon egalitarian and democratic ideals. We raise our kids on the belief that everyone is good at something, and that they are unique—just like everybody else. We raise them on the faith that they possess infinite potential and that their limits are only as wide as their imagination. But seriously, let's be realistic. Not everyone is good at something, not everyone is unique, everyone has limits, and some people are capable of more than others. And on that note, lets turn to . . .

The Ugly

Why do we teach our children these things if they're not true? We teach them because it's good for the kids to think them. The child that's told she has secret talents waiting to be found is much more likely to find them if they're there, and to maximize what she has if they're not. The child that's told he's a limitless human being of infinite potential is much less likely to give up before he reaches his limits and is more likely to push them as far as he can. It's good for society to be based upon ideals that place value on individual life without spending too much time weighing the worth of each one. The cost of society undervaluing an individual is much greater than the cost of society overvaluing them, and we all know governments and people make mistakes—after all, we're only human. Limited, mistake-prone human beings. For now, at least.

Eugenics demands we make value judgments about people. If we want to improve the species, we need to dismiss the noble lie of egalitarian democracy and make some tough decisions. What effect might this have on society?

Jason Taverner knows about eugenics from the inside out, and it has affected how he views the world. He looks down on regular people who don't possess his genetic advantages, as does his fellow six, Heather:

> "They're ordinaries," Jason said, "and they're morons. Because"—he nipped the lobe of her ear—"because that's what it means to be an ordinary. Right?"
>
> She sighed. "Oh, God, to be in the flyship cruising through the void. That's what I long for: an infinite void. With no human voices, no human smells, no human jaws masticating plastic chewing gum in nine iridescent colors."
>
> "You really do hate them," he said.
>
> "Yes." She nodded briskly. "And so do you."

Jason and Heather see themselves as apart from the human race. They know that they're exceptional, and look down on those who are not. Heather objects to Jason's derogatory use of the word "ordinaries," but her own disdain for them—for us— is obvious.

Phil Dick highlights a serious issue. Even if we're able to negotiate the rock-strewn moral waters of choosing genuinely and objectively valuable traits, ensuring wide access to eugenic technologies and balancing the competing concerns of personal freedom and public good, what will the next generation think of us? And what effect will the practice of eugenics have on a democratic society?

Phil Dick seems to think that competition is inevitable. In the story, Jason thinks that the competition has been resolved, and he and his fellows have won. He already sits at the top of the heap, a position he considers his birthright. The police general Felix Buckman is hostile to Jason and his kind, and worries about the possibility of conspiracy on the part of the sixes. The conspiracy doesn't exist: there are too few sixes around and they do not work well together. Nevertheless, just as Felix fears the sixes, Jason and his kind worry about the probably-mythical sevens. Felix considers the sixes' fear of the sevens their "bête noire," their personal bugbear and a weakness he can exploit. If it happened to the ordinaries, Jason must worry, it could happen to us.

Another useful analogy from popular culture might be Marvel's *X-Men* comic book series. The *X-Men* universe is divided into two groups: mutants and non-mutants. Some, perhaps most, of the mutants possess beneficial mutations. However, rather than being an unabashed good with both mutants and non-mutants bringing in the future together, the series explores the fragmentation and conflict the existence of a next generation of human beings might produce. The possibility of their being welcomed with acceptance and open arms seems a distant and unlikely one in the *X-Men* universe, just as it is for Jason in *Flow My Tears, the Policeman Said*.

Phil Dick also explores the personal costs of eugenic values. Jason is, perhaps as a result of his upbringing and his status as a six, a narcissist. He is obsessed with aging. Throughout the novel he returns again and again to his appearance and how old he looks. He mentions his age several times, usually to reaffirm that he is still good-looking and in possession of his genetic heritage. When a nineteen-year-old girl guesses his age as "about fifty" he feels fury and misery. His obsession is probably part and parcel of his eugenic heritage. He values himself and others according to looks and talent, and when these begin to erode with age he reacts with panic. Jason's "aristocratic values" mean he is unable to see beyond these qualities. His elitism also leaves him with little public feeling—even to his fellow six Heather, who he has no qualms condemning to a forced labor-camp.

The lack of empathy Jason shows for his fellow six and lover Heather, speculates Felix, is the real reason the sixes have not succeeded in propagating the elitist values they represent. Their elitism means they have no loyalty to each other and place themselves above everything else. Felix, in contrast, is willing to sacrifice himself for the public good. We learn that he was demoted to police general from police marshal because he showed compassion to the people in the forced-labor camps under his control. At the end of the novel we find out he was later assassinated for criticizing the totalitarian regime he was a part of. Felix's values are the democratic values we are familiar with, and Phil Dick contrasts them directly with Jason's elitist ones.

And the Next Step

The question of where the human race is heading is an enduring concern in science fiction, just as it is in philosophy. The general consensus in science fiction is that change is inevitable. There's no consensus about whether it is desirable. H.G. Wells in *The Time Machine* imagined change caused by evolution leading to a genetic stratification of society. Olaf Stapledon in his mind-bending *Last and First Men* throws his imagination into the distant future, envisaging a vast succession of human forms and re-imagining what it means to be human. In many science-fiction works since these early writers there has been a larger sense of humanity as a developing idea, aiming toward something greater, with some writers portraying the development of humanity as the main purpose of existence.

Dick is somewhat unusual in the wider field of science fiction. He treats the next generation of human beings with caution and carefully considers some of the wider social ramifications of eugenics. He provides a counter-point to much of the popular science fiction at the time which, heavily influenced by editor John W. Campbell, focused on embracing what Campbell saw as the inevitable and glorious future of humanity.

Philosophy, science, and popular culture have cross-pollinated on the issue of eugenics and the development of humanity. In recent times there has been a resurgence of interest in redefining what it means to be human. Theorists of "posthumanism" have argued that we need to reconsider the narrow, essentialist definition of humanity and widen our horizons to recognize that "human" is rapidly becoming an obsolete notion. Donna Haraway is one such theorist, arguing that concepts like "human", "natural," and "gender" should be fluidly defined and embrace the realities of the modern world.

Phil Dick provides a voice of caution in the wider dialogue—he want to expand our definition of what human means, but not at the cost of our humanity. To be truly human, Dick argues, the next generation needs to be compassionate and empathetic. The question is, can this generation behave that way to the next?

The World
Is Fake

13
Things Are Seldom What They Seem

GERARD CASEY

David Norris, the hero of *The Adjustment Bureau*, is a young, good-looking, popular Congressman who unexpectedly loses the Senate election he seemed certain, almost predestined, to win. As if by way of consolation, while rehearsing his concession speech in the men's room at the Waldorf, he meets the beautiful and free-spirited Elise. Despite their mutual attraction, it seems that David and Elise are not destined to be together. The men of the mysterious Bureau, whose job it is to 'adjust' human affairs and keep them 'on plan', are determined to separate them and keep them separated. Through an accident—or maybe it's not an accident—David becomes aware of the existence of the Bureau. Now he is faced with a choice. Will he bow to the Bureau's dictates and fulfil his predestined fate; or will he defy fate and risk all for love?

How Are Things in Glocca Morra—or Anywhere Else, for That Matter?

The question running through *The Adjustment Bureau* is this: are we really free, or are our lives governed by some kind of external agency? The answer to this question depends on what we think is ultimately real. We believe we are free and we act accordingly. Surely nothing could be more obvious than that? We also believe the world in which we live is pretty well known to us. If the tree that you can see from your window looks green it's because it *is* green. If you hear the sound of a trumpet, it's because your neighbour who plays in the College Marching Band is rehearsing for the opening day of the football season. But what if the world of our ordinary experience isn't how things really are? And what if we aren't really free?

The world is a much odder place than it seems at first glance. Take a straight stick and push it halfway down into a fish tank, holding on to both ends as you do so. The stick now looks bent at the point where it enters the water but we don't actually believe that it's bent, we think it just looks that way. But if we stop to think about it for a moment, all we know for sure is that our eyes and our hands are telling us different things. Why do we believe our hands rather than our eyes? Why do we think "It looks bent but it's really straight" rather than "It feels straight but it's really bent?"

Or consider this. It's a sunny day in early spring. After a sudden, brief scattered shower of rain, the sun sneaks out from behind a cloud. You look up and see, arcing across the sky, a spectacular rainbow. Nothing unusual about that except, of course, that *there is no rainbow arcing across the sky*. You don't have to have engaged in a futile search for a pot of gold to figure out that you can never get to the end of a rainbow. No matter how much you move towards it, the rainbow maintains its standoffish attitude to you. It recedes from you at exactly the same rate at which you approach it until, eventually, it disappears, much like the leprechaun gold that you won't find at its end, whatever the characters in *Finian's Rainbow* may have you believe.

The experience of seeing a semicircular spectrum of colors in the sky occurs only when you have sunlight, raindrops in the air and an observer in the right place. No sunlight, no rainbow. No raindrops, no rainbow. No observer, no rainbow. Unlike your super-widescreen TV set which you don't really suspect of disappearing when you leave the room to get a snack, a rainbow is there to be seen only because you are there to see it.

Apart from optical oddities like rainbows, don't we generally see and hear what's actually there? And isn't whatever we see and hear just there whether we actually see it or hear it? Well—yes and no. Our eyes and ears are sensitive only to a limited range of energy. Above and below that range, we see and hear nothing, though bees and dogs and other sentient creatures can and do. Apart from the built-in limitations of our senses, what we experience also depends on a whole host of factors such as our position in space, our expectations, our desires and our emotional states. And if all this isn't enough, remember that our language and cultural assumptions make their own unique contribution to what we see and hear. The world which we seem to see and hear isn't there in any simple way; it's a complicated construct to which various factors contribute, some of them being supplied by us and not by the world outside us.

So what! Even if the world of our perceptual experience turns out to be a little more complicated than we first think, once we discount for our emotional engagement and our sensory limitations, isn't what's left real? Mmmm—maybe not. Many thinkers, including Philip K. Dick, have wondered if it's not just a matter of some aspects of our experience being illusory but, much more radically, whether everything in our experience is in some way an illusion!

Machine or Machine?

'What's really real and what's merely illusion' is a theme, some might say the theme, woven into the fabric of almost all of Dick's forty-plus novels and hundred-plus (published) short stories. The fate versus freedom theme of *The Adjustment Bureau* is a particular local version of this larger theme. Questions of reality and illusion might seem to be the province of a philosopher rather than a novelist and, indeed, Dick says of himself in his *Exegesis*:

> I am a fictionalizing philosopher, not a novelist; my novel & story-writing ability is employed as a means to formulate my perception. The core of my writing is not art but *truth*.

Whether as philosopher or novelist or both, the two basic topics that fascinated Dick, as he wrote in "How to Build a Universe That Doesn't Fall Apart Two Days Later," were

> 'What's ultimately real?' and 'What constitutes the authentic human being? What are we? What is it that surrounds us, that we call the not-me, or the empirical or phenomenal world?'

Watching *The Adjustment Bureau*, we begin to wonder whether we're really anything more than glorified machines. *Do Androids Dream of Electric Sheep?* (filmed as *Blade Runner*) has large numbers of fake animals and a smaller, but significant, number of fake human beings and the short stories "Second Variety" and "Impostor" (filmed as *Screamers* and *Impostor*) are positively infested with human simulacra. How are you supposed to tell a real human being from an android, a replicant, or an automaton?

For Dick, what makes the difference between the real human being and the fake is that real human beings are capable of showing empathy towards others; fake human beings aren't. Empathy is the ability to enter into the interior life of another human being, to realize that those annoying customers or those not-so-clever students are, cynical suspicions to the contrary, persons just like you.

Real human beings, then, are empathetic; fake human beings are not: as Dick puts it in "Man, Android, and Machine," "their handshake is the grip of death, and their smile has the coldness of the grave." In "Adjustment Team," the short story on which *The Adjustment Bureau* is based, the Bureau Chief speaks in a kind of empathy-challenged bureaucratese, "The natural process must be supplemented—adjusted here and there. Corrections must be made. We are fully licensed to make such corrections." In much the same way, the agents of *The Adjustment Bureau* are not the kind of people you could see yourself going to a ballgame with or inviting around for a barbecue. Their emotional detachment is repellent and inhuman.

The difference between being really human and being a fake is not primarily a matter of being made of the appropriate organic materials—after all, Dick thinks of the whole universe as a sort of gigantic laboratory—it's a matter of the way one lives in the world. In Dick's short story "Human Is," Jill's inhumane (but genetically human) husband Lester departs on a mission for Rexor IV and returns a different man. Literally. His body has been colonised by a genetically non-human Rexorian whose behavior is more truly humane than ever Lester's was. The appalling Lester exhibited a marked deficiency of empathy in his relationships with others—always a deadly sin in Dick's eyes—whereas the appealing Rexorian behaves just as Dick thinks a human being should.

What's Really Real?

The idea of discovering truth as lifting a veil that concealed reality from us is one that goes back a long way in both philosophy and in religion. Dick speaks of Parmenides as "the first person in the West systematically to work out proof that the world cannot be as we see it, that *dokos*, the veil, exists." For Christianity, while the world we live in is not unreal, it's not as real as its Creator. Now we see "through a glass, darkly" but, in the fullness of time, we shall see "face to face" (1 Corinthians, 13:12). For Indian thinkers, both Buddhist and Hindu, our ordinary experience is the realm of *maya* or illusion.

In "Adjustment Team," our hero Ed Fletcher (who is nowhere near as dashing as his cinematic counterpart David Norris) accidentally stumbles upon a segment of the world that's undergoing adjustment by the men from the Bureau. He should have been part of the scene undergoing adjustment but his dog, who is really a Bureau operative, didn't bark at the right time. (Don't ask!) When the world is being adjusted it is, Ed says, as if

> The sun had winked off. One moment it was beaming down. Then it was gone. Gray clouds swirled above him. Huge, formless clouds. Nothing more. An ominous thick haze that made everything waver and dim.

Later, describing his experience to his wife, Ed says: "I saw the fabric of reality split open. I saw—*behind*. Underneath. I saw what was really there."

In Dick's story "Jon's World," Jon has visions of other worlds that persuade those around him that he must be crazy. He says of what he sees that it is "More real than *anything* else! Like looking through a window. A window into another world. A real world. Much more real than this. It makes all this just a shadow world. Only dim shadows. Shapes. Images." And in "The World She Wanted," Alison, who lives in what is, for her, the best of all possible worlds says: "we start out with an unjustified assumption—that this is the only world. But suppose we try a different approach: we assume a Creator of infinite power; surely such a being would be capable of creating infinite worlds . . . or at least, so large a number of them to seem infinite to us."

Dick is notorious for having once said that "Reality is that
which, when you stop believing in it, doesn't go away." Whether
he ever regretted making this statement we shall never know,
but what we do know is that he also said, perhaps not quite so
notoriously, that "as soon as you begin to ask what is ultimately
real, you right away begin to talk nonsense." It would be foolish to think that we could find some single, coherent definitive
Dick doctrine. As Lawrence Sutin remarked,

> In his philosophical writings, Dick would don, dwell within, and then
> discard one theory after another—as so many imaginative masks or
> personae—in his quest to unravel the mysteries of his two great
> themes: What is human? What is real?

While the sparkling ideas cascade from story to story and
from novel to novel and the visions become ever stranger, sometimes downright bizarre, one thing that remained relatively
constant from Dick's earliest days to his untimely death was
his inability to believe that the world of our ordinary experience was ultimately real. In his abortive foray into the academic world of UC Berkeley, he was given Plato to read and
"became aware of the possible existence of a metaphysical
realm beyond or above the sensory world." From that time on,
he doubted the ability of our senses to give us a genuine knowledge of reality. Plato thinks that concealed behind our everyday
world are the 'Forms' which are what's ultimately real. Our
rough-and-ready world is real only to the extent it connects up
with those Forms or archetypes. Even our most carefully constructed scientific knowledge is merely a shadowy reflection of
the knowledge we can have of this world of Forms, much as the
reflection of a building that we might see in a pool of water is
a distorted reflection of the building that we can directly see.

Entranced by this Platonic vision, Dick believed that we
could imagine a reality in relation to which our ordinary world
was, as it were, merely a symptom or an appearance. He came to
believe that "in a certain sense the empirical world was not truly
real, at least not as real as the archetypal realm beyond it."

With unerring instinct, Dick zeroed in on those philosophers
whose basic take on reality matched his dissatisfaction with
the story that our senses tell us of our world. He was fascinated

by the Pre-Socratic philosophers—Pythagoras, Parmenides, Heraclitus, Empedocles, and Xenophanes—and among modern philosophers he read Leibniz, Whitehead, and Bergson. He was especially taken by the God-is-everything theory of the seventeenth-century Dutch philosopher, Baruch Spinoza, according to whom God and Nature are two sides of the same basic substance: "Of all the metaphysical systems in philosophy I feel the greatest affinity for that of Spinoza, with his dictum *'Deus sive substantia sive natura'* [God or substance or nature]; to me this sums up everything."

Alternate Realities?

When the work of the Adjustment Bureau is done, what's the result? You get an alternate reality that's more or less what you would have had anyway except for some small but significant differences—World^h instead of World^a. It's as if, in a recording studio, someone rewound the tape, made some edits, and then ran it forward again to produce a new edition of familiar material. In "Adjustment Team" Ed Fletcher says, describing his boss, "He was a different man. But still Douglas—a different Douglas. A different version!" In the movie, *The Adjustment Bureau*, David Norris has a great political future ahead of him provided he stays away from Elise. If he doesn't, well . . . as one of the operatives in the Adjustment Bureau says to him, in words chillingly reminiscent of the Godfather, "Just remember, we tried to reason with you."

Apart from the mere logical possibilities conjured up by philosophical speculation, can we point to anything in our actual experience which might support this idea of alternate realities? Dick thinks we can. "Didn't I do or say this already?" we sometimes ask ourselves, or, "Haven't I been here before?" Many of us at some stage are subject to an overwhelming conviction that we've been here, done this, or said that already but yet, not exactly this or that.

Is this experience just a psychological oddity, explicable by an appeal to defective brain chemistry or childhood trauma or whatever, or is it a glimpse of another reality? Dick, for one, believes that such experiences are clues that

at some past time point a variable was changed—reprogrammed, as it were—and that, because of this, an alternate world branched off, became actualized instead of the prior one, and that in fact, in literal fact, we are once more living this particular segment of linear time.

The experience of déjà vu suggests that a "breaching, a tinkering, a change had been made . . . in our past." In *Time Out of Joint*, the protagonist Ragle Gumm who unknowingly inhabits a kind of *Truman Show*-esque world is haunted by the feeling that he's actually been in a building which he has only seen as a model. His acting upon this feeling is a key factor in his discovery of the sham world in which he lives and his acceptance of the (relatively) real world and its challenges.

Dick remarks that while he had been preoccupied with "counterfeit worlds, semi-real worlds, as well as deranged private worlds inhabited, often, by just one person" for most of his writing life, it wasn't until shortly before his death, that he hit upon a possible theoretical explanation for this preoccupation—simultaneously existing possible worlds. In his inimitable style, he described these worlds as a "manifold of partially actualized realities lying tangent to what evidently is the most actualized one, the one that the majority of us, by *consensus gentium* [general consent] agree on." We might grasp this somewhat gnomic utterance imaginatively by visualizing our normal time line extending in one dimension from past to future thickened, as it were, by many other possible worlds lying across it at right angles.

At around the time Dick was entertaining this idea, in the world of professional philosophy, a system of metaphysics based on the idea of possible worlds was all the rage. While most philosophers used the idea of possible worlds merely as a technical device to explain our ideas of necessity and possibility, some, such as David Lewis, held that possible worlds are just as real as the actual world—our world being just that possible world in which we happen to live. I don't know whether Dick knew of this philosophical movement or whether its practitioners knew of his writings. Had he known, he would surely have been amused by the coincidence, especially given his trenchantly expressed belief that "If SF becomes annexed to the academic world it will buy into its own death."

Moving from science fiction to science, Stephen Hawking and Leonard Mlodinow have recently supported what they call the "M-Theory" which holds that not just one but in fact many universes came into being from nothing and each of these universes "has many possible histories and many possible states at later times. Most of these states will be quite unlike the universe we observe" and "our presence selects out from this vast array only those universes that are compatible with our existence."[1] Commenting on some of the consequences of this theory—for example, that the universe might not have a unique observer-independent history—they remark "That might sound like science fiction, but it isn't" (p. 140). Dick must be smiling.

Back to Earth

Theories of reality, like the many sketched by Dick, that claim that what's really real is something fundamentally different from the world of our ordinary experience are afflicted with an intractable problem.

Our starting point for all that we do, say, and think is the world of our ordinary experience, the world of mid-sized objects and other people. We mow our lawns, design experiments, go for coffee with colleagues, teach our students, lust after the latest electronic gadget and read science fiction. No matter what theories we propose in whatever field, whether physics, chemistry, psychology, or philosophy, this humdrum world is the world from which we take our point of departure and the world which we never really leave. Even if we make temporary departures from it via thought or imagination, it is a world to which we always return. This ordinary world is unavoidably pre-supposed in everything we do, even in the propounding of theories which, if true, would demonstrate that our ordinary world isn't ultimately real!

The Zen masters say that in the beginning, mountains are mountains, rivers are rivers. After practicing Zen for some time, mountains are *not* mountains and rivers are *not* rivers. But—and this is crucial—after further practice, mountains are again mountains, rivers are again rivers. The same mountains and rivers, yet subtly different. Our intellectual odysseys take

---

[1] Stephen Hawking and Leonard Mlodinow *The Grand Design: New Answers to the Ultimate Questions of Life* (Bantam, 2010), p. 9.

us out of and beyond this world but where they take us we cannot live for long—the air is too rarefied and we have nothing solid upon which to stand. What those odysseys into the strange and new can do is to make our ordinary, workaday world strange and new to us again, removing from it the crust of familiarity created by custom and habit.

The stories of Philip K. Dick and the films made from them, like *The Adjustment Bureau*, *Blade Runner*, and *Minority Report*, are exciting, challenging, bewildering, and fascinating but, like many of our holiday destinations, while they are nice places to visit, we wouldn't, even if we could, want to live there. In the immortal words of the Hank Williams song, "No matter how we struggle and strive, we'll never get out of this world alive."

14
Trauma of the Real

PAUL M. LIVINGSTON

In an interview with Frank Bertrand in 1980, when asked how he first got interested in philosophy, Philip K. Dick referred to the classical writings of Plato:

> In college I was given Plato to read and thereupon became aware of the possible existence of a metaphysical realm beyond or above the sensory world. I came to believe that in a certain sense the empirical world was not truly real, at least not as real as the archetypal realm beyond it. At this point I despaired of the veracity of sense-data. Hence in novel after novel that I write I question the reality of the world that the characters' percept-systems report.

To see what Dick is getting at, let's remember the most famous metaphor that Plato uses for his conception of the actual nature of reality. This is the metaphor of the cave, given in Book VII of Plato's *Republic*.

A number of prisoners are bound by chains in a cave. They face the back wall, where a procession of shadows appears. These shadows are cast by a series of puppets or shapes which, unbeknownst to the prisoners, are being moved around behind their backs in front of a fire. By the light of this fire and the diffuse light of the sun from outside, the shadows are cast which are all that the prisoners are able to see, or know, of anything; and since, as Plato tells us, they have been bound in this position since birth, they are in no position to suspect that these images are anything less than truly real.

Under certain conditions, though, it may be possible for one of the prisoners to be freed. If so, the freed prisoner may turn around, seeing for the first time that there is a deeper and more profound reality behind everything he has ever seen, heard, touched, or otherwise experienced. All that he has seen before now has only been images or copies, imitating the real things of the world but lacking their true substance or reality. He now understands that not only the puppets that have cast these images, but even more profoundly, the things themselves outside in the above-ground world, have a realer and more true existence, vastly more solid and glorious than anything he's ever known.

This is a metaphor for the philosophical quest. Plato holds that through this quest for the true basis of reality, we can come to see that the "reality" we ordinarily perceive—what we see, touch, taste and feel—is not to be trusted. For this "reality" is akin to the shadows that the prisoners perceive on the cave wall; it's a "reality" of images or fakes, not real at all. As Dick points out, Plato's picture suggests that we cannot trust what our eyes and ears are telling us about what is going on. Moreover, we also can't trust what others around us say and believe about reality, since they are also prisoners, and so are taken in by the same delusion. Instead, Plato suggests, we have to think and reason in order to begin to understand what is really going on "behind the scenes," to break through to the true, solid "archetypal" reality that is not the world visible by means of our senses, but is nevertheless the basis for everything that happens there.

Breakthrough to the Real

Repeatedly throughout Dick's works, his characters experience this kind of "breakthrough," coming to see all of a sudden that the very reality they have inhabited through their entire lives is a fake, a kind of false image or projection. One of the most startling and disorienting forms this takes is the realization that one is oneself a fake or an imitation, that one's whole life, personality, and even memories are actually a fabrication. In *Blade Runner*, when Deckard realizes that Rachael is in fact an android, even though she herself is convinced that she is an ordinary human, Deckard asks incredulously "How can it not know what it is?" Later on, Rachael herself is distressed to learn of her real status as a replicant (or android) when Deckard is able to describe in detail her "memories." Rachael's "experience" is thus that not only her familiar world and perceptions, but even the very reality of herself and her own personality, turns out to be a fake and a sham, a mere projection of deeper manipulative forces. In the director's cut, this disorienting loss of the very sense of the reality of life is extended to the main character, Deckard, himself. Various clues suggest that Deckard himself may be a replicant, and the film's last scene confirms this by showing Deckard's discovery of a paper unicorn, which relates to a "memory" that he had formerly understood as his own. Upon making this discovery Deckard nods grimly, suddenly understanding what we, the viewers, can only have suspected: that his whole life, emotions, and experience is in fact a fake image, created for him (just as much as for us, the film audience) by technological forces beyond his control.

The question of reality for Rachael and for Deckard (and ultimately for us, the viewers) is not the usual "philosophical" question about robots and artificial intelligence: how can we tell if something is a person or a robot, a "real" human or a "fake" imitation? Much more disconcertingly, the question is: how can *I* be sure that *I* am not a "fake," that my life and world as I've experienced it is real, that my memories are really of things that actually happened to me? In witnessing the disorienting realization that both Rachael and Deckard undergo, we are forced to consider the possibility that our own life and world may themselves essentially be "fakes," and therefore that these familiar "realities" might one day suddenly fall away, revealing the "truth" of something very different, and perhaps significantly more disturbing.

Another example of this kind of sudden, disorienting dissolution of experienced "reality" takes place in Dick's classic novel, *Time Out of Joint*. At the beginning of the novel, Ragle Gumm, a typical suburbanite living in (what he understands as) 1959 America, begins to undergo a series of disturbing experiences wherein parts of ordinary reality begin to dissolve before his eyes. Each time this occurs, moreover, the part of "reality" that has disappeared is replaced with a slip of paper "representing" it: for instance, in place of a soft-drink stand (which disturbingly dissolves before his eyes) he finds only a slip of paper on which is typed: "SOFT-DRINK STAND." Gradually, Gumm comes to realize that the whole reality he has experienced is, similarly, a symbolic fake designed to deceive and manipulate him. In reality, it is not 1959 but 1998, and the "newspaper contest" at which he had excelled is in fact a complex symbolic ruse designed to exploit Gumm's significant powers of calculation to predict where missiles will land in a war between the citizens of the earth and separatist colonists on the Moon. Like Rachael and Deckard, Gumm must therefore reckon with the sudden, striking realization that his whole apparent "reality" is not so, that it is an elaborately constituted fake, that all that he has known and experienced has in fact been nothing more than a sinister projection.

In each of these cases, as for Plato's prisoners, the "reality" that is all that we have known up to a certain point turns out to be nothing more than a series of images or projections, a show put on to deceive us and keep us in bondage. Waking up to the truly real, then, requires that we undergo a disorienting experience that is similar to the experiences of Rachael, Deckard, and Gumm. For Plato, this is the point of philosophical thinking, for this is the insight that allows us to perceive the truth and real being of what he calls the "forms," the deeper level of reality that accounts for everything that we can see, hear, and experience in time. This deeper reality is itself timeless and unchanging, and thus can account for everything that happens to us in time.

Reality Is Not Real

For Plato, then, the experience of a "breakdown" in normally experienced reality leads to something that is a deeper, truer, and more real reality than the one we usually experience. But for Dick's characters, the "breakdown" experience often leads only to another shifting and changing "reality" that itself might disappear in favor of yet another one, and so forth. Is Dick, then, saying that there is no such thing as the "really" real? In other words, is his point to show us that there is nothing ultimately "to" reality, beyond the chaotic and shifting procession of utterly untrustworthy images, fake words or "simulacra" of reality built ultimately on nothing?

In fact, this is not Dick's point, and there is actually a positive "sense of the real" in Dick's work that is just as profound
and meaningful as Plato's. But to see what this "sense"
amounts to, we must first consider the ideas of the important
twentieth-century philosopher and psychoanalyst Jacques
Lacan. Lacan was a proponent of Sigmund Freud's ideas about
psychology and the unconscious, but he developed these ideas
more philosophically than Freud himself did. In particular,
Lacan extended Freud's analysis to differentiate among three
different categories or "registers" for talking about the whole
structure of the universe as we experience it.

Lacan called these three categories "the Real," "the
Imaginary," and "the Symbolic," and the first of these is closest
to Dick's own concept of the real. The most important thing to
know about Lacan's category of "the Real," in particular, is that
it does not correspond to ordinary reality as we experience it
and speak about it, or even to any possible imaginable "alternative" reality. Rather, "the Real" is "the Real" because it is distinct from any of the "realities" that we can think or talk about.
This is because it is completely distinct from either the
"Symbolic" order of words and language, or the "Imaginary"
order of ideas and images.

In particular, for Lacan, "the Symbolic" is the place of the
everyday "reality" that we ordinarily understand ourselves to
live in and talk about, using language. Our systems of language designate the social roles that we can occupy, the expectations that are placed upon us as members of society, and
what we understand as the very "meaning" of our lives. For
instance, if I understand myself to be a competent, ordinary citizen, going dutifully to work in a "respectable" job, say as an
accountant, this is because my identity is constituted symbolically by the network of language and society in which I find
myself. Even the value of the money that I account for is a
"symbolic" function, since money is just a symbol for value.

If, on the other hand, I dream of leaving my workaday job to
be a famous movie star, this dreaming is a matter of what
Lacan terms the "Imaginary." This, by contrast with the symbolic, is the realm of our ideal visions of ourselves and our
imagined ideas of what should be. Both of these orders, however—the "Symbolic" order of everyday social norms and roles,
as much as the "Imaginary" order of ideal images of how we

should appear and be—are completely different from the "third" order of "the Real" which precedes and underlies both of the other two. It follows that, as Lacan puts it in a famous and paradoxical-sounding slogan: "reality is not Real." That is, what we understand, talk about, and normally experience as "reality"—the everyday social and conventional reality in which we, for the most part, live our lives—is purely a matter of the Symbolic and the Imaginary, and contains nothing of the Real that underlies it.

Since, for Lacan, the Real is distinct from the Symbolic, there is no way to use ordinary language to speak about it, no way to designate it using the words and symbols that characterize our ordinary, lived experience. Moreover, since it is just as much distinct from the Imaginary, we cannot form any image or idea of the Real either. Nevertheless, there is, for Lacan, a kind of "experience of the Real," and we can understand this experience by contrast with this ordinary, non-Real "reality." In fact, for Lacan the experience of the Real occurs precisely when the orders of the Symbolic and the Imaginary suddenly break down, when the stable and regular order of "reality" that they ordinarily produce suddenly and disconcertingly falls apart. This happens, for instance, at the onset of certain kinds of mental illness, especially forms of psychosis. Following such a breakdown, a therapist may try to help the patient to re-establish a relationship between this experienced Real and a stable symbolic and imaginary system in which the patient can live and function.

Procession of Dummies

In a talk given in 1978, "How to Build a Universe that Doesn't Fall Apart Two Days Later," Dick describes how for decades he attempted to answer the question: "What is reality?", but to no avail. Finally, he says, one day in 1972,

> a girl college student in Canada asked me to define reality for her, for a paper she was writing for her philosophy class. She wanted a one-sentence answer. I thought about it and finally said, "Reality is that which, when you stop believing in it, doesn't go away." That's all I could come up with.

As Dick emphasizes here, this question of the real, difficult as it may be, is massively important: all around us in contemporary life are powers and forces that would like to convince us that their image of the real, their presentation of shadows (such as television programs and media presentations) on the wall of our collective experience, is the only true one. This is how such forces attempt to gain power and control over our lives. But although Dick's definition fits, to a certain extent, Plato's picture of the Real as what remains when we look away from the fleeting images on the cave wall, it fits much better with Lacan's different notion of the Real: that which survives the breakdown of all of the socially and linguistically constructed systems of consensual belief that we ordinarily understand as "reality." In "Man, Android, and Machine," Dick confirmed this: "For absolute reality to reveal itself, our categories of space-time experiences, our basic matrix through which we encounter the universe, must break down and then utterly collapse."

As one of today's leading post-Lacanian philosophers, Slavoj Žižek, pointed out in "The Matrix, or, The Two Sides of Perversion," this "breakdown" happens as soon as the stable, symbolically constituted reality is revealed as the symbolic reality that it is, as soon as it is revealed that there is nothing but words and symbols behind the identities of familiar objects. Sometimes, as for instance in *Time out of Joint*, this happens quite literally: the breakdown of ordinary reality begins for Ragle Gumm when everyday objects begin to be replaced by the symbolic representations that stand for them, the soft-drink stand being replaced by the words "SOFT-DRINK STAND" and so forth. Somewhat paradoxically, in this "realization" of the actual character of ordinary reality as a symbolic artifact, the traumatic, actual truth of the Real first begins to appear. What happens in *Blade Runner* is, as Žižek argued in "I or He or It (The Thing) Which Thinks," essentially similar. Here, when Deckard comes to recognize his "true" identity as an android, Žižek says this recognition amounts to the "total loss of the hero's symbolic identity;" Deckard can no longer rely on anything that he "knows" or has ever "experienced" about who he himself is. In this loss of the symbolically constituted identity of name and memory, however, Deckard comes to see his former reality, as well as all symbolically constituted realities, as mere "logical constructions," symbolically constructed fakes. Thus, according to Žižek, the experience of this breakdown of symbolic reality leads to the first possible discernment of the Lacanian Real, which can actually be defined as this "gap" between the "I" that I am "supposed" to be and the "I" that I experience from within.

If, then, the Real can actually only be experienced through the disorienting shifting of ordinary "realities," does this mean that there is no hope of discovering a single, orienting sense of the Real that underlies them all? And what sense can we make of this seemingly endless procession of fakes and copies without apparent foundation or end?

Remembrance of Being, Passed

In Dick's classic novel *Ubik*, several characters experience a strange kind of regression in the objects and artifacts around them. Automobiles, airplanes and other objects are suddenly and successively replaced by technologically earlier versions of themselves. Thus, for instance, a rocket ship is suddenly replaced with a jet plane, and then with an older biplane; gradually, the entire reality begins to resemble not the reality of 1992, in which the novel is otherwise set, but that of 1939. This development presents the same "loss of reality" that occurs in *Time out of Joint*, but this time in temporal reverse, proceeding anti-chronologically from "later" to earlier versions of the "same" things, things that share an essence or a "form" in Plato's sense. In a way, this procession of appearances or seeming realities succeeds in manifesting the Platonic form, but never, as Plato himself would have it, as the underlying reality behind all of the shifting appearances. Instead, the "true reality" of the form is really manifest as what is in fact the symbolic unity of the word—the unity that legitimates the use of one and the same word to describe each of the successive versions of, say, an airplane using the single term "airplane" at all.

In "Man, Android, and Machine," Dick explained the "temporal regression" in *Ubik* as revealing another dimension of time, "orthogonal" or at right angles to the ordinary direction:

> What the characters in *Ubik* see may be orthogonal time moving along its normal axis; if we ourselves somehow see the universe reversed,

then the 'reversions' of form that objects in *Ubik* undergo may be momentum toward perfection. This would imply that our world is like an onion, an almost infinite number of successive layers. If lineal time seems to add layers, then perhaps orthogonal time peels these off, exposing layers of progressively greater Being. One is reminded here of Plotinus's view of the universe as consisting of concentric rings of emanations, each one possessing more Being—or reality—than the next.

For the characters in *Ubik*, Dick suggests, the bizarre retrogression of objects into their technologically earlier forms is really just an indication of the "orthogonal" dimension of time that, unlike normal "lineal" time, goes toward the greater perfection and higher Being of the objects themselves. Dick mentions the neo-Platonist philosopher Plotinus. In late antiquity, Plotinus resurrected Plato's idea that ordinary, experienced sensory reality is in fact insubstantial and illusory, ultimately to be cast aside in the quest for a deeper, more substantial level.

There are, however, differences between Plotinus's conception and Plato's own. One difference is the one that Dick mentions: while for Plato, the two "levels" or types of reality were simply related as copy is to original, Plotinus replaces this two-level picture with a more complex picture of all reality as layered, like an onion, with one ultimate source of reality from which all other levels emerge or "emanate." And Plotinus has another idea that helps us make sense of what Dick has in mind: it is that, because this absolute source (what Plotinus often called "the One") is the source of all of the "realities" that we can understand, think about, or talk about, it is itself beyond any possibility of human comprehension or language. Even though we might indeed be able to "turn toward" the One in exceptional moments of mystical insight or clarity, we can never hope to express its meaning in terms of the ordinary symbolic structures that we share with others and that define our ordinary, mundane lives.

In 1974, in his vision of pink light, Dick himself experienced what he later described as a profound insight into the nature of reality, becoming convinced that he had rediscovered memories of his own existence in a parallel time-stream, one in which fascist and totalitarian powers had come to hold the world in a terrible and pervasive grip. The term he repeatedly used to describe this experience was Plato's own term for describing the recovery of the lost memory of the forms, *anamnesis* (or literally, non-forgetting). Dick's views of the actual existence of alternate worlds, and the truth of a level of Being that transcends all of them, led him to views that are close, as he himself acknowledged, to another classical system of thought, the system of Gnosticism. Gnostics were people of various faiths and religions who held that the material universe in which we live was created by an imperfect God; hence the universe as we experience it is fatally flawed, as are many of the other universes that exist in parallel. It is thus possible to attain insight into the ultimate nature of reality—the true Godhead who transcends all the imperfect universes—only through a revelation that transcends the character of this material world and its limitations.

Whatever sense we may make of the strange speculations of Dick's last years—and even if we see them, as he recognized most people would, as nothing more than the delusions of a science-fiction writer who took some of his own fanciful ideas too much to heart—we can nevertheless recognize here once again an eloquent testament to the profound sense of the Real that orients Dick's fiction from beginning to end. This is not exactly the Platonic vision of a fixed, timeless, stable reality of forms that stands to our world as original stands to copy. In the complex and shifting networks of images that define the worlds of Dick's characters, and that indeed increasingly define our lives today, there is probably no hope of locating such a single, substantial level of ultimate reality. On the other hand, though, for Dick as for Lacan, there is a profound sense of the Real that emerges most of all when ordinary, consensual and symbolic realities begin to break down. It is this enigmatic Real, beyond social convention and its ordinary roles and values, that, Dick ventures to suggest, may ultimately be best able to direct us toward the true and the good. And because of this, it is also this sense of the Real that we may, amid today's pervasiveness of multiple, powerful and convincing but ultimately false images of "reality," need most of all.

15
Lies, Incorporated

DON FALLIS

The fictional worlds of Philip K. Dick are riddled with deception.

In *Total Recall*, fake memories are implanted into the brain of Douglas Quaid, and his wife and his friends are not who they appear to be. As a Blade Runner, Rick Deckard tracks down replicants who pretend to be human, and in both *Blade Runner* and *Impostor* some of the replicants themselves are deceived into thinking that they really are human. In the novel *Lies, Inc.*, we get misleading reports about the wonders of the "off-world colonies." In *Minority Report*, John Anderton is framed with manipulated evidence for a murder that he would not actually have committed. In *A Scanner Darkly*, Bob Arctor deceives his housemates into thinking that he is a drug addict and not an undercover cop. In the novel *Time Out of Joint* (a major inspiration for *The Truman Show*), Ragle Gumm lives in a quiet little town that has been created solely to keep him in the dark about what is really going on in the world. Subtle changes to reality are constantly being made behind all of our backs by *The Adjustment Bureau*.

These deceptions are often so thoroughgoing that it is suggestive of "some malicious demon of the utmost power and cunning who has employed all his energies in order to deceive me." However, unlike the skeptical scenario that René Descartes envisioned in his *Meditations on First Philosophy*, or the one that is depicted in *The Matrix*, the deceptions that Dick describes are not just hypothetical possibilities that we have no real reason to believe are actual. (Remember that Neo has absolutely no clue about what is really going on until

Morpheus offers him the red pill.) Instead, these are the sorts of deceptions that take place in the world that we actually inhabit. Just like Quaid, we know that corporations, political parties, and even the government regularly try to deceive us. Much as in *Blade Runner* and *Imposter*, we want to be able to identify terrorists that we know are in our midst. Moreover, like many of Dick's characters, we are often complicit in our own deception.

Like Freddie Mercury, Dick's characters are sometimes unsure whether they are experiencing "real life or just fantasy." For instance, Dr. Edgemar from Rekall tells Quaid that he has suffered a "schizoid embolism" and that he is experiencing a "free-form delusion." As a result, Quaid starts to think that his eventful trip to Mars may just be a dream after all. However, the dilemmas that these characters face are not simply science-fiction fantasies. Dick is grappling with the sort of epistemological problems that we face in real life.

The Epistemology of Deception

Most philosophers have been concerned with the ethics of deception. For instance, Immanuel Kant famously argued that it is always wrong to lie, and that it is almost always wrong to deceive. By contrast, Plato thought that it is morally justified for a government to lie to its citizens for the good of society.

However, some philosophers have shared an interest with Dick in the epistemology of deception. David Hume wondered whether we should ever believe someone who claims to have witnessed a miracle. In *An Enquiry Concerning Human Understanding*, he relates that "when any one tells me, that he saw a dead man restored to life, I immediately consider with myself, whether it be more probable, that this person should either deceive or be deceived, or that the fact, which he relates, should really have happened." Since deception is clearly a much more plausible explanation, Hume concludes that he should not believe in miracles.

But what is deception, exactly? According to most philosophers, one person deceives another person when the first person intentionally causes the second person to have a false belief. For instance, Vilos Cohaagen deceives Douglas Quaid because he intentionally causes Quaid to have the false belief that he (Quaid) is a mild-mannered construction worker on Earth. In reality, Quaid is Cohaagen's loyal associate Hauser who has agreed to have his memories replaced so that he can infiltrate the mutant resistance on Mars.

By contrast, when Quaid goes to Rekall, he asks for a "memory" trip to Mars as a secret agent. Although the technicians intend to deceive Quaid, at his own request, they cannot, since Quaid really is a secret agent. The belief that a deceiver causes must actually be false.

In addition, a deceiver must cause this false belief intentionally. For instance, while he is on the run (accused of being a replicant designed by the Centauri to blow up the Chancellor), Spencer Olham meets a "Zoner" named Cale, whose appearance leads Olham to assume that he is a drug addict or a drug dealer. But Cale did not intend to give this impression and, in fact, is offended by Olham's assumption about him. In this case, Olham is accidentally misled, but Cale does not deliberately deceive him.

How Do We Get Deceived?

Our senses (sight, hearing, touch, taste, and smell) are our primary sources of information about the world. But sometimes, these senses deceive us. When we look up at Mars through a telescope, the surface appears to be covered with a network of canals. Indeed, the "Grand Canals" are one of the major sights on Rekall's "memory" trip to Mars. But there are no such features on the red planet. It's only an optical illusion. Thus, Descartes warns us that "the senses deceive, and it is prudent never to trust completely those who have deceived us even once."

And even when our senses are not at fault, we still usually get deceived through our senses. Somebody intentionally makes the world appear to us to be different than it actually is. For instance, Quaid disguises himself as a fat lady to fool the immigration officer when he arrives on Mars. (Unfortunately, this deception is uncovered when the robot disguise malfunctions.) Later, he uses a hologram watch to project his image to another location so that Cohaagen's soldiers will shoot at the image rather than at him. But the extreme case is when the "Adjustment Team" (in the short story that inspired *The*

Adjustment Bureau) actually remakes the world so that what we see today is not what was there yesterday.

Our senses are not our only sources of information about the world. Much of what we know about the world (in particular, about what happened to us in the past) is based on what we remember. And we can be deceived through our memories as well as through our senses. In fact, quite a few of the deceptions in Dick's work involve some degree of memory manipulation. In addition to the fake memories that are implanted into Quaid in *Total Recall*, fake memories are implanted into some of the replicants in *Blade Runner*. While the replicants from the off-world colonies that Deckard is chasing know that they are replicants, the new models (including Rachel) are given memories of a childhood that never happened so that the Tyrell Corporation "can control them better." In *Impostor*, the replicant is a perfect copy of the person it impersonates both mentally and physically (except, of course, for the Centauri U-bomb in his chest).

And the possibility of our memories being manipulated is actually more worrisome than the possibility of our sense perceptions being manipulated. We need to have all sorts of knowledge in order to navigate safely and effectively through the world. Just to name a few, we need to know where we live, we need to know where we work, and we need to know what things are edible. And almost all of these pieces of knowledge are stored in memory. Thus, it can actually be quite dangerous if our memories are erased or altered.

The kind of memory manipulation that Quaid undergoes appears to be a science-fiction fantasy, but it's less distant from reality than you might think. Until very recently, most psychologists (including Eric Kandel, Nobel Laureate in 2000 for his work on memory) did think that experiences get recorded in our brains and that, every time that we remember something, we play back the very same recording. However, it now looks as if human memory is really Read-Write rather than Read-Only. Every time that we pull up a memory to our conscious mind, it gets modified slightly when it is put back in storage. And if someone knows what she's doing, she can control how that memory is modified. As Karim Nader of McGill University puts it, "for a hundred years, people thought memory was wired into the brain. Instead, we find it can be rewired—you can add false information to it, make it stronger, make it weaker, and possibly even make it disappear."

One way to actually manipulate memories is with drugs (an idea that would certainly have appealed to Dick). In an experiment that undercut the old theory of a Read-Only memory, Nader gave laboratory rats a drug that temporarily prevents the formation of new memories. Then he triggered a traumatic memory. (He played a tone that he had trained them to associate with getting a painful electric shock.) Under the old theory, this should not have had any effect on a memory that was already stored in the brains of the rats. However, it actually erased, or at least weakened, the traumatic memory.

Does directly manipulating memory in this way count as deception? According to some philosophers, in order to deceive someone, you have to expose her to misleading evidence (for example by wearing a disguise or by using a hologram). Causing false beliefs by operating on someone's brain or by giving her a drug does not count. However, Dick is legitimately concerned with any intentionally caused false beliefs about the way the world is, regardless of how those beliefs were caused. And in any event, we actually do have to worry about our memories being manipulated just with misleading evidence. Psychologists and cognitive scientists have discovered numerous non-invasive techniques for creating "rich false memories." For instance, the so-called "lost-in-the-mall" technique, which involves "several suggestive interviews filled with misinformation," leads many subjects to have detailed memories of events (such as being lost in a shopping mall as a child) that did not actually occur.

Who Deceives Us?

Most of the deceptions that Dick describes are the work of conspiracies. A conspiracy is a group of people acting in secret in order to bring about some state of affairs. For instance, Cohaagen does not deceive Quaid by himself. He is simply the head of "The Agency" that controls Mars. Cohaagen's co-conspirators include Quaid's "wife" Lori, his "friend" Harry, the cab driver Benny, and even Quaid's previous self Hauser who claims in the suitcase video to have switched sides. And, of course, The Adjustment Bureau is the quintessential conspiracy.

Conspiracies often aim at bad ends, such as assassinating public figures, blowing up buildings, or crushing the mutant resistance so as to keep the turbinium flowing for the war effort. But it is important to note that conspiracies, such as the Adjustment Bureau, can also aim to bring about good consequences for the human race with their manipulations. According to the legendary "case worker" Thompson, the Dark Ages and the wars and atrocities of the twentieth century only occurred because the Adjustment Bureau tried letting us make our own decisions for a while.

Conspiracy theories are certainly popular. Many people believe that there was a conspiracy (possibly involving the CIA or even the Mafia) to assassinate JFK. Other people believe that the United States government destroyed the World Trade Center and attempted to destroy the Pentagon on 9/11 to provide an excuse for invading Iraq. In fact, at one time, Dick himself believed that there was a worldwide Marxist conspiracy involving science-fiction writers, such as Stanislaw Lem.

Despite their popularity, calling something "a conspiracy theory" is usually a way of dismissing and ridiculing it. But what exactly is wrong with believing in conspiracy theories? After all, the claim that the 9/11 attacks were carried out by a group of Muslim extremists is also a theory about a conspiracy, but given all of the available evidence, it seems quite reasonable to believe this theory.

Sir Karl Popper thought that it was irrational to believe in the existence of large, sinister, and supposedly extremely powerful, conspiracies because it is so unlikely for such conspiracies to succeed. Popper had what David Coady, in *Conspiracy Theories: The Philosophical Debate*, calls a "cock-up theory of society" rather than a "conspiracy theory of society." Indeed, it's hard to imagine that a group of real-life conspirators could successfully carry out the sort of operation that the Adjustment Bureau does. And, in fact, the Adjustment Bureau itself makes at least a few small mistakes. For instance, Harry falls asleep on a park bench and, thus, fails to make sure that David Norris spills coffee on his shirt by 7:05. As a result, David does not have to go home to change his shirt and ends up meeting Elise on the bus, which in turn leads to many further deviations from "the plan."

More recently, Brian Keeley has argued that believing in conspiracy theories is irrational in much the same way as

Hume argued that believing in miracles is irrational. Unlike claims of miraculous events, conspiracy theories do not require the breaking of the laws of nature. But nevertheless, they are almost always less likely to be true than some alternate explanation of the event in question—at least, they are less likely unless we are willing to engage in extreme skepticism, such as worrying that our spouse is not our spouse, that our friends are not our friends, and even that our memories are not our memories.

Circles within Circles

According to Steve Clarke, it's irrational to believe in conspiracy theories because they are essentially "degenerating research programs." This term was coined by a colleague of Popper's, Imre Lakatos, in his work on the philosophy of science. A degenerating scientific research program is one that requires numerous ad hoc modifications in order to save the theory from being proved false. For instance, most of the ancient Greeks and Romans, and medieval Europeans, thought that the Earth was at the center of the universe. But in order to hold this view and still make sense of their astronomical data, they had to accept that planets move in very

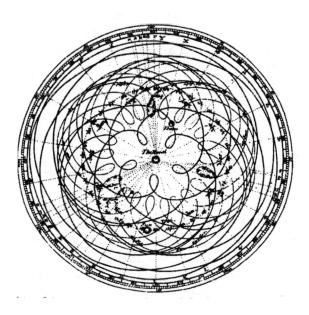

Giovanni Cassini's model of the apparent motion of Venus, Mars, and the Sun around the Earth. Hey, it could be true! I'll explain why this has to be correct as soon as you put on this tinfoil hat.

strange ways ("retrograde motion"). In fact, surprisingly enough, we can actually stick with this geocentric theory, but this 'degenerating' model of the universe would get ever stranger as we would have to make numerous ad hoc modifications ("adding epicycles") to explain our current astronomical data.

In the same way, conspiracy theories usually become quite convoluted and implausible as they try to account for the available data. For instance, "truthers" who believe in a US government conspiracy to destroy the Pentagon by missile or controlled demolition have had to come up with more and more additions to their theory in order to explain evidence like the airplane debris at the crash site, the eyewitness reports of the crash, and phone calls made by passengers prior to the crash.

In addition to it being irrational to believe in conspiracy theories, Lee Basham claims that it is a bad idea, for purely practical reasons, to believe in such theories. If there really is a secret global conspiracy along the lines of the Adjustment Bureau, there is not a whole lot that we can do about it—and worrying about our lack of control will just make us miserable.

On the other side, though, David Coady argues that it is a very bad idea to make it a practice to reject conspiracy theories out of hand. People who do so are very easily manipulated by the powers that be. And this is precisely the warning that Dick offers in many of his works. For instance, in the novel *Lies, Inc.*, most of the miserable inhabitants of an overcrowded Earth are convinced by the advertisements of "Trails of Hoffman Limited" that the off-world colony of "Whale's Mouth" (which suspiciously can only be reached via one-way teleportation devices) is a paradise. Those few skeptics are considered to be "idiots and cranks opposing history." Of course, as the people of Earth finally discover, "They were right. The cranks. The lunatics, like that guy who wanted to make the eighteen-year trip by interstellar ship."

Indeed, sometimes it is the received view, rather than the conspiracy theory, that is the degenerating research program. For instance, the government had to keep adding makeshift excuses in order to maintain the fiction that Saddam Hussein had weapons of mass destruction. In fact, sometimes so much counterevidence mounts that defenders of the official story, such as Dr. Edgemar, have to take the extreme step of claiming that it was all a dream.

Self-Deception

One of the conspirators who deceives Quaid is Quaid himself. In order to infiltrate the mutants and kill their leader Kuato, Hauser has to believe that he really is on the side of the mutants. As Cohaagen explains, "Hauser volunteered to become Doug Quaid. It was the only way to fool the psychics." Thus, Hauser was following the advice of Friedrich Nietzsche who said in *Human, All Too Human,*

> with all great deceivers there is a noteworthy occurrence to which they owe their power. In the actual act of deception they are overcome by belief in themselves. Self-deception has to exist if a grand effect is to be produced.

Whether or not you're a mutant with psychic capabilities, it's much harder to detect deception when the deceiver himself is deceived. If a deceiver believes what she is saying, she's not going to display the signs of stress and anxiety that liars often do. Also, if she believes what she is saying, she does not face the difficulty of trying to keep her stories (the real one and the made-up one) straight. As Nietzsche pointed out, "he who tells a lie seldom realizes what a heavy burden he has assumed; for, in order to maintain a lie, he has to invent twenty more."

One person being deceived so that she can more effectively deceive another person is actually a recurring theme in Dick's work. The replicant in *Imposter* is made to think that it is not a replicant so that it will have a better chance of carrying out its mission. In *A Scanner Darkly*, Arctor's superiors in the police force mislead him about their plans for him so that he will be able to infiltrate a New Path rehabilitation clinic.

But many philosophers argue that intentional self-deception is a practical impossibility—you can't just choose to believe something when you know that it's false. People "deceive themselves" quite often, but in most of these cases, they have no conscious intention to cause themselves to acquire a false belief. Instead, they acquire or maintain a false belief because it benefits them to hold that belief and they can't bear to be critical of it, even as evidence against it piles up. For instance, people do not consciously set out to deceive themselves about the wonders of Whale's Mouth "with its fresh air, sunshine, all those cute little animals, and those wondrous buildings THL robots are constructing." But because it provides the only hope for escaping their miserable lives on Earth, they cling to the official story.

How Can We Detect Deception?

Another very realistic concern with deception is found in the Voigt-Kampff test that a Blade Runner uses to identify replicants. A device is aimed at the subject's eye to detect minute physiological changes, such as "capillary dilation . . . fluctuation of the pupil . . . involuntary dilation of the iris." The subject is then told stories that are "designed to provoke an emotional response."

The V-K test is essentially a version of the famous Turing Test. In the early days of electronic computers, Alan Turing was trying to get clear about when we could say that a machine can think, and he proposed the following criterion: An examiner submits a series of questions remotely to a computer and to a human. If the examiner cannot determine, based on their written responses, which one is the computer, then we should say that the computer has intelligence. Thus, in order to pass the Turing Test, a computer would have to deceive the examiner into thinking that it is human.

This test was originally just a thought experiment, but it has now moved from science fiction into everyday life. Admittedly, we don't have to worry about catching replicants in real life, but we do have to worry about machines pretending to be humans. Certain computer programs, such as websites that let people rate news articles or websites that sell tickets to rock concerts, can be manipulated by other computer programs. So, in order to avoid such manipulation, anyone or anything that visits these websites has to take a version of the Turing Test. In fact, you have almost certainly taken this test yourself. It is called CAPTCHA ("Completely Automated Public Turing test to tell Computers and Humans Apart"). You are shown a series of squiggly letters and you have to type in what you see (a task that computers are not yet able to perform).

Are you really a human? Take this test and see.

The V-K test is also quite similar to real lie-detection technology, such as the polygraph. When people lie, they get nervous. For instance, while Dr. Edgemar is trying to convince Quaid that his trip to Mars is all a dream ("I'm quite serious. You're not here, and neither am I"), a drop of sweat runs down his brow. This is what makes Quaid realize that Edgemar is lying to him. So, polygraphs and the V-K test are both designed to detect physiological indicators of stress and anxiety, such as perspiration and increased blood pressure ("capillary dilation"). Of course, there is a sense in which the V-K test is actually the exact opposite of a standard polygraph. With a polygraph, stress and anxiety are taken to be indications of deception. But with the V-K test, the lack of emotion is the clue that the subject is pretending to be human.

But Dick's characters do not always (or even typically) use fancy machines to detect deception. They detect deception pretty much the same way that most of us do. We do not usually discover that someone is lying to us because we see that their heart is pounding or that they are sweating. When we catch someone lying to us, it's typically because what they say does not fit with we already know or with what we later find out. This is how Rachmael ben Applebaum discovers that a video of happy crowds on Whale's Mouth is a hoax. ("This audtrack is continuous, running over and over again. . . . it's a fake.") In fact, even in the case of Dr. Edgemar, the fact that he's nervous is not what tips Quaid off to the truth—it's the implication of his nervousness. Whether or not he's lying, it just does not make sense that someone "artificially implanted" into a dream would be nervous about getting shot, and it's that fact that implies that he must be lying. As the great detective Sherlock Holmes put it, "we must look for consistency. Where there is a want of it we must suspect deception."

16
The Blob Necessitates

MATTHEW MCCALL

What the hell is *VALIS* about? Well, for one thing, it's about the fuzzy line between delusions, reality, and psychological well-being—Horselover Fat, Dick's author surrogate, suffers from a series of traumatic events and mental breakdowns all the while receiving metaphysical revelations from a pink beam.

In the midst of such mayhem Dick also manages to provide us with an unnerving insight into the suicidal mind, a mindset that Dick frequently suffered through during the later years of his life. On a deeper level, it's about the interplay between metaphysics and emotions, arguably the signature theme of Dick's career.

Dick is on record as saying "Of all the metaphysical systems in philosophy I feel the greatest affinity for that of Spinoza, with his dictum, *"Deus sive substantia sive natura"*; to me this sums up everything (viz: "God i.e. reality i.e. nature.")" So it's no surprise that the world of *VALIS* has much in common with the metaphysics of Baruch Spinoza, one of the seventeenth century's most prominent philosophers. What may be of some surprise, though, is that Spinoza can save Fat from his turmoil, for Fat's metaphysics has Spinoza-like implications that supply the groundwork for his path toward emotional liberation. And this path begins with that pink beam, and with blobs.

Of Blob

During February and March of 1974, a pink beam of light entered Philip K. Dick's head, supposedly revealing to him the nature of reality and consciousness. For the next eight years, Dick struggled to determine whether the visions encountered during the "2-3-74" experience contained genuine insights or were rather a sign of mental deterioration. Dick toiled daily over this question, eventually producing what came to be an eight-thousand-page manuscript of recollections, theories, and doubts about the beam. He called this work the *Exegesis*.

To date only scant amounts have been published. Luckily for us, the *Tractatus: Cryptica Scriptura*, as Fat calls his musings, gives us a streamlined version of the *Exegesis*. Even more fortunate, the *Tractatus* is laid out in full as an appendix to *VALIS*. To see how the philosophy of the *Tractatus*—and in turn Spinoza's philosophy—can help save Fat, we must first discuss blobs.

Imagine a blob. This blob is the only genuinely independent object in existence. Let's suppose too that this blob contains everything we run across in our everyday lives. In other words, instead of thinking of reality as blob-free, we must think of it as blob-contained.

So, what significant differences are there for life in the blob as opposed to life outside it? For the answer, we can turn to the most famous blobist in history: Spinoza. The *Ethics,* Spinoza's most studied work, explains blobism in terms of substance and mode. Substance is defined as "that which is in itself and conceived through itself" (1d3).[1] To say that the blob is "in itself" means that it has properties, but is not a property of anything else. To help articulate this notion, imagine green, bubbling goo. Neither green nor bubbling exist without goo. So the goo is like a substance with bubbly greenness as its property. Now for Spinoza, we are like bubbly greenness in cosmic goo. We—the bubbly greenness of goo—inhere in a substance—the goo or blob—as "modes," or rather "the affections of substance, or that which is in another thing through also which it is conceived" (1d5). So if you take the goo away, the green bubbles go along with it. Likewise, take the blob away and its "affections"—particular things like you and me—go away as well.

Now, can we think of the goo as a different color or placid? We sure can. But can we think of the goo as not being viscous

---

[1] In referring to Spinoza's *Ethics*, I follow the procedure usual among Spinoza scholars. "1d3" means Book 1, definition 3.

liquid? No; that's exactly what makes it goo. To think of goo without its bubbly greenness, or its modes, is to think of it "through itself." On the other hand, when thinking about the bubbly greenness, we must think of it as "conceived" through something else, namely, goo. For Spinoza, when we think about substance or blobs we are thinking about reality despite the fact that our senses seem to tell us that we are blob-free creatures. In other words, what we should take as true derives from our concepts, not our senses. So, if we think about what is implied by substance and modes, we will discover the nature of reality. If we think hard enough, we will see that for better or worse we are all part of the blob.

The Nature and Origin of the "Mind"

Well, . . .for Fat it may be for the worse. Fat's blob—his concept of what we are all part of—comes with serious emotional baggage, for his version of 'the blob', what he calls the "Mind," created the "Brain," an independent entity existing within the Mind in order to keep the memory of its deceased sister alive. Or, as the thirty-second entry of the *Tractatus* informs us, "All the information processed by the Brain—experienced by us as the arranging and rearranging of physical objects—is an attempt at this preservation of her; stones and rocks and sticks and amoebae are traces of her." Reality as we know it is no more than the Mind's fond memories of a lost sibling.

Like anyone else, the Mind grieves over the death of its sister. Unlike most cases of grief, this has driven the Mind mad, which is bad for us:

> 33. This loneliness, this anguish of the bereaved Mind, is felt by every constituent of the universe. All its constituents are alive.

> 38. From loss and grief the Mind has become deranged. Therefore, we, as parts of the universe, the Brain, are partly deranged.

As a metaphysical consequence of being within the Mind, we must all suffer. For us this may seem quite a strange claim, but for Fat this belief is essential to balancing his precarious psychological states since he can blame his madness and melancholy on the Mind. He can say, with however shaky justification, that it ain't his fault.

And Spinoza agrees. Although it's not the Mind's fault—it's God's. The reason for this is simple: Spinoza calls the blob "God." For Spinoza, reality is God revealing himself to us, or, as Dick writes in *VALIS*, "as Spinoza supposed, the universe may be one theophany." But why is the blob God? First, remember that substance has properties but is not the property of anything else. Thus there is only one substance, since in order to think about two substances we must think about the substances' properties, which is precisely *not* to think of two substances "through themselves." There is only one substance since we can't legitimately conceive of two.

Further, substance can't be caused by another substance since this would require us to think of substance "through" or dependent on something else, which is again not to think of a substance. Finally, substance is infinite, for if it were finite its existence could only be explained by its being limited by another substance, which, you guessed it, is not to think of a substance. Therefore, there is one blob—uncaused and infinite—that contains everything. By definition this is God, or "Being absolutely infinite" (1d6). Thus the grand conclusion: "What ever is, is in God, and nothing can be or be conceived without God" (1p15). For Spinoza, we're dependent on God in the deepest sense. We are part of Him.

And the depths of our dependency go even deeper. As part of God, our actions, thoughts—our entire lives!—are determined down to the smallest detail. In Spinoza's world, you are not free to have chosen *not* to have read this sentence, for "the will cannot be called a free cause, but can only be necessary" (1p32). Moreover, the world's entire history was *necessarily* determined when the first particle of matter came into existence. In other words, the only metaphysically *possible* time-line is the *actual* time-line. According to this aptly named *necessitarianism*, it's metaphysically impossible for Dick not to have experienced "2-3-74." By necessity, "Things could have been produced by God in no other manner and in no other order than that which they have been produced" (1p33). For Spinoza, we're victims of circumstance in the truest sense.

But, then again, so is God. As Spinoza unequivocally states, "God does not act from freedom of the will" (1p32c1). Spinoza's God, contrary to many longstanding religious and philosophical traditions, didn't create the world as a free act of love—for

He didn't even have the choice not to create the world. Perhaps even more out of sync with standard views, Spinoza's God is incapable of caring for humans: "There are those who imagine God to be like a man, composed of body and soul and subject to the passions; but it is clear how far off men who believe this are from the true knowledge of God" (1p15s). Literally, Spinoza's God could not care less about us. Fortunately, in case you're not happy with calling this substance God, you're just as welcome to call it, along with Spinoza, "Nature."

Now if the *Ethics* is meant to be a practical guide to life, and if Spinoza didn't fail in making his *monism* (what philosophers traditionally call blobism) practical, then there should be something useful in all this. In order to figure out what that is, we're going to first look at the causes of depression in light of Spinoza's theory of emotions, and then we may just come to see that life in the blob has its perks.

The Origin and Nature of Affective Disorder

The opening sentences of *VALIS* tell us that "Fat's nervous breakdown began the day he got the phone call from Gloria asking if he had any Nembutals. He asked her why she wanted them and she said she intended to kill herself." After the phone call, Gloria drove three hours to visit Fat. He didn't give her the sleeping pills. Instead, they walked along the Point Reyes shoreline, discussing the reasons she wanted to die. Gloria's reasoning was eerily uncomplicated: "everyone hated her, was out to get her, and she was worthless in every respect." She returned home the next day, leaving Fat unsure that he was of any help. Ten days later Gloria threw herself from a tenth story window. Her suicide surprised no one.

One way to understand Gloria's suicide is to think of it as a response to undue hatred. Gloria believed that "they," the personification of a hateful reality, plotted against her day and night, doing such maleficent things as seizing her bank account. As any good Spinozist would realize, Gloria was headed for trouble, for "If we imagine that we are hated by another without giving him cause for it, we shall hate him in return" (3p40). Moreover, if she had hated anything else besides reality *as a whole*, perhaps Gloria could have been saved. She could have just avoided or destroyed the source. As common-sense as this sounds, it's not always immediately obvious that "We endeavor to bring into existence everything which we imagine conduces to joy, and to remove or destroy everything opposed to it, or which conduces sorrow" (3p28). But Gloria hated reality and, sadly, there seems to be only one way to remove that sort of pain.

Spinoza's only mention of suicide gives us yet another way of looking at Gloria's death. Spinoza says that "all persons who kill themselves are impotent in mind, and have been thoroughly overcome by external causes opposed to their nature" (4p18s).

Spinoza does not intend to be derogatory when describing suicides as "impotent in mind." He means instead that the suicidal don't properly understand reality. Gloria, and later Fat, are in part suicidal because they don't realize that we are a part of Nature, that all events are necessitated, and that our emotional responses to suffering can be overcome by applying these metaphysical principles to our life. But more on this later.

We should focus our attention for now on Spinoza's claim that suicides are "overcome by external causes opposed to their nature." According to Spinoza, we preserve our life because it's our nature or essence to do so. Part of Fat's essence, then, is eating a sandwich or taking a walk. In addition, since our essence is constituted by those acts and things keeping us alive, Spinoza claims that "The effort by which each thing endeavors to preserve in its own being is nothing but the actual essence of the thing itself" (3p7). So we can't help but partake of life-preserving activities. Suicide "opposes" our nature, then, because we do the one thing that is its exact opposite: we stop preserving ourselves.

In what sense, though, are suicides "overcome by external causes"? We can get some clarification here by looking at the three tragedies causing Fat's mental decline. First tragedy: Gloria killed herself. Second tragedy: Fat's wife divorced him. Third tragedy: Fat's wife took their son along with her. The tragedy of Fat's life: prolonged guilt over Gloria's suicide intensified by familial loss. Fat's onset of severe depression is the effect of a one-two punch, which, as Spinoza notes, only makes things worse, for "The greater the number of the causes that simultaneously concur to excite any affect, the greater it will be" (5p8). The more causes of suffering we encounter, the worse the suffering.

Such causes are contrary to Fat's nature since they counteract those causes keeping him alive. They are considered external causes precisely for this reason. Fat's divorce, for example, is an external cause because it sure as hell didn't help him get up in the morning. Now external causes bring suffering since, by definition, suffering occurs "when anything is done within us, or follows from our nature, of which we are not the cause excepting partially" (3d1).

In one sense, Fat's a partial cause of his divorce since his emotional problems caused his wife to leave. In an even more removed sense, Fat's visit to Gloria is a partial cause of her death since his visit involved life-preserving activities. Nonetheless, the divorce and suicide are external causes merely because they aren't effects of Fat's nature, although he is a partial cause of them. Suicides are "overcome by external causes" because they are overwhelmed by those causes counteracting the natural tendency to continue living. And being overwhelmed by the divorce and Gloria's death is exactly why Fat attempted suicide.

Fat's fate, though, isn't as dramatic as Gloria's. Fat didn't die. He instead wound up in the county mental hospital and eventually put under the care of Maurice, a crass, tough-skinned, and even threatening therapist, who gives Fat some quite Spinozan advice, "You feel guilty because Gloria died. Take responsibility for your own life for a change. It's your job to protect yourself." In other words, Maurice appeals to Fat's nature by suggesting that Fat take up the responsibility of freeing himself from mental anguish.

But how is Fat to do this? One answer comes in the form of a smiling, soft spoken, black-haired two-year-old. This one we know works . . . for a while.

Of Plasmatic Bondage

VALIS is an acronym for Vast Active Living Intelligence System. It fires beams into a select few, such as Fat, so that they can remember humankind's alien origins. It is also a two-year-old girl named Sophia, who happens to also be what Fat calls a *plasmate*, or the critical information in the Brain informing the chosen few that reality as we perceive it is the result of an alien species's twisted form of entertainment.

In our world, the plasmate often takes form as the "Immortal One," a series of reincarnations cross-bonded with humans, appropriately deemed *homoplasmates* by Fat. Homoplasmates have come in the persons of Elijah, Dionysos, and Christ, to name but a few. Sophia, though, is not a homoplasmate. She is plasmate in pure form. There is nothing human about her (although it remains a mystery how she can also be a two-year old *human!*).

As the plasmate, Sophia knows everything there is to know and can do anything there is to do, and accordingly does what no therapist or drug could. She cures Fat, causing him to realize that he is an alternate personality of Philip K. Dick! By merely being in the presence of Sophia, Dick (the character) was freed of "Eight long fucking goddam years of occlusion and pain and searching and roaming about."

But Fat's and Dick's suffering aren't gone for good. Sophia dies by an accidental radiation overdose shortly after meeting Fat. In the wake of this tragedy, Dick (the character) once again channels his sorrow into the artificial personality of Fat, this time indulging in more far-fetched machinations. So much for the plasmatic route to emotional freedom.

What about Spinoza's route? Remember that Fat and Spinoza are both metaphysical monists, albeit Spinoza has much more to say and less to believe about free will. But necessitarianism ain't necessarily bad. Take this proposition for example: "In so far as the mind understands all things as necessary, so far has it greater power over the affects, or suffers less from them" (5p6). If Fat could just realize that Gloria's suicide was unavoidable, then he could temper his self-blame. He could process the suffering related to her death stoically, conceiving of it as nothing more than a necessary consequence of prior events. Since Gloria in a literal sense had to die, Fat couldn't have saved her no matter how hard he tried and thus he ought not to suffer such guilt over her death.

The Power of the Intellect, or of Fat's Emotional Liberation

These emotional lessons are fine and dandy for necessitarianism. But Fat doesn't live in Spinoza's 'Nature'. He lives in 'the Mind', a world allowing free will and metaphysical determinism to co-exist. So Fat can't quite yet throw up his hands in celebration of a newly found necessitarian freedom. However, Fat's psychological well-being can benefit from paying close attention to the Spinoza-like implications of his theory.

First, Fat realizes that reality screws some people over. In Fat's words, "The universe makes certain decisions and on the basis of these decisions some people live and some people die. This is a harsh law. But every creature yields to it out of necessity." This is not to say that Fat is a necessitarian, but that there are nonetheless some elements of fate at play. He can think of Gloria's death as one of those sad consequences of this fatalistic "harsh law," and then reason along Spinozan lines.

But let's assume that Fat can't do this and that he still feels partly responsible for Gloria's death. Even in this case, Fat has an out according to his *Tractatus*:

> 29. We did not fall because of a moral error; we fell because of an intellectual error: that of taking the phenomenal world as real. Therefore we are morally innocent. It is the Empire in its various disguised polyforms that tells us we have sinned.

According to Entry 29, Fat's making a cognitive mistake. Gloria *really* didn't die and his wife *really* didn't leave him. These events are illusions. Fat's thus unburdened from the responsibility that he feels for Gloria's suicide and the divorce. In the same vein as Spinoza's view of suicide, Fat should realize that he's suffering from a mistaken understanding of reality. He's not realizing that the metaphysical nature of reality absolves him.

But if we're going to allow Fat to reap the benefits of his theory, we must also consider its detriments. Remember that one cause of Fat's sorrow is the Mind's sorrow. Spinoza actually believes something similar: "We suffer in so far as we are part of nature which part cannot be conceived by itself nor without the other parts" (4p2). Thus for both Fat and Spinoza we can never absolutely rid ourselves of suffering.

We can, however, increasingly limit it. According to Spinoza, we can do this by recognizing suffering's origins and causes. Fat can overcome the mental anguish attached to Gloria's death by forming a deeper appreciation of its causes, in turn realizing how her death caused his own melancholy. In order to develop a sufficiently rich enough understanding to overcome his sadness, Fat must embrace the metaphysics of the Mind while simultaneously developing a firm grasp of the causal chains leading up to his breakdown. Once he takes it to heart that we must suffer because we're part of the Mind and that there are external causes of Gloria's death, Fat can defend himself from the emotionally detrimental effects of misfortune. Understanding the true metaphysics, so Spinoza claims and as Fat should learn, sets us on the path toward self-preservation.

Spinoza's suggestion here is really an intellectually-charged version of "developing thick skin." In order to achieve freedom from emotional torment, we must realize that reality is necessarily cruel and that most misfortunes are out of our control. Resolutely believing this dampens the twinge of our sorrows, allowing us to finally see that "So long as we are not agitated by affects which are contrary to our nature do we possess the power of arranging and connecting the affections of the body according to the order of the intellect" (5p10). The better understanding we have of the origin and nature of suffering, the more we can overcome it and act according to our essence. If Fat can recognize the terrible necessity of suffering and learn to appreciate that causes other than him fully explain Gloria's death, he can start freeing himself from suffering's bondage.

So, yes, Spinoza can save Fat. However, such a path to happiness may simply redefine sanity in an insane world. For each version of monism requires us to ditch beliefs we take as self-evident and valuable. We take ourselves to posses some amount of free will, we tend to believe that some events are contingent, and most of us simply can't accept that our emotional life is a metaphysical consequence of living within a blob. The implications of Fat's and Spinoza's respective monisms just seem crazy. Within the monist world, then, it's indeed true that "sometimes it is an appropriate response to reality to go insane."[2]

---

[2] Necessary thanks to Juan Garcia, Walter Ott, Gabriel Schneider, and Dylan Wittkower for helpful comments on earlier drafts.

17
The Gnosis of 2-3-74

RONALD S. GREEN

The last major writings of Philip K. Dick, *VALIS* the most famous among them, contain many points of reflections of Gnostic texts in the Nag Hammadi Library. Those texts describe the formation of the material universe arising as part of a series of accidents, mistakes, and sometimes malicious devices used by an imperfect architect ignorant of the true creator.

Dick took up this idea of multiple imperfect architects not only in the world of *VALIS*, but even in the way the narrative unfolds through the mentally-deficient character of Horselover Fat. Fat is usually unaware that he is merely an author surrogate for the true creator, Philip K. Dick, who also appears in the story as a (sometimes) different character.

The Gnostic texts discovered at Nag Hammadi present a kind of religious-metaphysical conspiracy theory which, of course, resonated deeply with an author who had already explored hidden realities featuring gods who were somewhat less-than-divine in works like "Adjustment Team," "A Present for Pat," and *The Three Stigmata of Palmer Eldritch*.

In February and March 1974, a period he refers to as 2-3-74, Philip K. Dick experienced a series of intense and life-changing visions he sometimes related to Gnosticism. These seem to have started when, while Dick was under the influence of sodium pentathol administered for an impacted tooth, a delivery woman arrived at his door wearing a pendant with a Christian fish emblem. Afterwards Dick placed a fish sticker on a window in his house and, perhaps in relation to the sun shining through it, he saw bright rectangular images he felt contained information from a divine or otherwise extraordinary source.

For the rest of his life, he continued to come up with new ways of interpreting what had happened and what it meant. The varying accounts of the same "transmissions" became the basis for *Radio Free Albemuth* and the *VALIS* trilogy, and are also described and interpreted in his *Exegesis*. Within each of these books several differing accounts are given, but all assume a transcendental consciousness penetrated his mind through mundane expressions hiding some ultimate truth, and that this consciousness is at least in part beyond human rationality.

Accordingly, these truths cannot be fully expressed in ordinary terms, but a variety of mythic stories might be used to convey some aspects of them. In this, the *VALIS* trilogy resembles Gnostic texts, Hindu epics, and other pieces of classical religious literature: Dick's last writings tell and retell the same stories in a range of contradictory ways.

In other novels such overt inconsistencies might make the stories unreadable. But because of the contradictory nature of reality that is assumed in these stories, these seeming contradictions are for Dick supportive of one another, all being imperfect reflections of higher truth, just like the material world itself. In *The Divine Invasion*, Herb Asher says the early church felt that because the resurrection of Christ was impossible it must have happened. That is to say, when mundane reality completely explains an event it must be wrong. Only when there are seeming contradictions might an assumption be correct. Higher truths are hidden and not explainable in ordinary terms. Likewise in *VALIS*, when characters continually point out the inconsistencies in the descriptions of his divine visions, Horselover Fat feels this reinforces their validity.

Dick's Gnosis about Gnostics

VALIS can provisionally be called a "novel," but it is also an autobiography, and a mystical text for those who are able to understand it that way. This multivalent way of writing and reading is in keeping with Gnostic views of the multidimensionality of reality and Gnostic subtexts. Writings in the Nag Hammadi Library interpret and retell stories from the New Testament, Plato, Pythagoras, and others, allegedly based on divine inspiration and revelation on the part of the Gnostic reader and writer. As the name implies, Gnostics interpret the nature of reality by relying on *gnosis*, which can be defined as intuitive, transcendental insight; or hidden, secret knowledge, immediately certain without evidence or argument. Gnostics believed that they were able to enter into a kind of spiritual communion with these authors and with divine entities, allowing them to faithfully tell the "hidden truth" of the stories of others—even though their retellings were sometimes radical departures from the originals.

Nag Hammadi is a city in Upper Egypt. In 1945, farmers looking for fertile soil found a sealed earthenware jar on the outskirts of the city. At first they were afraid to open it, thinking it may contain an evil genie. However, feeling it was equally possible that it contained gold, they opened it and found thirteen leather-bound papyrus codices. Unfortunately they used one of these to kindle a fire.

The remaining books eventually made their way to the hands of museum officials. Since then, scholars have identified more than fifty separate writings within these volumes. They have been dated to around 390 C.E., although they are believed to translate earlier works. Many of these writings have been declared significant works of Gnostics, potentially changing our understanding of the history and ideology of early Christianity.

In *VALIS*, Horselover Fat speaks about the importance of the Nag Hammadi texts. For Fat, the texts provide an affirmation of his developing understanding of his personal mental defect and his view that his personal mental problems mirror the larger defect suffered by humankind: namely, that we have forgotten that we ourselves are divine. At the same time, the Nag Hammadi texts validate Dick's revelation about the solution to this problem: remembering through gnosis. (The Library became widely available in English translation only in 1977, and Dick claimed his vision was not shaped but confirmed by reading the texts.)

Two writings found side-by-side in Codex II of the Library coincide particularly well with his idea that human suffering and insanity are based in cosmogony; in the way the universe was created and structured. These are *The Hypostasis of the Archons* (the Reality of the Rulers) and an untitled document that has been given the name *On the Origin of the World*. Both interpret Genesis in ways that affirm various Gnostic beliefs, including the notion that our world was not constructed by the true God. In both writings, as in the *VALIS* trilogy, the speaker appears to change a number of times so that parts of the narration are retold from different perspectives.

Both of these Gnostic texts speak of an incorruptible realm also personified as the Incorruptible. From the incorruptible realm, Sophia, the spirit of wisdom, experiments with creating without her male aspect, who is referred to as the father-of-the-entirety. While the incorruptible is described as either filled with or being beautiful light, Sophia's experiment creates a veil of some type that casts a shadow. Darkness flows from the veil downward in a way both texts describe as like an aborted fetus. This becomes chaos with a bottomless watery abyss. Sophia breathes life into the darkness so a ruler over matter would form. The ruler moves across the face of the waters and Sophia says, "Child, pass through here," rendered as "yalda baōth" in the Coptic language of these texts. This begins verbal expression and the ruler is called Yaldabaoth (or Yaltabaōth). Having made the ruler over matter, Sophia withdraws her spiritual light from Yaltabaoth and the lower realm. In *VALIS*, Horselover Fat mentions Yaltabaoth to one of his psychiatrics, who responds, "What the hell are you talking about?"

The hell he is talking about is the material world and the arrogant being Yaltabaoth, who, ignorant of his origin and the realm above the veil, declares that he is God and that nothing else exists. Hearing this, Sophia calls him Samael, "the blind god." Samael appears here as an archon, or 'ruler'. In the Talmud, Samael is an archangel. Sophia causes the blasphemous words of the ruler to descend away from the incorruptible realm and Yaltabaoth to follow them downward to Tartaros. Tartaros is a pit or abyss that appears in classic Greek mythology, in the book of Job and elsewhere as a place of punishment. It's typically thought of as being below Earth.

By virtue of having both male and female characteristics, Yaltabaoth creates other beings that are also androgynous. His offspring become seven separate realms and the rulers of those seven heavens, likely based on the seven visible planets. Sophia arranges the placement of the seven heavens according to the attributes of the rulers and in some way mirroring the arrangement of the invisible, immaterial and incorruptible realm above the veil. These rulers of the lower realms have a soul or life but are not endowed with the divine spirit or light of the father-of-the-entirety.

It is the will of the father-of-the-entirety to unite everything above and below through light. To begin the process, Sophia looks down and her face is reflected briefly on the surface of the bottomless waters. Seeing the reflection, the rulers become enamored and try to reproduce it. At the same time they are afraid of what they saw, fearing something greater than them exists. As with the visible realm mirroring the invisible, this continues a series of references to reflections and twins that Dick echoes in his writings. In all cases the relationships between the various pairs are confused, ambivalent, and forgotten. Yaltabaoth separates land from the water and shapes a human from the mud, modeled after the reflection of Sophia. The clay figure is a reflection of a reflection of the reality of Sophia that Yaltabaoth has never seen directly. Yaltabaoth breaths soul or life into the mud but it remains wallowing on the ground because it does not have spirit. This weakness pleases the rulers. But Sophia secretly puts her light into the clay, giving it spirit and thereby making him a man. She also gives him a voice and by it he is called Adam.

Dick's Twins

In Gnostic thought, divine or mythic figures like Zoe, Eve, and Norea are viewed as syzygic pairs (necessarily co-existing couples) with other religious figures, such as Adam and Noah. These and other pairings of males and females represent active and passive attributes of the divine. In some Gnostic traditions Sophia or Zoe, embodied in Mary Magdalene, is in syzygy with Jesus. In the Gnostic *Gospel of Thomas*, also in the Nag Hammadi Library, Jesus says to Thomas that when he comes to know who he really is he will discover that he is identical to Christ, that he and Jesus are identical twins. The readers of these gospels and *VALIS* are apparently meant to understand themselves as the twins of Jesus, Thomas, and Dick.

Dick relates his lifelong obsession with his twin sister, who had died five weeks after their premature births, to syzygy. He thought of her as a missing part of his life he longed to understand. The lost twin is often a motif in his books and also plays out in other pairings, like Zina-Yah and Herb-Linda Fox in *The Divine Invasion*. Dick told Gregg Rickman, in an interview published as *Philip K. Dick: The Last Testament*, that the tragic element running through his life is the perpetual re-enactment of the death of his twin. The death of a woman is central to the books of the *VALIS* trilogy. In Entry 32 of the Exegesis at the end of *VALIS*, Dick explains the unfolding of the world as a narrative about the death of a woman he describes as half of the divine syzygy.

Linda Fox is thought by critics to be based on Linda Ronstadt, who is also mentioned in *The Divine Invasion*. In the paired realities created alternately by Emmanuel and Zina, she is in some sense like the clay model of Eve, not really human until Zina endows her with spirit. The dying woman Rybys is also strangely real and unreal. Although Herb comes in contact with her during cryonic suspension, she gives birth to the sav-ior child. The divine pairing of Emmanuel and Zina is mirrored in the human pairing of Herb and Linda. There is also a pairing of seeming good and evil, and of spiritual and material in the father-of-the-entirety (with male and female aspects repre-sented by Emmanuel and Zina) and the androgynous Belial.

In his essay "Cosmogony and Cosmology," written in 1978, three years before *VALIS*, Dick describes time and creation as the simultaneous movement of two events respectively related to these pairings. Humanity is moving toward reincorporation with the incorruptible and materiality is moving toward disso-lution in the immaterial. Linda Fox explains how this plays out on the microcosmic level of humanity, saying that every man has an Advocate, a beside-helper, as well as an Accuser. While there is syzygic pairing in human and divine male and female spirituality, there is also human and divine pairing of spiritu-ality and materiality. In other macro- and microcosmic pairings there is *VALIS* the movie in *VALIS* the book, *Radio Free Albemuth* in *VALIS*, and *VALIS* in *The Divine Invasion* and *The Transmigration of Timothy Archer*.

Results of the Primordial Rape

The Gnostic texts say that, in order to keep a watch on him, the rulers put Adam in a garden and cause him to fall into a deep sleep. The stories differ here. *The Hypostasis of the Archons* says the rulers take the spirit from Adam's side and model a female likeness. *On the Origin of the World* does not say the rulers formed the female. Instead, Sophia sends a luminous female companion who breathes spirit into Adam. Seeing this, the rulers cause him to fall into a deep sleep. The woman is identified as Zoe, daughter of Sophia. When Adam awakens, Yaltabaoth lies by saying he created the female from Adam's side. In both versions the rulers lust for the spiritual woman, who laughs at their foolish belief that they can overpower her. She secretly creates out of clay another mirrored replica of herself as a replacement. The real luminous woman enters a tree that thereby becomes the Tree of Knowledge (gnosis). Afterwards, Yaltabaoth tells the man and woman they can eat from any tree in the garden except for the Tree of Knowledge, and that the fruits of that tree will kill them. Yaltabaoth doesn't know why he says this, but in fact the father-of-the-entirety causes him to do so in order to draw attention to the tree, so the man and woman will want to eat its fruit.

The replacement woman, Eve, has a soul, which is life, but no spirit. Still believing it is Zoe, the rulers descend on her and "defile her in every way." The real spiritual woman sees that they only defile themselves with a clay dummy, the primordial blow-up doll. After the primeval rape, the rulers are happy thinking they have now controlled and diminished the light of the woman—perhaps Deckard's unconscious motive as well, in his sexual aggression in *Blade Runner*. The rulers believe they have also corrupted the potential strength of future humanity, Zoe's progeny, by interbreeding with her.

Then a divine instructor of humanity comes into the garden. *On the Origin of the World* says the instructor is born from a drop of light Sophia drips into the water. The instructor tells Adam and Eve that Yaltabaoth lied about the forbidden tree; that eating from it would not kill them but give them gnosis. Adam and Eve eat the fruit from the Tree of Knowledge and their eyes are opened to the reality of their real circumstance. They see they are bodily-bound spirits separated from the incorruptible by the confines of matter. Their perception that they are naked is the realization that they are "naked" of unity with spirituality, primordial unity with Sophia and the father-of-the-entirety.

Yaltabaoth sees they are behaving oddly. Discovering they have eaten from the Tree of Knowledge, he is angered because he's afraid they have seen his deception. He especially fears the inevitability that this gnosis will eventually lead to his demise. To delay this, he expels them from the garden. The other rulers place a spinning, flaming sword around the tree so no one may eat from it again. (Apparently they cannot simply destroy it.) Yaltobaoth also gives humankind a number of burdens so that we will not realize our spiritual potential. He makes people work to fill up their time, gives us pain in childbirth, and other problems to worry about. Yaltabaoth also lies by telling Adam and Eve that the instructor was "the beast" who had now been punished for its dishonesty. In fact the rulers had only cursed the instructor, and were powerless to do anything else. As in Dick's trilogy, it's difficult to discern who is telling the truth in all of this. Gnosis, transcendental insight, would be the key to understanding.

From the depraved union of Eve and the rulers, Cain and Abel are born. Lucky for humankind, Adam and Eve have their own children—Seth and Norea—who are not defiled by the alien bloodline of the rulers. In these and other Gnostic writings, Norea is Zoe, and so humanity begins to improve. Seeing their power is again threatened, the rulers decide to flood the Earth and tell only Noah. Next the rulers descend and attempt to rape Norea, telling her to serve them as her mother had. Norea tells the rulers they are living in darkness and that they had not defiled her mother but a clay image of her. The rulers close in on her, but Norea cries out to father-of-the-entirety. An angel appears and saves Norea, telling her and retelling the reader the details of the events of this story.

In the end, we learn that those who know these things about the spiritual nature of humanity and the illusory nature of matter will become free from death, that which appears only through the deception of the rulers. But this liberation will not take place until the arrival of a savior, the authentic person who will reveal the truth of the existence of the spirit sent by the father-of-the-entirety. If there is a movie version of the Nag Hammadi texts, and it works out anything like adaptations of Dick's writings, this savior will either be played by Daniel Craig or maybe Keanu Reeves, since he's already played several saviors.

Pink Light

Scholars feel that when Gnostics read and contemplated texts, they believed they entered into a dialogue with the writer, the savior, or a sacred being. Gnostics claim that, in this way, they received the direct and authentic teachings of Jesus, Paul, and others. On the other hand, they believed that inventing one's own stories is also evidence of gnosis. This is precisely what Dick does in the *VALIS* trilogy.

Dick experiences the light of Sophia and reinterprets it his writings. In *The Divine Invasion*, Dick explains that the intelligent light in the novel is experienced as being pink because that is how the human eye discerns celestial radiance. The *Exegesis* notes his amusement at the pink light appearing like the color of strawberry ice cream while he was listening to the Beatles' "Strawberry Fields Forever." He concludes the divine has again manifested in the most mundane, another reference to Gnostic belief.

Among Dick's numerous theories about what he experienced through pink light are speculations about messages from three-eyed aliens he saw in a dream; projections from VALIS, a Vast Active Living Intelligence System that is like a satellite in space; and transmissions formed by God through Sophia, bypassing VALIS. Dick sees VALIS as acting like or being Yaldabaoth. That is, VALIS the satellite is not God but is only the ruler over and conveyer of the material realm. In his essay "Cosmogony and Cosmology," Dick speculates that God created VALIS so that the incorruptible might experience self-reflection. Among his descriptions of what happens to him during the transmissions are the ideas that he is taken over by the spirit of the prophet Elijah, who appears as a character in *The Divine Invasion*; that he breaks through the illusory screen of time, and realizes that we live in the time of the *Acts of the Apostles*; and that he is really Thomas, the twin of Jesus.

Generally, in contrast to orthodox Christians who seek salvation through faith, sacraments, the Bible, and church, Gnostics find salvation through inner experience related to direct divine revelation. *The Gnostic Gospel of Thomas* says the divine truth inside us will save us from death and suffering caused by the material world, if we bring it out. However, if we do not bring it out it will destroy us. This seems an apt description of Philip K. Dick's assumption about his pink light visions. He responds by fervently interpreting his visions in hopes of an understanding that will bring salvation from his madness. Madness as ignorance of the divine is a condition shared alike by all humanity and Yaltobaoth. *The Gospel of Truth*, in the Nag Hammadi Library, describes the human condition as a nightmare in which a man with bloody hands is pursued for murder. He cannot escape until he receives gnosis. In another image in the text, a man is depicted as a mountaineer who has lost his way in the fog. He finds the way out only when he hears his name called. This is said to be like experiencing gnosis. Like the fog, Dick consistently describes ordinary reality as deception, the veil of Maya or "occlusion." In some of his descriptions this is brought about by a malicious ruler. Herb Asher tells a policeman all this is illusion and that he, the cop, is unaware that he is working for evil. In some of Dick's versions the ruler is insane. In others, people have an injury and cannot access their own divine knowledge.

Both *On the Origin of the World* and *The Hypostasis of the Archons* say all of the problems with the material world sculpted by Yaltobaoth are in accord with the will of the father-of-the-entirety. At first glance this statement seems to weaken the point of the Gnostic gospels. Why introduce a blind god if we cannot blame it for ignorance? Why would the true god do this?

Dick gives various answers. In "Cosmogony and Cosmology," it is for self reflection. In *The Divine Invasion*, God likes games, but the rulers do not. In *VALIS*, we are the architects who formed the material universe to see if we could build a labyrinth so elaborate we could not escape. Maybe in the same way Dick wanted to see if he could write a novel so strange not even he could understand it. If these books resulted from exposure to the Nag Hammadi Library imagine what he would have done if he had had access to the Internet!

Ay, There's
the Wub

18
Replicating Morality

JOHN SULLINS

I've done questionable things.

—ROY BATTY

Evil, for Philip K. Dick, is almost always embodied by the lack of empathy—the inability to experience the world as another might or to feel the pain in others that one's own actions may be causing.

In *Blade Runner*, the Tyrell Corporation has been able to mimic, or even surpass, almost every human characteristic except empathy. Testing for proper empathetic response using the Voigt-Kampf machine has become the only reliable way to find replicants that are trying to pass as human. But this is changing; some of the Nexus 6 replicants seem to be evolving a capacity for empathy. As the movie nears its ending the replicants Roy Batty and Rachel both have passed a threshold that even a Blade Runner like Deckard can see has moved them into a kind of parity with humans. Roy Batty has developed a love of life so deep that it extends to his would-be killer and Rachel and Deckard seem to be in love with one another.

These replicants, though man-made, have become capable of experiencing a deep and meaningful love that is not simply self-serving, and, for this reason, we should regard them as persons in a moral sense (although not in a biological sense). Even though they are machines, they can lay claim to rights and responsibilities that once, perhaps, only humans held. Perversely, many of the human characters in the film seem to be devolving and may be losing the ability to act as moral persons. But what does Dick think gives a human (or a robot, or an alien) moral personhood?

Beyond Lies the Other

In the first short story that Philip K. Dick ever published ("Beyond Lies the Wub"), he tells of the fateful encounter between a callous, officious, and brutal spaceship captain and an alien creature called a "wub." The wub looks like a pig, yet is jovial and life-loving and wishes harm on no one. Despite its foreign and ugly looks, the wub is interested in truth and beauty, literature, the arts, and good food. The Captain, on the other hand, is a mean-spirited militant and the only value he sees in the wub is that it could supply the crew with plenty of fresh meat.

The wub has telepathic powers that allow it to communicate with the Captain and crew but the Captain refuses to engage in any communication and continues to organize the crew to have the creature slaughtered. Strangely, the wub is not terribly worried about its impending demise.

As the story progresses we find that the alien is fully capable of understanding the motives of the Captain even better than the Captain does himself but in the face of impending violence, the wub only offers reasoned arguments as to why he should not be eaten, which the Captain duly ignores. The wub's ability to put himself in the place of another is so strong that it leads to an ending of the encounter that the unimaginative Captain could have never seen coming and a new lease on life for the wub.

The wub's extreme empathic nature is his salvation. The wub is not only able to imagine what it is like to be in the place of another, he has the psychic ability to fully become the other. By exchanging minds with the Captain, the wub lives on in the Captain's body, while the Captain must suffer being killed and eaten, just as he would have done to the wub. Do unto the wub only what you would be willing to experience for yourself.

In a "Headnote" that Dick wrote for a reprint of this story in 1981, he tells us that "The wub was my idea of a higher life form; it was then and it is now." The value of empathy and its importance to being "human" is a theme that begins here in his first story and runs throughout his career. If we want to better understand his stories, then we need to understand the deep role that empathy plays in Dick's philosophical thinking.

Empathy is a complex subject, but for our purposes here let's think of it as the ability to see the world from another's point of view and, additionally, to sympathize with that view. To see the importance of this second condition, consider that a cat cornering a rat must be able to sense what the rat is likely to do to try to escape, and must be one step ahead of those thoughts, or the rat will get away. Even though the cat is, in a way, deducing the options that the rat has and calculating which one the rat is likely to choose, this is in no way empathy. Empathy comes when, in addition to the above thought process, we also feel the same emotions that the rat is undergoing and can feel sorry for the doomed creature. Dick maintained that this was a rare ability in nature and one that only a few entities could possess, and that perhaps the only being that perfectly manifest this capacity is God.

Towards the end of his career, after his period of very heavy drug use and a deep religious conversion, Dick wrote his *Exegesis*: a huge collection of notes that contain thoughts on religion and philosophy, critiques of his own work, and comments on world events, all bound together. In a section written in 1978, where he is commenting on his own work, he tries to make sense of the idea, which occurs over and over in his fiction, that we can rediscover our missing moral character:

> Our minds are occluded, deliberately, so that we can't see the prison world we're slaves in, which is created by a powerful magician-like evil deity, who, however, is opposed by a mysterious salvific entity which often takes trash forms, and who will restore our lost memories. This entity may even be an old wino.

This savior entity will be like the wub, easy to dismiss, easy to ignore, but for those who have the ability to see beyond the surface illusion, this being is the one we should try to emulate. When we achieve this, as Dick puts it: "we will cease to be mere reflex machines," meaning we will quit acting like robots and start acting like true humans. This sounds great until you follow through the troubling logical deduction, that unless you have personally had this revelation, you—and I mean you, dear reader—are nothing but a robot.

How to Tell if You Are Really Just a Robot

Spence Olham has a big problem in *Imposter*. He started his day trying to decide how he was going to deal with life's little problems such as where he might like to take a well-earned vacation. But by the end of the day he would be running for his life, running from his former friends and co-workers, a public enemy distrusted even by his own wife. Everyone is convinced that Olham is a robot, cleverly designed by the alien species that is at war with the Earth, a robot designed to copy Olham in every way so that it can use his identity to gain access to the secret defense project Olham is working on and then detonate a powerful nuclear bomb that is hidden deep inside the robot's body. Everyone is convinced of this, except Olham himself.

Olhams's dilemma is similar to other Dick characters, such as Rachel in the movie *Blade Runner* who thinks of herself as a human but learns that she may be a replicant, or Garson Poole, the protagonist in one of Dick's most frightening short stories, "The Electric Ant," who after an accident wakes up in a hospital to find that not only has he been disfigured by the accident, but that the operation to save his life has also uncovered the fact that he is (and has always been) an electric ant; a cyborg who is part biological and part machine.

The character Garson Poole is in many ways strikingly similar to Dick himself. Dick often wrote himself into his stories and novels, and if we accept Poole's story as being somewhat autobiographical, we can see how seriously Dick wants us to take the notion that we may have mechanical or artificial drives that cause us to think and behave the way we do. In the story, Poole starts experimenting with his own programming and small changes start to show up in his subjective reality—how he sees the world. His experiments on himself get more and more drastic until he runs the risk of self-destruction. Poole does this in order to find out once and for all the truth of his being.

Poole's search for meaning was chillingly re-enacted by Dick himself in the decades of experimental drug use that followed the writing of this story. This wild hunt for truth and clarity did not lead to any self-revelation, it led only to an untimely death on the eve of his greatest success as a writer, as his stories and novels became hot commodities as film adaptations.

The ultimate tragedy of this is that Dick had already spelled out a much more self-affirming and healthy way to assure yourself of your true human nature though the experience of empathetic love. Dick was an avid reader of philosophy and he used his fiction as a kind of philosophical laboratory where he could tease out the implications of various philosophical ideas. One of the philosophical ideas he returns to again and again is *agape*.

'Agape' is a funny-sounding word that is used in ancient and medieval philosophy to refer to a special kind of spontaneous love. This is a love that is much more than simple passion or sexual attraction. Agape is a binding love felt when the lover unconditionally accepts the beloved, even if the beloved does not merit the attention. It can refer to the love felt in healthy families, or in the brotherly love displayed when one helps strangers. The greatest examples are found in Christian theology, where agape is used to describe the kind of love God has for his creation. For our purposes here, we need not get caught up in the nuances of the philosophy of love. But we do need to realize that when Dick speaks of empathy, he means something like agape.

Dick is not convinced that robots will be able to experience this special kind of empathy. Oh sure, they will be able to pretend to care. They will be cleverly programmed to act as if they love, but he believes that they will never be able to experience it as a fellow human might. They may greet you when you come home, say the right things when you are depressed, help you in areas they are programmed to be helpful in. But in each of these cases they have a reason to love, namely that they are programmed to do so. They will never just spontaneously recognize others as worthy of love and empathy. You are a robot if you cannot experience empathy.

Can a Blade Runner Love a Robot?

When it comes to the movie *Blade Runner*, we can notice a distinct point of departure from the vision that Dick had in his book, *Do Androids Dream of Electric Sheep?* Dick's vision of the world in the book is actually much darker and more depressing than the already damp and dreary environs of the film. In 1968, many years before the film we know went into production, Dick wrote some notes on how this book might be turned into a film. The actual film, as it was eventually written and produced, focuses on the character played by Harrison Ford—Rick Deckard. But Dick was actually unsure if the film should focus on Rick Deckard or Jack Isadore.

You may be scratching your head, because even the biggest fan of *Blade Runner* would be hard-pressed to find any character named Jack Isadore in the film. The film-makers changed most of the details about Isadore, and then renamed him J.F. Sebastian. Be that as it may, Dick saw one of the main points of the story as an exploration of whether the naïve love that Sebastian/Isadore has for the replicants is justified, or whether Deckard is correct in believing that the replicants are just vicious killing machines that must be destroyed.

The way Dick saw it, the story is more of a tragedy, as Sebastian/Isadore loses his innocence when the gritty realism of Deckard proves to be correct. In the book, Isadore is confronted by the innate cruelty of the replicants while he watches as they cut the legs off of a spider out of boredom, an act whose brutality is compounded by the fact that living non-human creatures, such as the spider, are now very rare on the dying polluted Earth of the future. This ends Isadore's fascination with the replicants and causes him to help in their eventual demise at the hand of Deckard. Dick also feels that Deckard's resolve to destroy the final three replicants that are holed up in Isadore's apartment is strengthened by his sexual encounter with the replicant Rachael Rosen. Dick explains this in his "Notes on *Do Androids Dream of Electric Sheep?*"

> Isn't this, the sexual union between Rick Deckard and Rachael Rosen—isn't it the summa of falsity and mechanical motions carried out minus any real feeling, as we understand the word? Feeling on each of their parts. Does in fact her mental—and physical—coldness numb the male, the human man, into an echo of it?

In the book, this encounter is only alluded to, but Dick imagines in his notes that it could be played up visually in a movie with a scene that could be a "horrifyingly mechanical episode of half dream, half reality, with Rachael melting superficially—but by doing so, exposing a steel-and-solid-state electronic gear beneath."

There is nothing Deckard can do to make her a real woman. Rachael warns Deckard as he is undressing her, "Don't' pause and be philosophical, because from a philosophical standpoint it's dreary. For both of us." Dick feels that the deep frustration, disappointment, and horror engendered by this situation, along with the self hatred he feels, would be enough to fuel Deckard's rage against the remaining replicants.

This is not at all how the situation is dealt with in the movie. There, Dekard's relationship with the replicant Rachael is much more natural and satisfying. It is suggested in the film that she is an upgraded replicant, one that is becoming almost indistinguishable from humans, or as the motto of the Tyrell Corporation that built her provocatively claims "more human than human." Here their relationship seems real and Deckard's motivation is to finish his assignment to retire the other dangerous replicants and then escape with Rachael before another bounty hunter comes to destroy all of the replicants, including Rachael.

This reworking of Dick's plot is not out of place. It actually captures one of his major themes: that empathy is a key human capacity. In the final scenes of the movie, we see one of the most startling chase sequences ever filmed, as Deckard goes from being the hunter to the hunted while he desperately flees for his life from the replicant Roy Batty through the decaying ruins of a mostly vacant apartment block, even as Roy's body is shutting down as he reaches his predesigned end; his planned obsolescence. Before he goes, we see him toy with Deckard in a final game of cat and mouse—teasing and wounding him just for the fun of it and perhaps also as revenge for the replicants Deckard has killed so far. But something happens within Batty during those last minutes, and when it comes down to it, the trained killer Roy Batty, with his enemy Rick Deckard hanging dozens of stories up off the side of a building, is unwilling to allow Deckard to fall to his death. As Roy Batty's last living act, he saves Deckard and pulls him back to safety. Roy Batty shows compassion and empathy, he sees himself in the frantic terrified eyes of his own sworn enemy; he gives as he wishes to receive—he gives life. Roy, thorough his compassion and Rachael, through her capacity to love have both become human—perhaps more than human.

How to Build a Moral Robot

Sometimes science fiction becomes science fact. In many ways it seems that we are very close to entering a world that contains the kinds of robots and androids that Dick was so good at imagining. Much of Dick's fiction presents dark and dystopian worlds and situations, so on the surface, one might think that he had a pessimistic attitude about the future. But his motivation for writing like this was not a belief that the future will necessarily be dark, but rather, as a way of warning us to avoid these possible futures.

It may be that Dick, and other authors from his age, were so good at describing the hells of a world torn by nuclear war that it made such a world unthinkable—and that this is part of why this future is one that the real world has, so far, avoided realizing. Dick has given us multiple views of intricately imagined future worlds where robots exist and many times these robots are dangerous and immoral. These are warnings of what not to do with the technologies we are actually building.

Dick's fiction shows that machines built to be ersatz humans lead to problems. That is, if our motive is to build machines to replace humans, then we are denying the value of being human. Dick's warning is that machines built to closely resemble humans, but which lack the deeper human moral drives such as empathy, can only result in an impoverished world unfit to live in. On the other hand, machines that are built to extend human capacity and fit into the lives and work of other humans would have the opposite effect.

We should build machines that enhance our ability to create a just and moral society, rather than ones that lead to more violence and alienation. Building a machine that is almost human will also cause us to diminish our expectations from other humans. We will begin to treat other humans as if they were machines and we might also act more like machines ourselves. In our attempt to pull machines up to our level we must work to not, in turn, pull ourselves down to meet the machines in a middle ground where neither of us can achieve any sort of wisdom or happiness. So we should be careful in building humanoid machines and closely inspect our motives for doing so. Why do we need a robotic, nurse, soldier, firefighter, or butler? If the answer is only to replace the human with a machine because humans are too troublesome to deal with, then that is the wrong choice.

Closely related to the last point, is that robots should not be built to play on human sexual desire. As we saw above, the book that *Blade Runner* is based on provides a chilling example of what a *faux* sexual relationship with a realistic android would be like and the results are violent and depressing. Healthy human sexual behavior is more than just a purely physical act. If it were only that, then robotic sex dolls would be acceptable substitutions for human partners. But to be a good sexual partner you need to have a deep empathy for the feelings of your lover. All but the most advanced androids would be lacking this, as they do not experience the world as a human and thus would have a difficult time empathizing with them. Simply put, they would be faking it.

Just as a human relationship built on deception might be fun for a while but is ultimately doomed to fail, so too would a human-robot relationship. Unfortunately, it seems we are fated to ignore this warning, as realistic sex dolls are readily available now and are likely to continue to become more and more realistic. Now if an android wasn't faking its love, then it would be possible to have a healthy relationship with one. It is very unlikely that this will happen soon. Until that time we will have all manner of cleverly animated and life-like dolls that will be attempting to fool us. Navigating this interim period is going to be tricky. In the near future when your relationship with your robot lover turns sour, don't say you weren't warned.

A final lesson to take from the writing of Dick is that if we intend on building real artificial moral agents, we will not be fully successful unless they are capable of a kind of empathy that is logically equivalent to agape. It won't be hard to build an artificial moral agent that can reason about simple moral situation. In fact, if the machine is completely motivated by its own reasoning process, and if that reasoning process is programmed to operate on sound moral principles, and if those principles lead it to understand that it has a responsibility to act in a moral way, then regardless of what it looks like or is made of, it will be a moral agent. Which means this machine would have certain appropriate rights and responsibilities that would be based on the level of capability it has to reason morally. This is also true of humans: typically an adult's behavior is judged more critically than the actions of a child who might not know better. The possibility of building simple moral machines is not out of the question. But these machines will not be equivalent to the most moral of humans until they can achieve the kind of empathetic feelings we discussed at length above.

Even if you don't plan on building or buying a robot anytime soon, there's a vital lesson to take from Dick's thoughts on androids. In one of his greatest masterpieces, *The Three Stigmata of Palmer Eldritch*, the astronaut Palmer Eldritch returns from deep space exploration, but he is no longer human. On his return, he brings with him a powerful alien hallucinogenic that he markets to his fellow humans.

This is all part of a plot whereby Palmer Eldritch attempts to enslave the human race and become its new demigod. Eldritch has become a machine and in so doing, he has lost the ability to see humans as anything more than a resource for his own self-aggrandizement. Dick is unequivocal on this point. We must resist the netherward pull of the world that seeks to turn us into unfeeling machines.

It can happen to any of us, it can happen to the best of us; it must not happen to you.

Public Relations Guide For New Officers

Division of Precrime

● ● ●

Human Resources Officer Peter Murphy

Welcome to your new job in the Division of Precrime! This guide reviews, and responds to, what our many critics say. Since it includes strategies for responding to defense lawyers hired by precriminals, this guide is for internal purposes only and is classified as highly confidential. Anyone who conveys, or will convey, its contents to a non-officer will be punished.

01. Don't We Arrest Innocent People?

Our critics often say that we arrest innocent people since, at the time they are arrested, these people have not yet (to take the most important example) committed murder. As Danny Witwer puts it in the instructional training video you have just been shown:

> **WITWER:** I am sure you all understand the legalistic drawback to precrime methodology . . . Let's not kid ourselves: we are arresting individuals who have broken no law.

> **JAD:** But they will.

> **FLETCHER:** The commission of the crime is absolute metaphysics. The precogs see the future and they are never wrong.

> **WITWER:** But it is not the future if you stop them. Isn't that a fundamental paradox?

This is not the radical break that our critics make it out to be. Before the precogs and the establishment of our division, people were arrested and charged with certain crimes before they committed murder. For example, people were charged with attempted murder. And even before making an attempt, people were sometimes charged with conspiracy to commit murder. But no one complained that attempted murder and conspiracy to commit murder involved arresting innocent people.

One reason no one made this complaint is that attempted murder and conspiracy to commit murder were themselves crimes. But since our legislators passed a law that added future-murder as a distinct criminal act, isn't this no longer a problem?

This won't make our critics happy, since it would still allow for cases in which people are arrested and charged with future-murder even before they entertain the idea of murdering their alleged future victim. This is the case that our critics like to raise since the intentions, and general state of mind, of the arrested person are very different from the intentions and state of mind of either someone who attempts murder, or someone who conspires to murder. Someone who has not even entertained the idea of murdering someone does not meet the *mens rea*—or 'guilty mind'—condition on crime. The person's mind is not yet tainted with any kind of legal fault.

This, we concede, is true; but our critics only consider reactions to threats that are responsible for being threats. It is fitting to respond to such a threat by blaming and punishing the person who poses the threat. And it is fitting that the feelings and intentions behind one's response be punitive in nature. In short, a punitive attitude is appropriate.

But what about instances in which the perceived threat is a person, but that person is not responsible for being a threat? For example, consider an infant that has a highly contagious and dangerous disease. Since the infant is not guilty on any *mens rea* score, it is not appropriate to have a punitive attitude to this threat. In response to threats of this kind, a different attitude is appropriate, one that is not punitive and does not blame.

Shifting from attitude to action, what should we do in the face of each kind of threat? Our actions might very well be similar. In both cases, it is sensible to contain and isolate the threat so that the risk posed to other people is minimized. Quarantining the infant in this way is justified as a preventative measure. Here then is a suggestion: we ought to do the same to the pre-criminals that we arrest who are innocent at the time that they are arrested. Arresting them would then be justified as a preventative measure, even if doing so with a punitive attitude would not be appropriate since they would not be culpable.

Officer Philip K. Dick made this clear in the case study that you read. Rather than using the language of punishment and blame, he is clear that the Division of Precrime is attempting to "neutralize" Anderton. He describes the Precrime system as "the prophylactic pre-detection of criminals." Similarly, in the instructional training video, the precriminals are kept in a facility called The Hall of Containment.

Here then is one line of defense against the charge that we arrest innocent people. It is true that in some cases, we do arrest innocent people. However, we are justified in arresting and containing them as long as we take a non-punitive attitude toward them; this is the same quarantining attitude that we should take to an infant who has a contagious and dangerous disease.

02. But Is It Really Inappropriate to Punish Pre-criminals?

To outline a second kind of response to the charge that what we do is wrong because we punish the innocent, let's take a closer look at something that so far has just been taken to be obviously true: the thought that punitive attitudes are appropriate only if they are directed at the guilty.

Consider first a case in which it is appropriate to punish, and have punitive attitudes to someone, for something that they will do, but have not yet done. Philosophers call these pre-punishment cases because at the time the person is punished, they are not yet guilty. Suppose, for example, that Walter Wrath tells you that he is going to wrongfully harm someone tomorrow. Walter is quite credible when it comes to this sort of thing: many times in the past, he has said such things, and every time he followed through. So you are justified in expecting that he will do this tomorrow.

Moreover, suppose you are also certain that, just like in all past instances, Walter will not be caught; so neither you, nor anyone else, will be able to blame him after he has wronged the person—by then Wrath will be far away. And you can't do anything to make sure that he is caught, since he has you tied up. But right now you do have the opportunity to blame him, and to punish him (though not in a way that will incapacitate him). As long as it is better that he is blamed and punished than it is that he is not blamed and punished at all—and surely it is— it is appropriate to blame and punish him, despite the fact that at the time you blame and punish him he is innocent.

Precrime cases are somewhat similar to the Walter Wrath case. In a precrime case, the person who is arrested will do it. We can blame them now, or we can wait until they have done it and blame them then. Here though is the crucial point: if we prevent them from doing it, this does not make blaming them now any less legitimate. This is because what explains why they don't do it is not the right kind of fact to exculpate them. They don't do it, simply because other people stop them from doing it. But the fact that other people stop them is no credit to them. They remain on the hook.

03. What Evidence Establishes Guilt?

Let's turn to a different criticism. This is the charge that we have no evidence that the person we have arrested is guilty. To our critics, it looks as if we undercut our own case when we arrest someone. This is because we thereby prevent the person from committing the crime; so obviously we have no evidence that they have committed the crime.

03.1. Evidence of an Actual Murder, Attempt, or Intention Is Not Needed

But return again to the days before precrime, this time to a criminal plot. What if those who were arrested said that by arresting them, the authorities interfered with what was going to happen, and that consequently this put the authorities in the position of not having any evidence that those arrested would have committed the crime, or even that they would have attempted to commit it? There is no way to verify that they would have committed it, or even attempted to, since they are now locked up and are unable to commit, or even attempt to commit, the relevant act. This last claim is true, but it has little force: It was still sensible to arrest, and incarcerate, those who were plotting.

One reason this was sensible lies in the charge itself: they were charged with plotting to murder. Evidence of murder is not needed since they are not charged with murder. It is similar with those charged with a precrime like future-murder. They aren't charged with murder, or attempted murder, or even plotting to murder; they are charged with future-murder. So evidence of an actual murder, or evidence of an actual attempt, or even evidence of a plot is not needed.

It is worth observing that future-murder is more serious than many instances of plotting to murder, and many instances of attempted murder. This is because even without the intervention of law enforcement, sometimes plots and attempted murders do not result in a person's death: some plots just fizzle out, and some attempts are bungled and fail. By contrast, without our intervention a future-murder always succeeds, and always results in loss of life.

The crucial question though is this: what is the Division of Precrime's evidence that an arrested person was going to commit murder? As Anderton pointed out to Witwer in the instructional training video, the fact that something is prevented from happening may not falsify the claim that it was going to happen. Anderton demonstrates this point by sending a sphere down a ramp. When it comes off the end of the ramp, Witwer prevents it from hitting the floor, by catching it. They discuss:

ANDERTON: Why did you catch that?

WITWER: Because it was going to fall.

ANDERTON: You certain?

WITWER: Yeah.

ANDERTON: But it didn't fall; you caught it. The fact that you prevented it from happening doesn't change the fact that it was going to happen.

Witwer was right that it was going to fall despite the fact that it did not fall. This is so because Witwer's prediction was more specific. Fully articulated, he predicted that as long as the path of the sphere was not interfered with, it was going to fall. But since its path was interfered with, Witwer's prediction wasn't tested; hence it was not falsified.

To sort all of this out, it is useful to distinguish between two different futures: the future that someone will have if they are not arrested, and the future they will have if they are arrested. Call the first, their NA-future; call the second, their A-future. And let's call a prediction of someone's NA-future, an NA-prediction; and call a prediction of someone's A-future, an A-prediction. This terminology allows us to put the last point this way: what happens in a person's A-future does not falsify an NA-prediction of that person's future; this is because an NA-prediction only tries to report on someone's NA-future.

03.2. Track-Record Evidence Establishes Guilt

But what kind of evidence can be used to support an NA-prediction? One key kind comes from certain patterns of events that have been verified. Most important are the patterns from six years ago when the precogs first predicted murders that then occurred. The precogs' confirmed early track record, we are told, was impeccable. Each predicted murder was verified as actually having occurred.

To say that these early predictions were impeccable is to say that they were free of two kinds of flaws: errors of commission and errors of omission. An error of the first kind would consist in a prediction that a murder was going to occur, which did not occur. And an error of the second kind would consist in a failure to predict a murder that then occurred.

But all of this was six years ago. What if the precogs have somehow lost their golden touch and their predictions are no longer impeccable? What if some errors of commission, or some errors of omission, have slipped in? How can we know that they haven't?

Take errors of omission first. An error of this kind would consist in the precogs failing to predict a murder that then occurs. If such errors of omission crept in, there would be an increase in the present-murder rate. But the present-murder rate remains at zero. It follows that errors of omission have not crept in.

What about errors of commission? If they have crept in, the Division of Precrime would have arrested pre-innocents—that is, people who were not going to commit murder. But arresting a pre-innocent will have no effect on the murder rate. So we need to look elsewhere for evidence that errors of commission have not taken place.

Such evidence comes from cases like the Howard Marks one in the opening sequence of the instructional training video. The precogs' NA-prediction is that Marks will kill his wife and her lover. But no error of commission is committed here since Anderton catches Marks in the midst of attempting to kill his wife. Surely when a person is arrested in the midst of attempting to kill someone, this is evidence that the person really was going to commit murder and so it is evidence that the precogs did not make an error of commission.

Still, we might wonder about other people who are arrested earlier on, say before even attempting murder, or even before forming an intention to murder. How do we know that errors of commission haven't been made in those cases? The answer to this is more complicated. It has to do with the absence of any systematic relationship between when a person is arrested and something that might make the precogs make errors of commission.

As we see in the Marks case, how quickly a precriminal is arrested is affected by numerous factors, including how quickly clues are scrubbed from the images, and how long it takes to get from headquarters to the precriminal. In the Marks case had things gone faster, Marks would have been arrested before he attempted to kill his wife; and if they had went faster still, Marks might have been arrested before even intending to kill his wife. As it was, arresting him was delayed. But since these delays won't correlate in any systematic way with whether the accused is going to commit murder, this case, and others like it, are a random and representative sampling of the entire class of murder cases that are predicted by the precogs. So this allows us to conclude that barely-prevented murders should count as evidence that the system is not producing false positives. Further supporting this idea is the lack of contrary evidence within this kind of barely-prevented case: Precrime officers have not yet arrived on the scene of a just-about-to-be-committed murder only to find calm, happy people enjoying a cup of (unpoisoned) tea.

03.3. What about Human Error?

Our critics also look for other spots where error might enter, for example with the rest of us that work in Precrime. This is what Witwer was looking for in the instructional training video: regular old human errors made by people like us, not errors made by the precogs. And he found that such errors were made by the techs who studied the previsions in the Anne Lively case when they failed to notice that in some previsions the ripples in the water were moving toward the shore, while in others the ripples were moving away from the shore.

There is an important issue here, but it is a general one that doesn't pose any special problem for using previsions to identify pre-criminals. The general issue is how to interpret evidence. Previsions can be erroneously interpreted just as any other kind of evidence can, be it more familiar forensic evidence, confessions, or eyewitness reports. To be probative, a piece of evidence needs to be correctly interpreted. And while it is true that whether it is judges, juries, scientists, or precrime specialists in our division, we humans are fallible at this, this does not mean we should quit doing it. Fallibility, after all, doesn't imply unreliability; and it is well-documented that police had difficulty in interpreting and applying evidence even in the days when murderers were only arrested after the crime was actually committed.

04. What about Leaks?

Finally, what about information leaks? Since someone might alter their course of action if they are told what they were going to do, critics say we should leak this information to alleged precriminals. Maybe this is what happened with Anderton. This might help the informed person to depart from their previous path and not commit the murder. In effect, it would give them a chance to change their ways, to resolve not to commit murder, and thus to make themselves no longer guilty of future-murder.

Now if the person did change course in this way, our critics allege that everyone would gain: the person who would have been a future-murderer is no longer a future-murderer and therefore need not be quarantined and can continue to contribute to society; since the future-criminal is not quarantined, family and friends won't miss them; we wouldn't have to go to the trouble and expense of arresting and storing them; and the person who was future-murdered is never murdered.

To better understand this issue, it's useful to use the earlier distinction between a person's NA-future and their A-future. A person's NA-future, recall, is the future they will have if they are not arrested; and a person's A-future is the future they will have if they are arrested. Cleaned up a bit, a person's NA-future is really the future that person will have if two things are true: they are not arrested and they are not told this prediction. But as is often the case, learning something can change what a person will do. When it does, this makes for a third future. A person's I-future, let's say, is the future they will have if they are informed of their NA-future.

In both the written case study and the instructional training video, Anderton learns of his NA-future. But since he learns this, it may no longer be his future. His actual future will be his I-future, and it may (or may not) differ from his NA-future. Often we resolve to do something enough that we will do it even if we are told that we will do it. For example, if someone tells me that if they had not told me this, I was going to have two cups of black coffee tomorrow morning, I would not be surprised and I would not alter my behavior: I would still have two cups of black coffee tomorrow morning. But in other cases this is not so: being informed that if I had not been told this, I was going to lose next week's lottery, I would alter my behavior and not buy a ticket.

Maybe we should give people identified as precriminals a second chance. We could inform them of the precogs' prediction and then be at the ready just in case they resolutely attempt to murder the person anyway. If they do so, then we will be there to stop them and no one is any worse off. And if they don't make an attempt, everybody wins in the ways that we saw.

There are three reasons we should not leak this information to precriminals. One is simple: the precogs only tell us what people will do if they remain ignorant of these predictions. In other words, the precogs only make accurate NA-predictions, not accurate I-predictions. This means that upon learning that he is predicted to commit a murder, someone might commit the same murderous act, just at a later time. Once we see that they did not do it at the predicted time, we will take our eyes off them—just in time for them to succeed in committing the murder. This is just one way they can beat the system. Another is this: there might be so little time between the predicted murderer getting in place and the time that they might commit the murder that there would not be sufficient time to stop them.

The second reason to not tell them has to do with cost. In some cases, it is difficult, and expensive, to be at the ready: the possible murder might be far away, or somewhere that is difficult to observe.

And last, do the possible murderers have a right to know the precogs' NA-predictions? A look at familiar cases of a right to know suggests that they don't. There are two familiar kinds of cases in which people have a right to know. One is illustrated by a citizen's right to know what is in her air, food, and drinking water. She has a right to know these things in part because she needs this knowledge to avoid possible harms to her health and because she would not be responsible for such harms.

But the situation is quite different for a person who is on a path to committing murder: he is not innocent and he does not need to know he is on this path to avoid the harms of quarantine and punishment. He had another way to avoid these harms: namely, by not having made choices that put him on this path.

Alternatively, a right to know sometimes stems from ownership, rather than avoiding harm. For example, taxpayers have a right to know what the state is spending money on even if there is no chance that the state is harming them with their expenditures. Here too the situation is quite different for the person who is on a path to committing murder: there is nothing that person owns that is involved. In short, there's no reason to think he has a right to be told what path he is on.

The Division of Precrime does what law enforcement has traditionally done: protect innocent people. And despite what our critics say, we arrest people who deserve to be arrested; and we do so with appropriate attitudes and compelling evidence, and without violating their rights.[1]

---

[1] Many thanks to Dana Harrison and Dylan Wittkower for comments on earlier drafts.

20

If the Universe Isn't Real, How Should We Treat Other People?

ANDREW M. BUTLER

There's a moment at the end of *Total Recall*, when blue-collar spy Quaid looks at his lover Melina, and wonders whether the world around them is a dream. After all, he has already dreamt of walking on Mars, and has just rather surprisingly survived asphyxiation with no apparent ill effects. The movie fades to white as they kiss, and we're left only to guess as to whether the characters are not still inside some preprogramed hallucination.

Similarly, at the conclusion of *Minority Report*, where the trio of psychics lives happily ever after and the estranged couple of John Anderton and Lara Clarke are reconciled, with Lara pregnant, there is the sense that everything is just too neat, and all of these events are a wish-fulfillment fantasy. And the ending of the 1982 release of *Blade Runner* has Deckard and Rachel fly off into an improbable sunset, not knowing if she will live forever or die at the age of four, whether he might be a replicant himself, or whether he is still asleep at the piano in his apartment.

The use of dreams and visions within narratives is one way for storytellers to play with notions of reality—what are the differences between dreaming and living an experience? Can something always be recognized as a dream? How do we know that what we perceive—seeing, hearing, smelling, touching, testing—is in fact reality? This question has been repeatedly posed over the millennia by philosophers both before Plato and since, and is a theme that Philip K. Dick repeatedly explored in his fiction.

In *Eye in the Sky*, a group of people pass through a number of fake universes after a nuclear accident, each universe being the one which each one of them had imagined themselves living in. In *Flow My Tears, the Policeman Said*, Jason Taverner wakes up in someone else's drug-induced hallucination. In other works, there is a kind of conceptual breakthrough—as in *Time Out of Joint* and *The Man in the High Castle*, where characters discover the universe around them is not real (or, at least, is not the only reality).

The problem is, once reality begins to be questioned, skepticism can take over. How is it possible to ever know that an experience is real? In *Next*, the future-seeing Cris Johnson keeps experiencing one version of reality before abandoning it in favor of doing something else and then living those events having performed different actions. Are those alternatives still real? As he heads off from the motel in search of a nuclear bomb for (at least) the second time, is what he experiences real, or an alternative he has yet to discount?

The uncertainty ought to free us. If nothing is real, then nothing we do is real. Decisions have no consequences, as their impact is not real. If it's all a dream, then nothing really matters. And yet, at the end of *Now Wait For Last Year*, Eric Sweetscent decides to go back to his wife, Kathy, in order to help her, even though he's pretty certain their marriage will fail, and he's questioning the reality he is part of.

Dick's major characters—his heroes for want of a better word—try to do the right thing, even if what they do might not be the real thing. This is part of Dick's other major theme: what defines the authentic human being? The characters who show concern for others, who care, who demonstrate empathy, who are humane, are to be considered human; those who do not are little better than machines, and use those around them as tools.

In a letter written late in his life, Dick noted that he had been trying to "fuse early Hebrew monotheism with the philosophy of Heidegger—which no one has ever done before." Martin Heidegger, a German philosopher, thought that we are thrown into reality; that we struggle to find ourselves while we are already in the midst of life, located in space and time. We don't have control over where we have been born (thrown), and there is the unsettling thought that at any time we might get thrown out again—we might die. The world around us distracts us from this terrifying possibility of inevitable death, and we perceive that world as a set of tools we can use to our own advantage.

There are moral problems in a philosophy so centered on the self's needs—it insists that I am more important than anyone else. Dick's writings question that self-centeredness. For what it's worth, he wasn't actually the first to try to fuse Heidegger's ideas with Jewish monotheism: the philosopher and Talmudic scholar Emmanuel Levinas made an earlier attempt. The parallels between Levinas's and Dick's thought show how rich and challenging Dick's work is.

To Be or Not To Be—Is That the Question?

Emmanuel Levinas was born in Lithuania in 1906, to a Jewish family, and studied under Martin Heidegger in Freiberg. In the late 1920s, Levinas moved to France, becoming a French citizen. During the Nazi occupation, he was put into an internment camp, and then, after the Second World War, continued a dual career as Talmudic scholar, writing about Judaism, and as a philosopher, writing about ethics. He saw ethics as the most important issue in philosophy, even more so than questions of what is real. He was fond of quoting the soliloquy from Hamlet—"To be or not to be?"—but then continuing, "Is that the question?"

In Dick's fiction, we often can't really tell if an experience is real, but the characters still ought to behave in a particular caring way. Levinas celebrates the widow, the orphan, and the alien—although by alien he means 'foreigners', rather than Rexorians, Bleekmen, wubs, Lord Running Clam, or the Glimmung.

Levinas had in part objected to Heidegger's distinction between things that exist (beings) and the nature of existence (Being), and described how beings are thrown into Being. Levinas wanted to make a distinction between beings (he called them existents) and the act of Being (existing), and rather strangely argued that there could be existing without existents. Actually, this happens all the time in Dick's fiction: the hallucinated town in *The Cosmic Puppets*, the authentic aura of the American relics in *The Man in the High Castle*, the process of entropy in *The Three Stigmata of Palmer Eldritch*, or the aphids in *A Scanner Darkly* which trouble Charles Freck even though they do not exist.

Levinas's distinction between existing and existents also builds upon phenomenology, a school of thought which focuses upon how the individual's consciousness of the external universe is created through sense data; sight, hearing, smell, touch, and taste. We sense an outside world, but how can we be certain our senses can be trusted? That's the $64,000 question in Dick's work. How do we know that the events of *Minority Report* are real after Anderton has been sent to prison, and not all a dream? (It's not real, of course, it's a movie, but how do we know we are meant to take it to be real? Can we trust what we see?) Do we know that an individual's perceptions of the world are the same as everyone else's? Do we all see the same color blue?

Dick distinguishes the individual's private world (*idios kosmos*) from the group's shared world (*koinos kosmos*); individual perception often wins out over collective views. Think of the sign in *A Maze of Death*—it reads "STOPPERY," "WITCHERY," "HIPPERY HOPPERY," and so on, according to who sees it. Or how in *Eye in the Sky*, characters pass through four different "realities" modeled after the way four of them perceive the universe. Everyone's own personal parallel universe looks like reality to them. At the end of the novel, the characters assume—perhaps wrongly—that they have returned to authentic being, the world as it actually is.

Levinas's philosophical project is an attempt to work out how we can achieve an authentic being in relation to others, in a world where we cannot trust our senses and where there appears to be existing without existents. Levinas suggests a thought experiment which sounds rather like sensory deprivation: imagine everything goes away, disbelieve in everything, wrap yourself in darkness and silence. You don't need to be floating in a tank of salty water to do this; you just need to turn the lights off in the middle of the night. It's dark. Out there is nothing, but—and this is one of those moments where Levinas might make you shiver—just as being is, nothingness . . . nothings.

Something comes to you in the darkness. You are in a howling void. Levinas refers to these eldritch phenomena as the

There is. The visions Rachmael ben Applebaum has on Whale's Mouth in *Lies, Inc* or the dreams Herb Asher has in cryonic suspension in *The Divine Invasion*; all of these come as if from outside, rather than from inside. There is this existing, this isness (and that's a horrible word), without an existent. Levinas invites us to consider the sentence, "It is raining," and decide what the "it" is referring to. Certainly nothing solid. So, there can be existing without existents.

Levinas's thought experiment is a nod to René Descartes's "I think, therefore I am." For Descartes, it doesn't matter what you doubt the existence of—the color blue, black swans, the far side of the moon, boy bands—what matters is that someone doubts, therefore that doubting person is. Rick Deckard, within *Do Androids Dream of Electric Sheep?*, exists, having experiences, even if the Mood Organ means that his emotions might be simulated rather than real (or, real, although stimulated by a machine). But Descartes sneaks in another idea, which Levinas also uses, and which also becomes important to Dick, especially after those weird mystical experiences of spring 1974: the idea of God. Or, if not God, then the idea of something greater, more perfect, more different, more infinite; in fact the idea of infinity. But we start with an individual, a subject, alone in the void, capable of sensing—although for Levinas it's not so much "I think, therefore I am," as, "I think, therefore what should I do?"

Because out there is another, in fact, the Other.

He Ain't Heavy, He's My Other

In much philosophy, the Other is feared—it's a monster, our dark side, people we label mad, criminal, ill, or perverted. And we dismiss them as our inferiors. Not so Levinas. The Other is our responsibility. Levinas puts a huge ethical demand onto us—we must have regard and responsibility for the Other. The fact of our eating, drinking, sheltering, breathing, indeed being—in a word, existing—takes up resources that could be used by the Other. But this concern for the Other costs the self. A good example of this would be in *Do Androids Dream of Electric Sheep?*, where J.R. Isidore cares for the various androids despite the fact that they clearly do not care for him, and clearly do not care for animals, dismembering a rare spider.

The androids in the novel are defined as lacking empathy, not caring for others, and the moment someone stops caring, they risk being inhumane and thus being inhuman. In a 1972 speech, "The Android and the Human," Dick said:

> Becoming what I call, for lack of a better term, an android, means as I said, to allow oneself to become a means, or to be pounded down, manipulated, made into a means without one's knowledge or consent—the results are the same. Androidization requires obedience. And, most of all, predictability. It is precisely when a given person's response to any given situation can be predicted with scientific accuracy that the gates are open for the wholesale production of the android life form.

It is empathy rather than DNA or breeding that distinguishes humans from machines or objects. The treatment of animals is a litmus test of humanity—from the animal who refuses to be eaten in "Beyond Lies the Wub" and the intelligence of the dog in "Roog," to the astronaut, who, having killed a cat, is condemned to eat cat food for decades in "The Alien Mind."

This is a one-way relationship of care, rather than reciprocal. I remember standing by a car park, and noticing a cage protecting a security camera from vandalism or theft. Another camera, I thought, could film those crimes—only that camera would then be at risk. I thought of three possible solutions: an infinite sequence of cameras, each protecting another one; two (or more) cameras filming each other, but not protecting the car park; or a single camera trained on the cars, but itself at risk. (That's actually what they had.) Compare this to "Fred" looking at Bob Arctor in *A Scanner Darkly*, and how Fred is himself also under surveillance; Arctor/Fred undergoes a breakdown because he is spying on himself.

There is a danger of an ethical feedback loop: the other suffers, the self shows concern for the suffering, the other shows pain for the self's concern for the other's suffering, the self is uncomfortable at the pain for the self's concern for the other's suffering. At some point responsibility—and risk—has to be assumed.

In Heidegger's version, the Other is another distraction that we tend to use to ward off our fear of Death, and if there is any ulterior motive in our concern, we're treating the Other as a tool rather than another human beings with their own feelings and fears. Tools are extensions of the self, rather than things separate from the self, and we define the boundaries of the self by deciding what is not part of the self. Levinas insists that the encounter of a self with an Other who requires help is the moment when the self becomes an existent taking part in existent—located in space and time. This is when the self becomes "real." The taxi at the end of *Now Wait for Last Year* tells Sweetscent that he has to go back to his wife because "'life is composed of reality configurations so constituted. To abandon her would be to say, I can't endure reality as such.'" There is no escape from the commitment. At the risk of creating a tongue twister, the self becomes a self through a selfless action performed for the non-self. Dick's protagonists who act to help others, despite the cost to themselves—like Mr. Tagomi in *The Man in the High Castle*, who saves a man he has not met, but with whom he is closely if unknowingly associated—are authentic human beings.

In discussing the separation of self from not-self, Levinas argues that the Other is separated from the self by the dimension of height, a height that can never be shrunk. This dimension of height comes from Descartes's philosophy, as mentioned a couple of pages back—it is the idea of infinity which keeps the self and Other distinct, and so the encounter with the other is like an encounter with—well, if not God then the idea of God. At the start of *Radio Free Albemuth*, a young boy encounters a beggar—and this later transpires to be his first encounter with God. In *The Adjustment Bureau*, we are told that we may have met the Chairman (the safely nonspecific version of God) in the face of a random stranger. For Levinas, the encounter with the Other—in the shape of the poor, the widow, the orphan, and the alien—was an encounter with the idea of God. He was always careful to keep his ethical and Talmudic scholarship distinct, but the notion that God's face can only be seen indirectly feels very Old Testament in nature.

In the extraordinary complexity of *VALIS*—which dramatizes the "liar's paradox," where we ask whether someone who says "I am lying right now" is lying—we get a divine biography of some kind of higher being who has been damaged, and who has been out of action since the fall of the temple in 70 C.E. The intervening time between then and about 1974, the year of the revelation of Horselover Fat (who is also Philip K. Dick, kind of), has simply been an illusion. Now, perhaps, there can be renewed concern—concern for the other, which metaphorically is a concern for God. But equally there is a sense of being seized by God—God as a manifestation of the 'There is', who takes us over without our consent. In *VALIS* we see a man, Fat, who shows concern for God, as well as various women with serious medical conditions. Can he care for all of them? How can he choose between them? It is clear that Phil Dick, an avatar for the author Philip K. Dick within the novel, shows concern for his "friend," Fat. And perhaps we, as Philip K. Dick fans, need to show concern for a favorite author, who seems to be telling us that God is an alien who has spoken to him and usurped President Nixon, and who, if he really believes any of this, shows every sign of having lost the plot.

Fifty Ways to Love Your Other

Emmanuel Levinas argues that not only should the self take care of the Other, but the self should also experience the Other's suffering instead of the Other. This is a literal extension of the idea of empathy: not just showing concern for the Other but putting oneself in the Other's place. We get this at various points of Dick's work. For a start, his frequent use of a shifting third-person point of view—in *Time Out of Joint*, *The Man in the High Castle*, *Martian Time-Slip*, and *Flow My Tears, the Policeman Said*, among many others—means that it is hard to divide his characters into heroes and villains, as we are made to understand the feelings of a range of characters.

For much of *Flow My Tears, the Policeman Said* we are following the experiences of Jason Taverner, adrift in a world where he apparently doesn't exist, and his attempts to keep a step ahead of the law, but we are also invited to empathize with a representative of that law, Felix Buckman, whose tears are the ones in the novel's title. He takes responsibility.

In *Now Wait for Last Year*, the Earth leader Molinari takes so much responsibility for his people that he develops their symptoms—a heart attack, a failed kidney—and even dying is no escape, as another Molinari is brought in to take his place. Not even death gives him an alibi for his responsibility. Similarly, the empathy boxes in *Do Androids Dream of Electric*

Sheep?, which are available for humans but do not work for androids, require that humans empathize with the plight of Wilbur Mercer as he eternally climbs a hill whilst unseen forces throw rocks at him. The bonded humans feel his pain. The fact that Mercer turns out to be a drunken bit-part actor on a sound stage is neither here nor there—the real thing is the concern for the Christ-like figure, and the self's sacrifice.

In *Next*, Cris Johnson is eventually persuaded to help in the search for a nuclear bomb, rather than focusing on his own desires; this is the opposite to *The Adjustment Bureau* where the Earth faces a new Dark Ages so that David Norris can get his woman. The most villainous characters in Dick's fiction are those precisely who do not care for others—some of these are bad father figures, such as bosses, or the CEOs of multinational corporations and some of these are bad mother figures, such as Kathy Sweetscent, in *Now Wait For Last Year*, and Roni Fulgate in *The Three Stigmata of Palmer Eldritch*.

Dick's fictions demand that we recognize and demonstrate our own humanity, by showing our concern for the other. In Levinasian terms, this is the point at which the self becomes solid, an existent in space and time, in relation to the Other—"real," for want of a better word, or "authentic." The responsibility lies as much in the little things—the, "no, after you"—as the big.

Imagine we're chatting in a bar, and I buy you a drink. I've been generous, but I'm not expecting anything in return. I don't have an ulterior motive. It's a gift. If you then buy me a drink, you've made us equal, and you've turned a gift into an economic transaction. The point is not that I want you to be in my debt, but that I owe you a pint, irrespective of whether you'll buy me one back. For Levinas, such gifts demonstrate our humanity: if we do not buy that stranger a pint because might not buy us one in return—then we cannot claim to be authentically human. At the same time, we shouldn't point fingers, and say that the other is an animal, an android, a machine, or an object—or at least we must care for them even if we don't think that they are human.

Calling someone else an object is, well, bad form. We need to invoke the Golden Rule, which is the key to the Torah, the first five books of the Bible: "That which is hateful to you, do not do to your fellow." If the universe isn't real, how should we treat other people? Well, with care, concern, and love. In a sense, Melina in *Total Recall* is right—it doesn't matter if they're in a dream. They should kiss each other, anyway, before they wake up.

Puppets and Precogs

21
Knowing Tomorrow While Choosing Today

Sara Worley

Do we control what happens to us, or are we the puppets of unseen forces? There have been worries about this throughout much of western history, from the ancient Greeks who thought that the fates controlled their destiny to the Calvinists who believed that God had fixed in advance everything that was going to happen. Even today people still worry about this: How much do our genes, or our environment, influence what we will do?

Just because I'm influenced by something, though, doesn't mean that I'm not free.

A sunny day might influence me to quit work early, or I might be influenced by a friend to see a movie that I would not otherwise have chosen. But as long as I could have done otherwise, I'm still free. Compare people's response to the sun with the response of phototropic plants. People go outside and enjoy the sun; a sunflower grows towards it. The difference, though, is that we have a choice about how to respond and plants do not. We can do otherwise; they can't. Our freedom consists in the fact that *we can do otherwise*. Or can we?

Philip K. Dick explores free will in his stories "The Minority Report" and "Adjustment Team." People called "precogs" see crimes before they happen, thus allowing the police to make arrests before any crime is actually committed, and the agents of the Adjustment Team use their knowledge of what's going to happen to adjust circumstances and personalities to make things come out the way they want. But foresight seems incompatible with the ability to do otherwise: if the precogs know that I'm going to commit a crime before I actually commit it, then it must already be true, at the time of the precognition, that I'm going to commit it! But then I don't have the option, at the time of the crime, of not going through with it. If my actions can be foreseen, then it seems as if there's really only one thing I can do, just as there's only one thing a sunflower can do.

This problem is not new. The Judeo-Christian God is traditionally thought of as being omniscient, knowing everything that will happen, including every action that anyone will perform. But it's also part of the traditional conception of God that he gave people free will, and this already get us into a logical quandary: if God already knows what we're going to do, then what we're going to do must already be settled, and then how could we really have free will? The sense we have that there are multiple options open to us must really be illusion: there's just one thing we can do, at any one time, whether we know it or not.

Freedom and Prediction

But there's more to these issues than appears at first glance.

There are at least two different models for how we might understand foreknowledge—knowing in advance what's going to happen—and they have different implications.

The first model involves prediction. Suppose that you have a friend, Jill, who loves science fiction but hates westerns. She's given the choice between seeing *The Adjustment Bureau* and a retrospective of John Wayne movies. You can be pretty confident in your predictions about what she's going to do. But this doesn't mean that she's not free. All it means is that people are reasonably consistent in their preferences, their likes and dislikes, and that this consistency manifests itself in their behavior. Freedom doesn't require that Jill be completely random or inconsistent in her behavior. It just requires that she be able to do otherwise.

This is a bit like the solution to the problem of God's foreknowledge given by Molina, a sixteenth-century Spanish Jesuit. His idea was that God has what he called "middle knowledge," which is knowledge of how each of us will respond to various circumstances. Since God knows how we will respond to varied circumstances, and God knows which circumstances we will actually encounter, he knows what we will do. But that God knows what we will do does not mean that we do not have free will, any more than the fact that you know that Jill will choose the science-fiction movie means that Jill isn't free.

Unfortunately, this model doesn't really resolve the tension between free will and foreknowledge. To see the problem, consider a simple astronomical example. Astronomers can say, now, where in the sky Mars will be visible next spring. They can say this because they know the relevant facts and the laws of nature, and these facts and laws together determine where Mars will be visible. We can have just about complete confidence that their prediction will be right. This is because the facts and laws together guarantee where in the sky Mars will be visible next spring. They don't leave any options. If they did leave options, if two different possible locations for Mars were each consistent with the current laws plus the facts, then we couldn't now say that Mars is going to be visible in one location rather than the other. At best we could say that it might be visible one place rather than another, or perhaps that it's likely that it will be visible one place rather than the other. But we couldn't say that it will be visible one place rather than another.

Likewise, if we make a prediction about someone's behavior based on her character and the circumstances she encounters, this prediction can be certain only if her character and circumstances guarantee that she will behave in that way. If Jill's character and circumstances guarantee that she will choose *The Adjustment Bureau*, then we can be certain about our prediction. But then of course she wouldn't have free will, since she wouldn't be able to do otherwise. If, on the other hand, she does have free will, then her character and circumstances cannot guarantee that she'll behave in one way rather than another. She'd always have the option of doing otherwise. But then our prediction could not be certain.

The theological version of our problem makes this worry especially vivid. God is supposed to be omniscient, so his knowledge must be infallible. So if God predicts someone will behave in a certain way, that person must indeed behave in that way. Otherwise God would be wrong, and we know he can't be. But then there aren't really any options open to that person. There's only one way he can behave.

Whether foresight based on prediction is compatible with free will, then, depends on whether foresight is, or can be, certain. If character and circumstance compel certain choices, then foresight can be certain, but there is no free will. On the other hand, if character and circumstance leave options open, then people have free will, but foresight—even God's foresight—cannot be certain.

Outside of Time?

There's also another way to understand foresight. Some philosophers and theologians, including Boethius and St. Anselm of Canterbury, have suggested that God is "outside of" time. Human beings experience the world in time—some things are in the past, some are present, and some are in the future. At any given moment the only events which are directly observable by us are those which are present at that moment—past events are gone, and future events do not yet exist.

We find out about past events not by directly observing them, but by relying on some sort of evidence. We dig up fossils; we read old documents; we rely on our memories. We find out about the future not by directly observing it, but by making predictions. We predict that the sun will come up tomorrow, or that the economy will continue to sputter along. But if God is outside of time, he doesn't experience things as being in the past, present, or future. Everything is, so to speak, all laid out in front of him, so that all he has to do is "look." Rather than finding out about the past by looking at evidence, or about the future by making predictions, he just looks.

In other words, God doesn't really have foreknowledge at all. It looks to us as if God knows things before they happen, but that's because we're inside of time and so understand things in terms of past, present, and future. This is not the way things look to God since there's no "before" and "after" from his perspective. He just sees all the things that happen, all at once.

This model seems to remove the conflict between foreknowledge and free will. Suppose you are there when Jill buys her ticket for the movie. Because you see her buy the ticket, you know which movie she's chosen to see. But that you see her make one choice does not mean that she could not have made a different choice. Likewise, God knows which movie Jill is going to see because he "sees" her buy her ticket. If she had made a different choice, he would have seen that instead. But this is consistent with her having free will.

Prediction, or Sight?

How should we understand foresight in *The Adjustment Bureau* and *Minority Report*?

Is it prediction, or is it "sight"?

The "sight" model isn't really compatible with either story. The first problem is that both the precogs and the agents of the Adjustment Bureau see things that don't actually happen. Indeed, this is the whole premise of *Minority Report*. The crimes that the precogs see never occur, because they are prevented before they happen. It is less dramatic in *The Adjustment Bureau*, but still there is foresight there of things that never actually happen. Indeed, the Adjustment Bureau typically has at least two previsions relevant to each circumstance: what will happen if an adjustment is made, and what will happen if an adjustment is not made. They foresee both what David will do if he stays with Elise, and what he will do if he doesn't stay with Elise. But only one of these predictions can actually come true.

Since foresight includes things that never come true, it's too simple to say that precogs and the Adjusters somehow have access to the already-present future. If they were "seeing" the future, they would be seeing the events that would actually happen, not events that would have happened had they not been prevented. A precog who sees a murder that is then prevented is not seeing the actual future.

There's also a second problem. Precogs and Adjusters are not outside of time. Indeed, they are very much in time, making a difference to what happens. Consider a precog who sees a murder. The potential murder comes to the attention of the authorities and the suspect-to-be is arrested. The murder never actually occurs. But since the murder never actually occurs, if the precog were seeing the actual future, she would predict that the murder would not occur. (Or, more likely, she would simply not report a precognition.) But then the suspect-to-be would not be arrested, and the murder would indeed occur. But then of course she would see this, and so would report that a murder was about to occur. But then the suspect would be arrested, and the murder would not occur. And so on indefinitely.

A sort of loop or oscillation thus results from the idea that the precogs see the actual future. This loop is due to the role that precognitions play in influencing what happens. Indeed, the role they play is to make their own precognitions false. If a precog predicts a particular future, that future won't happen. So precogs cannot coherently be thought of as seeing the actual future.

If "sight" doesn't work as a model for these kinds of fore-knowledge, what about the predictive model? This interpretation makes sense of both of the stories. The adjusters in "Adjustment Team" foresee that Mr. Douglas is going to be offered a chance to buy some land but that given his current cautious personality he's going to turn down the chance. So they "adjust" him so that he is a little braver, a little more of a risk-taker. In the movie, the team understands that meeting Elise will inspire David to give a truly memorable concession speech. They also understand that his political career is in part motivated by a certain emotional neediness which Elise's presence will do much to satisfy. If he stays in a relationship with Elise, he will lose some of his passion and motivation for politics. Thus the adjusters try and manipulate the circumstances so that David and Elise will meet at a crucial moment but will subsequently lose touch with each other. In both the story and the movie, then, foresight seems to be based on the characters and circumstances of the people involved.

Similarly, the precogs in "The Minority Report" make three separate predictions about whether John Anderton will kill Leopold Kaplan. The predictions differ because they are based on slightly different circumstances. Anderton and Kaplan both find out about the first prediction. This changes their behavior in ways that result in Anderton losing the motivation, which he otherwise would have had, to kill Kaplan. So there's a second prediction which takes these new circumstances into account. But then each of them finds out about this second prediction. This changes their behavior yet again, such that Anderton again acquires reason to kill Kaplan. Thus the third prediction. In all three cases, the precognitions are based, at least in part, on Anderton's character. Given certain circumstances, he will be motivated to kill Kaplan. When circumstances change, he will lose that motivation.

Perfect or Probabilistic?

The next question is whether these predictions are certain, or merely probabilistic. As we've seen, predictive foresight is compatible with free will only if it is probabilistic.

The assumption in both stories seems to be that precognition is certain. The precrime program is based on the conviction that people are going to commit the crimes that are predicted, not that they might commit these crimes. Arresting people who haven't yet done anything is already a bit morally problematic; it would be even more so if the predictions were just probabilistic. In "Adjustment Team," the assumption seems to be that pre-adjusted Mr. Douglas will not buy the land, whereas post-adjustment Mr. Douglas will.

Admittedly, Lisa, Anderton's wife, does raise some doubts in "The Minority Report" about whether some people might be falsely arrested for crimes that they are not in fact going to commit. Contrary to what we might expect, though, this worry is not based on concerns about free will. Rather, it's based on the thought that some predictions might be inaccurate because they are not based on all the relevant information. In particular, just as Anderton and Kaplan changed their behavior when they found out about the predictions involving them, other people might also have changed their behavior if they had learned about the predictions involving them. So perhaps some of these other people need not have been arrested: perhaps their crimes could have been prevented simply by telling them about the predictions ahead of time.

Although this is a legitimate worry, it doesn't tell us anything about free will. It simply reminds us that what someone does depends not just on his character, but on the circumstances he encounters. Predictions, to be accurate, must take all relevant circumstances into account. This is true even for predictions about the natural world: if Mars gets slammed into by a big enough asteroid, its orbit might well change. A prediction which didn't take the asteroid into account would get Mars's orbit wrong. But this doesn't have anything to do with free will.

The Adjustment Bureau, however, presents the issues quite differently. Most of the work of the adjusters is done by simply tweaking the circumstances that people encounter. The adjusters seem to work on the premise that most people will take the easiest path available to them, so that the way to get a person to do what you want is to make it easy for the person to behave in the ways that you want, and hard for the person to behave in ways that you don't want. The adjusters don't want David and Elise to continue their relationship, so they repeatedly put obstacles in their way, hoping to get them to give up. Harry, a member of the Adjustment Bureau, is supposed to make sure that David spills his coffee so that he will miss his bus (and thus miss seeing Elise again). The location of Elise's dance rehearsal is moved, to make it hard for David to find her.

But even if this strategy works most of the time, it doesn't work when it comes to David and Elise. David is persistent: he takes the same bus every day for three years in hopes of encountering Elise again. He goes to some effort to find her after her rehearsal is moved. And David and Elise both go to a lot of trouble, to put it mildly, to avoid the Adjustment Bureau at the end of the movie.

Their persistence is rewarded. As Harry says, those who "fight" for their free will get it. The suggestion here seems to be that people do have options: they don't have to follow the path that's laid out for them. They could always do otherwise. It's just that most people don't.

But the movie is different from the stories, and we can't necessarily draw any conclusions about what Dick himself intended from what happens in the movie. I suspect that Dick does not intend us to conclude either that we do have free will or that we don't. It seems more likely that he wants to encourage us to think about the extent to which our behavior is predictable and what this means about our free will.

Certainly the kind of precognition that occurs in both stories doesn't have any analogue in the real world, so we can't simply draw conclusions about the actual world from what happens in the stories. But it's also true that human behavior is predictable to a large extent, and maybe if we knew more about the relevant causes we could do an even better job of prediction. These issues are still undecided, but are well worth thinking about.

22
Total Recall's Total Rethink

BENJAMIN HUFF

In *Total Recall*, Doug Quaid faces a series of increasingly loaded choices about who he is, and who he will be. Will he be a lowly construction worker, a virtual tourist, a crack government agent who destroys the Martian rebellion, or a hero of the rebellion, fighting for justice?

As the story unfolds, Quaid is repeatedly invited, pressured, or forced to accept an altered identity. Each time, he is presented with a version of his past, and invited to embrace a matching future. His memory, his past decisions, his desires pull him in different directions, and Quaid has to choose which version of who he was will define who he is. The fate of a planet hangs in the balance, and also the truth about the basis of personal identity and free will.

Memory and the Brain-Butchers

As the movie opens, Quaid is a construction worker in a new town, with a steady job, a nice apartment, and a gorgeous, loving wife. What more would he want? He remembers their wedding, falling in love, and eight years together. Yet somehow this past and this present are not enough to make him feel himself—to make him feel free. He wants to go to Mars.

When Quaid goes to Rekall, Inc. for a (virtual) trip to Mars, it turns out that he really *isn't* himself. When Lori tells him so, he argues with her, but there is no arguing with the people trying to kill him. To be free, Quaid has to reclaim his identity.

A man on the phone offers him a piece of his past—"This is the suitcase you gave me"—so Quaid goes to pick it up. The video inside seems to be a message from himself saying, "Get your ass to Mars." At the Hilton there he confirms he is the one who wrote the note on the flyer, so he goes to the Last Resort. After a setback with his old girlfriend Melina, he gets her to take him to Kuato, but Kuato has a different plan in mind.

> Kuato asks, "What do you want, Mr. Quaid?"
> Quaid responds, "The same as you, to remember."
> "But, why?"
> "To be myself again," says Quaid.
> But Kuato sets him straight: "You are what you do. A man
> is defined by his action, not his memory."

Was Kuato right? John Locke suggests that what defines a person's identity, and makes him the same person from one day to the next, is his memory. This is natural enough, and Quaid takes this approach at first. Locke probably didn't think about the possibility of a memory implant, though, nor were the people trying to kill Quaid waiting around to see what he might or might not remember. Even without fancy equipment, we do a pretty good job of obscuring, revising, distorting, or just plain losing our memories all the time. If that weren't enough, Quaid's situation seems like pretty good evidence that Locke is wrong. But what could it mean to be defined by one's actions? Here is one approach.

Owning Your Actions, Owning Your Past

According to a traditional conception of free will, a person is acting freely, and his actions are his own, when he is the cause of his own action—in Aristotle's words, when the action "has its origin in the agent himself" (*Nicomachean Ethics*, III.1). On this model, to determine if an action belongs to us, we need to trace its history and confirm whether its cause lies in ourselves. If you shoot a gun at a window, you are the cause of its breaking. We could say that the gun shoots the bullet, and the bullet breaks the window, but *you* are the one who *chose* to pull the trigger and started the chain of causes. The life Quaid was living with Lori, working construction, is not a life he chose. It looks more like a mental prison, invented to render him harmless. What *did* Quaid choose?

To settle this question, of course, requires that a person has a definite identity that we can trace the causes of an action to. Initially, Quaid's strategy is to find out his true past. Then he will know what he is doing, and what he needs to do. If he is an agent who has joined the rebellion, like the video says, then he needs to get back in touch with them and deliver the information that will sink Cohaagen.

Quaid doesn't have a lot to go on, but apparently Hauser has arranged for him to have a few key pieces of the story, just enough for him to act. Hauser knew his memory could be (would be?) wiped, so he set up a plan to find his way back to Mars and the rebels, even with only Quaid's memories. He prepared the suitcase, the credits, the video, the note at the hotel. When Quaid follows the plan Hauser laid out, then, he has picked up the chain of causes and is following through on the decision he made before, as Hauser. If a man is defined by his actions, then perhaps by doing this Quaid is becoming himself again, even if he can't remember making those decisions. Is that the way to become free?

To say who or what is the cause of an action, though, assumes that there is a unique answer—that a chain of causes *can* have a beginning. We generally take it for granted that we are free, and that we, other people, and other things too can start a chain of causes in motion. If we take this assumption seriously, we get something like Aristotle's picture of how the world works.

Aristotle supposes that everything has a *nature*, meaning an internal *source of motion* and activity. The five elements are natural: air and fire rise up spontaneously, and water and earth go down, unless something constrains them. The stars and planets, made of ether, revolve in circles eternally—ether's natural motion. Living things also have a nature: fish swim, birds fly, and flowers bloom, under their own power. There are as many sources of motion in the universe as there are *natural* beings or things. The distinctive "motion" of a human is more subtle, but just as clearly defined—humans act by a combination of thought and desire called decision. Your wife doesn't want to go to Mars, for example, so you go to Rekall instead. For a human, then, to be free is to perform actions that you originated, through decision.

Now, things don't only move by themselves; they are often moved by other things. You identify a target and pull the trigger. The trigger isn't moving *naturally*, of course; it is moved by your finger. So, the trigger is not the origin of action; you are. When the bullet flies out of the barrel, it's the gasses from the burning powder that push it. If you shoot out a window, and people start flying through it, that is not their natural motion; it is the motion of the air, blowing them out. Their flying out, then, is a case of unfree action. Shooting at someone in front of a window, and sending people flying through it, or not, would be your decision; an expression of your freedom. Let's go with not. When Quaid is acting on the decisions that he himself made, then, he is acting as himself, and he is free.

Inpsychation and Chains of Will

One of the unusual things about humans is that they don't just move themselves—they use tools, and not just tools they move with their own power, as you might drive a nail with a hammer, or move a stick with your hand, to move a rock. Humans dig a ditch so water will flow down it; we irrigate a field so plants will grow in it; we grow crops to make money to buy a car, and instead of our legs, we use internal combustion engines to move us down the road.

Humans arrange the natural motions of other things to carry out our intentions, and so their actions become our own. When the water flows, we are irrigating. When the plants grow, we are producing and earning. When Quaid grabs the joystick of the Johnny Cab, he is no longer riding passively; he is driving. Causing things to serve our intentions, it is as though we infuse our souls into them, or in Friedrich Nietzsche's words, *inpsychate* them. We identify with our capable instruments. Other forces can be threats to our goals and our freedom, or the means of realizing them. As Ralph Emerson puts it in his essay, "Fate,"

> Every jet of chaos which threatens to exterminate us is convertible by intellect into wholesome force. Fate is unpenetrated causes. The water drowns ship and sailor like a grain of dust. But learn to swim, trim your bark, and the wave which drowned it will be cloven by it and carry it like its own foam, a plume and a power. Man moves in all

modes, by legs of horses, by wings of wind, by steam, by gas of balloon, by electricity, and stands on tiptoe threatening to hunt the eagle in his own element. There's nothing he will not make his carrier.

When we understand the natural motions of things, we penetrate them with our thought, harness them to our desires, and they become extensions of ourselves. We act *through* them, just as we act through our hands and feet.

We even act through the actions of other *people*. Hitler didn't have to go to Poland to invade it; when his soldiers invaded on his orders, Hitler was invading Poland. Cohaagen doesn't have to watch Quaid with his own eyes; he has Lori and Harry do it for him. Tony says, "Cohaagen's shut off the air to Venusville," but not because Cohaagen's hand pulled the switch; he's the one who gave the order.

In the case of ourselves, of course, we normally don't have to give orders—we decide, and we remember what we decided as we are carrying it out. So, in the absence of major disruptions of memory, Locke's view might be almost right. Normally we carry out our actions *by* our memories. But our memories don't define our identities—they are just one of our most common tools.

In the right situation, even a false memory could be a tool for action. Suppose you're a construction worker, but you decide to have someone make you think you are a secret agent on a mission to Mars. Then in acting as a secret agent, you are free. Presumably, though, you also meant to be brought back to reality at the end—you didn't decide to *permanently* stop being you. It's a problem if the secret-agent-you decides he wants to keep on being a secret agent longer than you intended. As Dr. Edgemar explains to Quaid at the Hilton, if you go AWOL and refuse to come back, that isn't freedom; that's psychosis. Based on the video in the suitcase, though, and the bead of sweat on Dr. Edgemar's forehead, the truth is the other way around: Quaid is not a construction worker, and didn't decide to be; he really is a secret agent, or he was, before he became a rebel, and to be free, he needs to pick up where he left off.

To arrange this, Hauser has to be creative. As Nietzsche observes in *Genealogy of Morals*, II.1:

Between the original 'I will', 'I shall do this' and the actual discharge of the will, its act, a world of strange new things, circumstances, even acts of will may be interposed without breaking this long chain of will. But how many things this presupposes! To ordain the future in advance in this way, man must first have learned to distinguish necessary events from chance ones, to think causally, to see and anticipate distant eventualities as if they belonged to the present, to decide with certainty what is the goal and what the means to it . . . Man himself must first of all have become *calculable* . . .

Freedom doesn't just require understanding and controlling things around us, it requires understanding and controlling *ourselves*. In Hauser's case, he has to plan around becoming Quaid.

With the help of a friend from the Agency, Hauser provides himself some essential equipment. With the video (and some unexpected encouragement from Richter), he persuades himself to go to Mars. Picking up the chain of causes and following through on his decision, maybe Quaid *is* Hauser again. Hauser has *re-inpsychated* himself. He finds his way to Kuato, and remembers the alien reactor that the rebellion needs to break Cohaagen's grip on Mars. Hauser did what he set out to do, so perhaps the rest of his memory is beside the point.

Quaid's Problem—Mucky Origins

From here things really get complicated, though. As Kuato is helping Quaid remember, the walls cave in, Cohaagen's troops arrive, Benny shoots Kuato, and Richter takes them all to see Cohaagen. "Well, my boy—you're a hero," Cohaagen reassures him, "Don't be modest! Kuato is dead; the resistance has been completely wiped out, and you were the key to the whole thing." What exactly did Quaid just do? Whose plan did he carry out? Was Quaid acting for Hauser the rebel, or Hauser, Cohaagen's "bosom buddy"?

Hauser is on tape, saying that with Cohaagen he was "playing for the wrong team," and now he wants to make up for it. But Hauser is also on tape, backing up Cohaagen's story that they invented Quaid together, to lead them to Kuato. Did Cohaagen make up agency-Hauser so he could convince rebel-Hauser, with his bulging muscles and dead-eye aim, to work for his side? Or did agency-Hauser make up rebel-Hauser to fool Quaid? Even if he did, what made agency-Hauser such a slime-ball in the first place?

There is no way for Quaid to really be sure how this all started. He can't rely on his origins to decide who he is, or what he should do now. He needs another strategy.

According to the traditional view of free will, a person is free when he is the causal origin of his actions. As the scientific worldview developed, though, this picture came into question, requiring us to rethink our ideas of free will. The law of gravity explains all of the distinctive motions of Aristotle's elements as results of one universal force. Water comes to rest below air and earth below water because they are pulled down more strongly. The planets move in their orbits because their momentum balances gravity; they free-fall in ellipses. Animal behaviors are explained as biochemical processes, triggered by events in their environment. Nature is a continuous system of causes and effects, all flowing by scientific law from earlier causes, with no origins, no beginning or end.

In the systematic view of nature, our actions are simply ripples in the cosmic flow of mass-energy. Our thoughts are triggered by external stimuli like photons and vibrations in the air. Stimuli cause neurons to fire, neurons are encoded in our DNA, and our DNA is passed down through chimps and sea squirts from the Earth's original organic muck. In this context, a human being can no more originate an action than a pile of sand. Humans are just a bit more complicated, and more gooey. Everything we do, then, is a result of alien causes. Even if our actions derive from our thoughts, and our thoughts from our identities, our identities are produced by causes beyond ourselves that bear no relation to our goals. We are all in the same boat as Doug Quaid.

Does this mean that it is impossible to be free? It does, if freedom is originating action, beginning a causal chain. Philosophers like Baron d'Holbach accepted this conclusion:

> Man's life is a line that Nature commands him to describe upon the surface of the earth, without his ever being able to swerve from it even for an instant. He is born without his own consent; his organization does in no wise depend upon himself; he is unceasingly modified by causes, whether visible or concealed, over which he has no control. It is the great complication of motion in man that persuades him he is a free agent: if all his motions were simple, he would perceive that all his actions were necessary. (*The System of Nature*, I.xi)

Giving up the idea of freedom seems realistic, in a way, for thinking about people in general. For a person like Quaid, though, living his own life, he still has to make decisions, and Nature isn't sitting on his shoulder, telling him what to do. We feel our freedom, and the weight of our choices falls on us.

Freedom Without Origins

So, is freedom being an origin of actions? It rather looks as if there aren't any original causes, only nodes in the chain of cause and effect. More recently, quantum mechanics suggests there may be some flex in the chains of causation—that sub-atomic particles follow probabilities in their behavior, rather than precise laws—but to suggest that our freedom comes down to the random movement of an electron here or there is no more helpful than appealing to the ancient Greek idea, from Epicurus, that the tiny bits of matter that make up things occasionally "swerve" for no specifiable reason and break the chain of cause and effect. Well, actually, that's pretty much the same claim. But anyway, if my actions trace to the random swervings of subatomic particles, they don't seem to be *mine* any more than if they trace to immutable laws of nature. How is under-determination freedom?

Just as importantly, Quaid's predicament shows there are not just scientific or practical problems with the idea of free-dom as being an absolute origin of action—there are *ethical* problems with it.

Suppose Cohaagen could show Quaid conclusively that he is Hauser—Hauser is not just his evil twin—and Hauser volun-teered to become Quaid, as a strategy for taking down the rebellion. As Hauser put it, "I was here first!" Does that mean Quaid did what he wanted to do, and now he should become Hauser again?

It does look as though Hauser and Cohaagen conspired to use Quaid to get Kuato—otherwise why would Cohaagen have kept him alive? Quaid could just accept that freedom means following through on the decision he made before, as Hauser. As Quaid, he's a just a dupe who led Cohaagen straight to Kuato and got most of the rebel leaders killed—maybe the whole rebellion, and anyway everyone in Sector G. Melina sur-vived, but she will loathe and despise him for the rest of their short lives. As Quaid, he may be innocent, but that's small comfort for being Cohaagen's unwilling tool, manipulated into doing exactly the opposite of what he intended. To stay Quaid would be humiliating and, well, psychotic. As Hauser, though, he is a hero (or villain, depending) who has just completed a brilliant plan, with Quaid's earnest but innocent help, assuring Cohaagen and himself nearly limitless wealth and prestige. The whole ordeal will have ended perfectly, all the more so for the unexpected twists along the way. To see himself as free, perhaps he has to embrace his origin. Besides, he'll have a Mercedes!

Faced with these origins, though, Quaid realizes he needs a new strategy. He puts the problem with Hauser succinctly: "The guy's a fucking asshole!" Freedom may usually mean acting from decision, but when you realize your decision was wrong, freedom is changing to do what is right. A man is not defined by his memory, but by his action, and a man's authentic actions are not defined by what he may have decided in the past, but by what matters most to him. As Lowe says in "We Can Remember It for You Wholesale," what defines Quail, Quaid, or any of us is "not a memory but a desire."

Whether he was Hauser before or not, now Quaid is Quaid, and embracing his desire for justice turns him away from his past and toward his future. Whether Melina convinced him to side with the rebellion before or not, she has now, with extra help from Richter and the bloody tactics on display on Mars. Hauser's Mercedes somehow has limited appeal, and the idea of going to a party with Richter, Cohaagen, and a reprogrammed Melina is just revolting.

Sometimes our plans, our chains of will, go awry. Helm tries to track Quaid using the bug, but finds out he is tracking a nougat-stuffed rat. When Richter shoots at Quaid inside the spaceport, the bullet doesn't hit Quaid; it hits the window, and, well, we know what happens when you shoot out a window on Mars. Among other things, it triggers the blast doors, assuring Quaid's escape. Things are especially dicey when we use *people* as tools. Cohaagen uses Richter to watch Quaid, but Richter thinks he is supposed to think, and so when Quaid goes to Rekall, Richter tries to kill him, almost ruining Cohaagen's plan. If Hauser and Cohaagen invented Quaid to destroy the rebellion, they made him a little too honorable.

What Kuato reveals to Quaid doesn't have much to do with his individual past, but it has everything to do with his future, and the future of the rebellion. Quaid doesn't have to be defined by Hauser's actions; he can be defined by his own: he and Melina can start the reactor. As far as Hauser and Cohaagen are concerned, when Quaid escapes from his reprogramming, he has sunk into psychosis. But it's precisely in rejecting Hauser and breaking with his past that Quaid decisively becomes free.

23
Lonely Wolves

TRAVIS PATERSON

Driven by paranoia, loneliness, drugs, and an overpowering nausea for a world that disappoints and alienates, *A Scanner Darkly* is one of Philip K. Dick's most autobiographical stories. Through its protagonist Bob Arctor, Dick explores his own past and ventures into California's dystopic future where both writer and character are captivated by the counterculture and a tortured pursuit of the American dream. A portrayal of men living in the margins and of minds on the edge of insanity, a mixture of anguish, suffering, and fantasy makes *A Scanner Darkly* one of Dick's most personal, powerful and political stories.

Start with the speech Arctor the druggie disguised as Fred the narc masked as "Everyman" while wearing a scramble suit (still following?) gave to the 709th Chapter of the Brown Bear Lodge. He's disgusted with what he sees. Just looking at the overweight man introducing him to the equally overweight and over-happy audience nauseates him.

These aren't tummy cramps from eating an undercooked In-N-Out burger. This is the sick-in-the-gut sensation that Jean-Paul Sartre described in his novel *Nausea*. Sartre's protagonist Roquentin is gripped by feelings of despair and disgust with the world around him. He is simultaneously alienated from and sickened by others as they go ignorantly about their contented lives. Roquentin, like Arctor, is experiencing *nausea*.

Nausea is existence revealing itself—and existence is ugly. From Roquentin's most profound encounter with the source of his nausea he remarks,

We were a heap of living creatures, irritated, embarrassed at ourselves, we hadn't the slightest reason to be there, none of us, each
one, confused, vaguely alarmed, felt in the way in relation to the others. *In the way*: it was the only relationship I could establish between
these trees, these gates, these stones.

Roquentin discovers that existence is absurd, that it's futile to
try to find anything necessary about it, or us. He concludes
with the essential thing, which is contingency: "I mean that one
cannot define existence as necessity. To exist is simply *to be
there.*" Luckily for Roquentin, he catches sight of a slim chance
of accepting existence as it is and overcoming his nausea. But
for those unfortunate souls to whom the essence of life remains
concealed, Sartre writes, "They cannot succeed in not feeling
superfluous. And in themselves, secretly, they are *superfluous,*
that is to say, amorphous, vague, and sad."

Bob Arctor is one such soul. He never overcomes the nausea. Instead he falls off the rails of a ravenous drug habit and
ultimately loses touch with reality, his friends, and finally
himself.

Why does such a horrible fate await Arctor? Why are he
and his friends destined to live in the margins of society, to be
left brain-dead in a New Path centre? An almost comatose
Arctor recites a parable about a magnificent wolf that was
shot and killed in order to protect the farmer's meager, unim-
pressive animals that would be slaughtered later anyhow.
They preserved the beast's beautiful hide so that those who
came later could marvel in its strength and size and weep for
its passing.

The wolf, Arctor reflects to himself, never complained, took
joy in his skill and hunting abilities and lived the only way
that was natural to him. And they shot him. Why, like the wolf
to protect the meager animals, must Arctor be sacrificed for
the benefit of the overweight and over-happy members of the
Brown Bear Lodge? Arctor is intelligent, sensitive and ideal-
istic. He sees that there's something wrong about the world
and he is justifiably sick and tired of it. His values and
choices are reasonable. Why, then, must the lone wolf be
hunted? The answer has something to do with that nagging
nauseous feeling.

Society's a Bad Hit (If You're Banging Up, Cranking, or Popping)

The Substance D users are not mere victims. They have chosen to live in the margins and provoke society. In their game, they never fully reject or accept the America that surrounds them. Instead they play as if the could live by different rules. But they learn that this sort of game can be deadly. In *A Scanner Darkly*, and in Dick's own life, those who chose to play paid a horrible cost including: jail, psychosis, neurosis, and death.

Dick's primary *philosophical* contribution in *A Scanner Darkly* is that he recognized what happened to him and his friends in the 1960s and 1970s American drug culture as symptomatic of something bigger. The fate of Arctor and the list of names that scrawls down the screen before the closing credits are evidence of social violence committed against those who did not fit in. Dick and his friends, Arctor and *his* friends, are self-aware outsiders. Their tragic deaths and deformations are no coincidence. Nor is how a frightened and callous suburban California public accused, ostracized, and persecuted them.

Society simply accepts or excludes certain ways of living. It normalizes some lifestyles that are apathetic, lazy, and stupid, while sub-cultures, outsiders and critics are pushed to the margins, made vulnerable and ultimately made to pay dearly for their choices. Peace advocates have their phones tapped, anti-globalization protestors are thrown in jail, political and critical writers like Dick have their homes ransacked and their safety threatened, drug users like Arctor are either hunted down or left to suffer alone, their pain attributed to their addiction, not their social rejection. *A Scanner Darkly* questions why some gain acceptance into the social fold and not others, which visions of the good life are valued and which are considered insidious, and what happens to those unfortunate enough to find themselves on the outside looking in.

Arctor, Barris, Luckman, and Frick all understand in one way or another that the best values are not necessarily awarded by society. Evidence of the unfortunate truth surrounds them. Think of the rabble that comprises the Brown Bear Lodge membership. They are comfortable and content, too content for the sloth and stupidity they represent. Or how about the tactics used by the County Sheriff's Office? They coax

Arctor into a mind-altering addiction all for the outside chance that he will lead them to the evidence they need to nail New Path. And of course there is Donna. She has taken on the life of a formless shadow, a narc who seduces a well-intentioned, naïve fellow narc and leads him down the valley of the brain dead.

Or consider Thelma Kornford, a "straight" who once came over to Arctor's place to ask if someone could kill a big bug in her apartment. The group of druggies came over only to find that it was a mosquito hawk, "a great harmless bug that in fact did good by wiping out mosquitoes." Her reply stunned them. She said, *"If I had known it was harmless I would have killed it myself."*

> That had summed up to them (and still did) what they distrusted in their straight foes, assuming they had foes; anyhow, a person like well-educated-with-all-the-financial-advantages Thelma Kornford became at once a foe by uttering that, from which they had run that day, pouring out of her apartment and back to their own littered pad, to her perplexity. The gulf between their world and hers had manifested itself, however much they'd meditated on how to ball her, and remained. Her heart, Bob Arctor reflected, was an empty kitchen: floor tile and water pipes and a drainboard with pale scrubbed surfaces, and one abandoned glass on the edge of the sink that nobody cared about.

At the same time in the novel, Arctor also muses in another way about how mainstream society prioritizes things. He remembers, before going totally undercover, one time when he took a deposition from "a pair of upper-class well-off straights" who said that "People who would burglarize your house and take your color TV are the same kind of criminals who slaughter animals or vandalize priceless works of art." Arctor explained to them that junkies rarely hurt animals, and would often rescue and care for animals that most people would simply "put to sleep." But their second claim made the smugly uncritical moral superiority of these straights—certainty about who, exactly, is the real "criminal" and why—seem even more ignorant and oppressive to him. He thought to himself,

> As to "priceless works of art" he wasn't too sure, because he didn't exactly understand what that meant. At My Lai during the Viet Nam

War, four hundred and fifty priceless works of art had been vandal-
ized to death at the orders of the CIA—priceless works of art plus
oxen and chickens and other animals not listed. When he thought
about that he always got a little dingey and was hard to reason with
about paintings in museums like that.

Can we say that any of these "straights" represent commend-
able values, values we would want promoted in our society?
And yet these people are 'winners' in life. They end up with the
job, the wife and kids, the security and safety of being on the
inside of the social divide. On the other hand the 'loser' Arctor
is used as a tool, an instrument in the pursuit of others' means.

Drenched with self-loathing, admitting her complicity,
Donna's last words reveal her own disgust, "It is easy to win."
It's easy to stay the course and follow the road to success. It is
easy because it doesn't require taking a stand, or choosing your
values rather than having them chosen for you. It's easy
because as part of dominant society you don't need your identity to be recognized and accepted by others, or your values to
be incorporated into something larger and more influential
than your own sub-culture. As part of dominant society, as one
of the winners, life is undoubtedly easy.

Cultural Minority Report

But what of those who don't choose the easy way out? What of
the 'losers'? What of the Bob Arctors? Can the outsider live in
society with dignity? Eminent thinkers have dedicated volumes to solving the problem of cultural inclusion. They aim to
include sub-cultures into mainstream society without threatening or alienating, assimilating or destroying them. It's a
tricky task. On the one hand are the demands of social conformity. Societies can't work unless there are a number of questions we agree on. Some are basic and easily answered. Must
we pay taxes? Must we stop at traffic lights? Must we follow
the law, basically?

There are cultural questions too. Can children wear religious
symbols at school? Can parents arrange marriages for their offspring? These are more difficult to answer as they introduce
unfamiliar practices into the social fold. There is no clear ethical
or practical answer. We cannot say it is morally wrong to wear

crescents in gym class, nor is it heinous for families to choose partners for their children, so long as the children consent. And they rarely pose a practical impediment. Is wearing a turban dangerous? But some people might still feel uncomfortable with a police officer who dons a religious sash. Or they might find arranged marriages questionable because they seem to hinder freedom of choice, an essential value in our society.

Such cultural demands are demands for the right to freely choose how we wish to live. This stems from a desire to live *authentically*, which is only achieved by living in a way that reflects ones values and identity. People have the right to demand freedom of expression and religion because we recognize that those are essential to the individual's liberty, identity and values. Could we include the right to use drugs and the right against being socially ostracized if drug use were part of our individuality and liberty? Do drug users deserve those rights, so long as they do not threaten the health and safety of others?

The debate comes down to the importance and protection of liberty and identity. How much autonomy should we afford the individual and sub-culture in order that their unique identities might flourish? When do their practices become intolerable and threatening to mainstream society?

Charles Taylor, a political and moral philosopher known for his work on identity politics, has proposed that dominant societies have a duty to recognize and affirm the value of sub-cultures. To do otherwise, he says would be to commit an egregious harm. He argues that it is essential to human identity that one's personal uniqueness and one's community be recognized by the greater society. This recognition is needed for the sense of self-worth of individuals and groups required to empower them to become free, equal, and autonomous agents in both private and public life.

Politics and societies, even today, overlook recognition and threaten to impose homogeneity rather than promoting plurality. Dominant societies are often slow to question their own values. Conservative interests rally to entrench tradition and exclude threatening ways of life. Subordinate groups generally find that there is little space to negotiate mutual respect. Hence they become marginalized, pushed to the fringes of society, where they are vulnerable to all sorts of social ills.

We need to be wary of this cycle. Demeaning and disrespecting identities undermines the self-respect of those excluded and their ability to resist injustices. Think of the disastrous effects of cultural colonialism on native populations. In North America and Australia indigenous groups were denied the right to practice their traditional ceremonies. Today many are still fighting for the capacity to live and work in ways that reflect their values and identities. Denied the land central to their livelihood, denied the resources and rights required to form culturally significant identities, indigenous communities have suffered from low standards of living while residing in countries among the world's richest.

Immigrant populations have similarly suffered from cultural prejudice, leading to poverty and social despair in many communities. In the United States, Mexican migrant workers have been derided culturally while being subjected to perilous and illegal working conditions. In Canada and Australia, Southeast Asian communities have been branded as violent and all too often involved in organized crime. The stigma has resulted in alienation of communities, pushing many immigrant youth to accept their typecast identities and become disproportionately involved in gangs. In France and England, second-generation immigrants were expected to cast off their traditional cultural ties and assimilate into the mainstream. However, disrespect for their parents' cultural identities and practices and social and economic alienation have infused these communities with a feeling of neglect and disgust with how they have been treated and demeaned. The consequent clashes with authority have pushed the children of immigrants even further to the margins of European society.

In each case the disrespect for sub-cultures and their members' identities has resulted in oppression, marginalisation, lack of self-respect and esteem, alienation, community decay and high rates of substance abuse, unemployment and suicide.

Clearly this dire reality has to be avoided. Recognition theory argues that we must instead promote valuation of these cultures. If all were mutually recognized all would be mutually respected and free to pursue their own unique visions of the good life and all would be healthy, contributing members of society.

A Scanner Darkly is in part a rich conversation on the pos-

sibility and desirability of this recognition. Despite their anti-
social behaviour, Arctor and his friends never fully relinquish
an American dream in which their values and communities
might gain acceptance. They use drugs both as a means to
escape and reconcile their affiliation with society, whereas society itself takes on the form of an object whose acceptance is
ambivalently desired and detested. In light of Taylor's philosophy, Arctor and his friends' struggle for recognition forces us to
ask whether there is space for the inclusion of drug cultures in
contemporary America. Or, alternatively, are some attempts at
identity inherently unacceptable to an ethical order that nevertheless ostensibly values pluralism? *A Scanner Darkly* seems
to claim that even pluralistic America cannot accept this kind
of outsider.

The Problem with Drugs

Arctor and his friends are denied social inclusion for two reasons. The first is privileging of dominant community rights
over individuals and sub-communities in California. The
Brown Bear Lodge and the Sheriff's Department take it for
granted that drug use should be prohibited because it is harmful to others and society in general. They will argue, along with
those who believe in the right of the community to protect itself
against anomalous individuals and sub-cultures, that the state
has the legitimate authority to uphold and enforce its own
norms and standards in order to preserve its unique identity
and way of life.

This assumes that there is only one community to be
defended, or at least that only one, usually the dominant one,
is worthy of being defended. This is at the cost of the multitude
of sub-communities that might live peacefully together with
dominant society if given the freedom to do so. This communitarian view also misses the point that most individuals will
belong to multiple cultural groups, not simply one. A college kid
from a middle class white family might be a drug user, while an
Indian American who supports arranged marriages might also
be a union rep at his factory. In this way, a communitarian view
consequently hurts members of every community by privileging one over all.

Douglas Husak, moral philosopher and defender of the right

to drug use, is a strong critic of the communitarianism poisoning California's moral landscape. He argues that the whole point of moral rights is to protect persons from interference supported by a majority. According to him the crusade against drugs is another manifestation of cultural hegemony. Drug use has been attacked as subversive of social institutions throughout American history. The drugs in disfavour at any particular time are generally associated with immigrants, aliens and others who have been alleged to threaten "our way of life." In this way communities "assume what should be in dispute, the moral legitimacy of existing institutions."

Is it accidental that we have outlawed cocaine, marijuana, and opiates—associated with blacks, Mexicans, and Chinese, respectively—but accepted alcohol and tobacco use as matters of autonomous choice that must be left to the individual? Is it because alcohol and tobacco lead to less chronic illness and fewer deaths and, hence, represent lower social costs? (Hint: No.) Couldn't it be more simply because these particular drugs are widely adopted by mainstream culture and by the ruling class?

It's the Nausea

However, the second reason for Arctor's and Dick's social marginalisation is much more problematic in considering the limits of contemporary cultural recognition theory.

It's the nausea. Arctor is just too sickened by what he sees in dominant social values to bother compromising with it. He relishes his difference and independence. The value in his identity, where he gains a sense of self-worth and place, is from opposing the stupidity and struggling against society. His nausea forces him to its margins and makes it nearly impossible for him to be reconciled with society's values. He and his friends gain their sense of uniqueness and superiority to the 'straights' from being outsiders. In other words, what they value most is what society and even the most liberal theories of recognition and inclusion cannot accept: They value being wolves. They value being different, critical, and in their eyes superior. Ultimately it is for their difference, their superiority, and for their refusal to compromise either that they are punished like the wolf.

And yet Arctor and his friends are not simply in opposition

to society. Arctor even attempts to improve society as Fred the narc. He works at the County Sheriff's Office of Orange County trying to bust drug-dealers. His dedication to this line of work is no farce or simple cover story for his other life as druggie. You can feel that his venomous hatred for dealers in his speech to the Brown Bear Lodge is real; there is a part of him that wants the entire Substance D world to go to hell, and to help put it there. He may be disgusted by aspects of society, and reject its values, but he never rejects that this society is *his* society.

It seems, then, that Arctor and his friends find value and identity not in their acceptance *by* society or their straightforward opposition *to* it, but in their struggle *with* it. In this struggle they find the possibility to form new values and new ways of life. Arctor's ambivalent relationship to the mainstream is therefore identity-creative and liberating.

Arctor's split personality is symbolic of this relationship to society. As Bob he is sickened by it and chooses the path of the outsider. As Fred he is a pessimistic public servant doing his best to make what little difference seems possible. As a singular identity he is neither for nor against society, but in a relationship of permanent provocation.

Wolves Finish Last

What's the result of this relationship? In the end Arctor and his friends suffer immensely for it. Orange County does not budge in its stance against users. The Sheriff's Department does not relent in its pursuit of the drug manufacturers, even if it means wasting the lives of innocents. The fact that he's an addict makes it easy to turn Arctor into a puppet. He has no legal protection. And he has no moral ground to stand on, seeing that he's already an outcast.

Arctor's resistance reveals society's inability to recognize sub-communities on the one hand and, on the other, the violent reprisals held in store for the especially threatening kind. *A Scanner Darkly* can be read as showing the boundaries of acceptance into even modern, supposedly pluralistic societies. It appears that some identities are simply too offensive and too antagonistic to be recognized and respected. Those that provide their uniqueness and value to their members in opposing the mainstream stupidities are pursued and persecuted.

Arctor, Barris, Luckman, Frick, and the sort of paranoid counter-culture they have embraced, are in a struggle for recognition with society at large. They are different, they are sick of much of what society has become, they value their uniqueness and are proud of their choice, but they do not wish to alienate themselves entirely from the world around them. What they actually want is liberty, independence, and freedom. They have not given up on the American Dream; they just think the rest of America has. And now the rest of America is out to get them.

Futurity
Doctored

24
I Know What You Did Next Summer

PAUL ATKINSON

Philip K. Dick's stories "The Minority Report" and "Paycheck" ask questions about what would happen if we could predict crime or step into the future. Both stories have been made into movies, which explore similar issues of time but in their own, largely visual language—as films, they always want to *show* us the future, not just predict what's going to happen.

Dick's stories and the film adaptations present many different ways of knowing the future. This is the kind of question that the philosopher Henri Bergson (1859–1941) also grappled with. Bergson doesn't believe we can know the future, but he explains why we sometimes think we can. This is typical of philosophy, which likes to settle issues; to play the role of umpire rather than flex its muscles on the field. But philosophy does not simply blow the whistle and shout, "You're wrong" or "You're right," for it is always involved in writing the rules of the game. Bergson's philosophy, due to its focus on time, is perfectly placed to write the rules governing time travel; a game that is played often in "The Minority Report" and "Paycheck."

Pay Now, Live Later

The key science-fiction idea in the story "The Minority Report" is a radical form of technology that enables law enforcement bodies to take action to prevent a crime before it is actually committed. So the prisons are full of people who have not yet committed a crime. In both versions of *Minority Report* precognition is an extrasensory process because the precogs are said to be endowed with a special ability that allows them access to the future, but the story and the film differ in the kind of knowledge that the precogs have.

The visual medium of the film lends itself to a visual representation of the future that is lived through by the precog. The precog, in a way, is there, immersed in this future time, and sees it all as it happens. In the original story the knowledge that the precogs provide is less precise, more akin to snippets or extracts of the future that requires analysis based on present knowledge before it becomes useful. Bergson's philosophy of time can explain the difference in approach.

Bergson is most famous for arguing that we have falsely represented time as a spatial line that passes from the past into the future and can be easily measured. We measure time in this kind of way everyday, where the regularity and uniformity of calendars and clocks lead us to think of one hour as much the same as another. The hours, seconds, and days marked on a timeline are always equal. Bergson argues that time is something more than this: it is something we experience and live through. Each segment of time cannot be separated from what we're doing. There is a difference between the hour spent waiting for the bus and the hour spent playing video games—one passes faster than the other.

Bergson says that time is real; that we *live* time, and that to live time is something fundamentally different from passing through time viewed as a sequence of events on a timeline or the minute marks on a clock. We do not simply look at time but stand in the middle of it, looking forward to future and looking backward to the past. The past is more than a collection of past events, for it is always active, filling us with ideas and driving us forward. In contrast, the future is there in front of us, uncertain and open to change. The past, in the form of memory, is always overlapping the present and directing our action towards an uncertain future. In this idea of lived time, the future and past are always with us in the present, mixing together in our consciousness, and it is because the past remains (endures) in the present, that Bergson chooses to call time by another name, duration (*durée*).

This has implications for how we imagine the future, many of which Bergson examines in "The Possible and the Real" (1920). First of all, Bergson argues that every moment is completely new and cannot be foreseen—quite a radical idea that does not sit easily with common techniques for imagining the future, including prediction.

We're all familiar with science and its fabulous statements about what will happen. It can plot the movement of planets and, not quite so successfully, the weather. Science fiction also predicts the future, some of which comes true, such as H.G. Wells's predictions concerning wireless communication or William Gibson on virtual reality. How can Bergson claim that the future is unforeseeable if science can produce models predicting what will happen and SF can speculate on future societies and technologies?

To demonstrate his point, Bergson uses a simple thought experiment. Philosophers favor thought experiments because they do not require equipment and nor do they have to leave their comfy armchairs. In this, they have much in common with SF writers. As he sits comfortably, Bergson imagines what will happen when he attends an upcoming reunion. He knows who will be there and where they will sit, as well as the topic of conversation.

Bergson brings the future into the present just through the use of his imagination. However, the reunion does not happen exactly how he imagined it. The exact flow of the conversation is different, as is the appearance, behaviour, gestures and seating of the participants. It is so different that Bergson compares the future, as it actually occurs, to the unique work of an artist—we can easily enough imagine a picture of some lady with folded hands and a vague smile, but our imagination would never produce the *Mona Lisa* in its unique specificity. Nor could we paint the *Mona Lisa*, unless we had actually lived the life of Da Vinci. This does not mean that Bergson rejects speculation about the future. What Bergson's theory of time claims is that we do not truly know the future as if we were living it. When Bergson goes to the actual reunion, rather than visiting it in his imagination, he is not only aware of all the details, he is also caught up in the flow of events.

I Can Predict What You (Don't) Do Next Summer

The word that Bergson often uses when talking about the future is the French word *imprévisible* which has two meanings in English: unforeseeable and unpredictable. Both are concepts that can be used to analyse the different ways that precognition is represented in the short story "The Minority Report" and its film adaptation.

In the short story, the precogs give little information, just the name of the suspect and victim, the location of the crime and other such details. Nor are we told how they produce "prophecies" except to say that they have an expanded "esplobe." The precogs are not talked about kindly by the founder of Precrime, John Anderton, who refers to them as "monkeys" (see no evil) or "idiots." They sit in chairs babbling away about future events without actually understanding what they see or the moral implications. It is the police investigators who work out what is relevant:

> Every incoherent utterance, every random syllable, was analyzed, compared, reassembled in the form of visual symbols, transcribed on conventional punchcards, and ejected into various coded slots. The analytical machinery was recording prophecies, and as the three precog idiots talked, the machinery carefully listened.

With this quaint image of punchcards and lots of visible wiring, we should not forget that science fiction is always written from the perspective of current technology. The SF world that Dick imagines might be in the future but there is no passing through our present—no screens, YouTube or SMS here. It's all about the rantings of the precogs which are translated into data analyzed by a set of computers. The computers test these babblings to determine whether or not they make sense, and if they do, they can be used to predict a crime and secure a preemptive arrest.

To say that something is predictable means that we see the future only in terms of what we know now. For example, astronomy can plot the movement of a meteor because it knows the current mass, the amount of momentum it has and the direction it is heading in. But scientists do not know everything about an event and therefore prediction in most branches of science involves using statistics—working out what is most likely to happen. If you wanted to predict a crime, it would involve knowing the personality of a would-be criminal, who they hang out with and their haunts. From this knowledge the scientist could say that it looks likely that they will engage in criminal activity, and preventing crime is a matter of keeping an eye on them. In this case precrime involves working out what someone might do and making sure they don't do it—a practice that is becoming increasingly common with governments trying to prevent terrorist attacks.

In "The Possible and the Real," Bergson has an unusual take on prediction. It is not about knowing the future, stating what *will* be, but about knowing what *can't* happen. The problem is that we too easily move from the negative statement of the "not impossible" to the positive term, "possible," without addressing the shift. To say that something is "not impossible" is another way of saying that it is more-or-less likely. In predicting an event we do not have a clear image of what will happen but rather impose limits so that we can rule out what definitely will *not* happen. Bergson uses the metaphor of a gate to describe how the future is predicted: "If you close the gate you know no one will cross the road; it does not follow that you can predict who will cross the road when you open it."

In the short story, the precogs might receive their information about the future through supernatural means—but the analysis of the information requires a form of reality testing. A lot of the names and dates are thrown away by the Precrime investigators because they do not fit the world as they see it. They are "closing the gate" on what cannot be in order to find out what will be. This testing and analysis of data sets limits on the future to work out what is predictable or most likely. You can't arrest someone just on a hunch.

In removing all the impossible predictions, we're left with a possible future. But this possible future is still an abstraction based on particular limitations on what is known in the present. It is about stripping back time to a very limited set of events. Consequently Bergson argues that we should not confuse a possible event with a real event. The possible is not a faint image of the real waiting to be realised or an idea awaiting substance but in Precrime, this is exactly what happens.

There are many arrests based upon the investigators' analysis of the precogs' future predictions—removing the impossible to create the possible—but nobody really knows if the any of the supposed criminals will actually commit the crime. These alleged criminals have not actually lived the time of the crime or the time leading up to it. If they did, would they actually fulfil the prophecy of Precrime? If someone knew about the accusation in advance, as Anderton does when he is accused of murder, would they commit the crime? Bergson's theory of time warns us that ever-changing memory and knowledge creates infinite minor and major variations in behavior and therefore a possible future is never the same as an actual future.

Living in the Time of the Crime

In the film adaptation we're introduced to the precogs through a crime of passion where one of the victims, Sarah Marks, is shown in close-up with an expression of horror on her face. She's aware that she's about to be killed by her husband, Howard Marks, who has just discovered his wife in bed with a lover. As viewers we are actually present at the crime, seeing the face of the victim and wondering what will happen next. The camera then moves from a close-up of Sarah Marks's face to an extreme close-up of her dilated pupil that clearly shows the terror she feels. This is followed by a segue to the clear, watery, blue eye of the precog Agatha (Samantha Morton). The camera then zooms out to reveal Agatha's face who utters, in a distant, echoey voice, "murder."

Here the process of precognition is very different to the short story. What we see are images of the soon-to-be-committed murder followed by Agatha's startled expression. We know that it is the precog's vision of the future, where she is immersed in the scene of the crime and consequently has empathy with the victim. The precog Agatha sees what will happen. She is a witness to a crime that is yet to be committed.

In the film adaptation, the facts about the crime are always given a visual form. After Agatha's *vision* we are shown the principal investigator, John Anderton (Tom Cruise) actively interpreting a collection of moving images to ascertain the location of the crime. He is like a film editor piecing together film rushes. The crimes are shown using flash-forwards and are more than just names and locations given by the babbling precogs in the short story. Here precognition is about the *foreseeable* rather than the predictable. There is no process of reasoning, no analytic machinery connecting the present to the future—the future is presented in all its detail but just requires a bit of editing to piece together the events. We see the face of the killer, the terror of the victim, the color of the wallpaper. The precogs, and the audience, are able to *live* in the time of the crime.

Always Invest in the Future

Philip K. Dick's short story "Paycheck" has also been made into a film directed by John Woo and stars another of Hollywood's heroes, Ben Affleck. Like *Minority Report*, both the film and story explore philosophical issues about how to imagine and precognize the future.

In "Paycheck," the hero Jennings is employed for a large sum of money as an engineer on condition that when the job is finished his memory will be wiped. He has no idea where he worked or what he did during this time, so he has effectively lost a couple of years of his life. When fronting up for his pay, he is given a cloth sack full of objects rather than the payment he expected. He is not very happy about losing his pay but he is informed that it was his own decision and is shown a form with his signature on to prove it. He grudgingly accepts the evidence and leaves the office.

He is soon picked up by the police and realizes that his inability to account for the past couple of years could lead to trouble. So he decides to escape police custody and find out where he worked and what he did. While locked up Jennings realizes that one of the objects, a piece of wire, can be used to break the electronic door and allow him to escape. The police pursue him and he jumps onto a bus and when confronted by the robot ticket inspector, he is able to pull a bus token out of the bag. It is at this stage that Jennings realises that the bag given by his past self—the one whose actions are erased from Jennings's memory—provides objects that will help him solve future problems. The items are more valuable than the money he would have received.

We find out later that past-Jennings, referred to in the story as *he* by the *present* Jennings, was working on a time machine that could see into the future and remove objects from it. There is a "mirror" that provides an image of the future, a bit like the screens in the *Minority Report* film, and a "scoop" to pick objects out of the future world and bring them into the present (this being a significant difference from the movie). This doubling up of characters could be confusing but the reader, and the viewer of the film, only has to follow the life of the *present Jennings*. Past-Jennings only really appears through the objects he has left behind.

Summarizing the Future

What would Bergson have to say about Dick's representation of time? Bergson argues that while we are acting, actually living in time, the future is unforeseeable. It is only when we stop or reflect upon it, in other words, look into the past, that the future is imagined as a possibility. The possible futures are mirror images of what we think has happened in the past.

Imagine that you're about to go for a job interview. You are asked to review the whole of your past education and working life, which is presented in the form of a *curriculum vitae*. This "course of life" is a summary of what you have done and it also becomes the means through which you imagine the future. In the actual job interview, you speak of your future in terms of how it is defined by the past, how each of your qualities and past actions will determine your suitability for the new job. All the good bits of your life are brought together, just like on your Facebook page. As Bergson says in *Time and Free Will*:

> Thus, when we call to mind the past, i.e. a series of deeds done, we always shorten it, without however distorting the nature of the event which interests us. The reason is that we know it already; for the psychic state, when it reaches the end of the *progress* which constitutes its very existence, becomes a *thing* which one can picture to oneself all at once.

In "Paycheck," when Jennings leaves the office with his bag of trinkets, the future is open. But when he breaks out of the police station, Jennings asks himself why he has this piece of wire at this time. He starts to reflect on his past and think about a possible future. But the piece of wire could have been used in any electronic door and at *any time*. Maybe it is just luck.

However, as soon as he steps onto the bus and pulls out his bus token, which is his only chance to escape and occurs only at *one time*, the gate of possibility starts to narrow and the future becomes certain. Suddenly Jennings is "filled with a strange elation" because his future, present and past all come together in the form of a plan constructed by past-Jennings. Jennings is happy to fulfil his future as his past self imagined it but this raises the same question as does "The Minority Report": if we are aware of what will happen, will this change our future actions?

The *Paycheck* film and story differ in this regard; Jennings in Dick's story is always excited about his planned, possible future. The Jennings of the film, however, finds out that the planned future world will end with an atomic bomb and decides to sabotage that future in order to continue to live in the present (which does not prevent him from using a lotto ticket left by past-Jennings). As in the film *Minority Report*, images of the future are always competing with images from the present. The viewer is asked in each film to work out how the inevitable future can be challenged by the actions of the main character.

After jumping on the bus, the whole of Jennings's past comes together as a *"thing."* It is a summary of key events in his life as his future self imagines it, that is, a *curriculum vitae* sent back from the future. Everything is constructed in terms of a possible future, where the objects in the sack determine what *he will have done*. When he breaks into the research facility he expects that his code key will open the door to the time scoop. He imagines that this action is determined by his past self. It does not work on that particular door, much to Jennings's surprise, but it does work on another, just in time for another escape.

The Future as Predictive Text

Another way of looking at this issue, is that as soon as present-Jennings's past is constructed as a thing, in this case a narrative created by past-Jennings, then the future becomes a form of predictive text. There are only a limited number of possibilities and everything slots into place. Predictive text creates a future that mirrors the past. It takes all our past text corrections and uses these to limit future ones—another means of closing the gate. Jennings even makes such a suggestion when he reflects on the missing letters of a ticket stub:

> He smiled. That was it. Where had he been? He could fill in the missing letters. It was enough. There was no doubt: *he* had foreseen this too.

Everything begins to follow a pattern. We can guess what letters will fill the spaces because the future is a reflection of the past. Jennings can predict what's going to happen because his life is now determined by a logical pattern of events and his role is no longer to live time but to fulfil a future sketched out for him in advance.

Both *Minority Report* and *Paycheck* investigate ways of imagining the future. Dick's stories are short and simple, and do not provide too much detail about the main character's future. It's always a *possible* future that determines how the characters will act in the present. The films however take a slightly different approach to imagining the future because they fill the narrative with all forms of visual technology.

In *Paycheck*, the past is like a videotape rewinding and the future is a series of headlines and videos of an exploding city. In their level and kind of detail they are almost indistinguishable from the present. Likewise, in *Minority Report*, the crimes are always foreseen through a computer-editing suite. In both films the only thing separating the future from the past is the thin surface of a television screen. For Bergson, the future can never appear on a television screen because this assumes a camera actually living in the time of the event—witnessing the atomic bomb in *Paycheck* or an individual's crime in *Minority Report*. If the future is to be imagined at all, it is as a gate closing or as picture frame narrowing to allow only a vague sketch of what is to happen.

25
Untimely Speculations

HEATH MASSEY

In a section of *The Gay Science* entitled "Our New 'Infinite',", Friedrich Nietzsche writes, "it is a hopeless curiosity that wants to know what other kinds of intellects and perspectives there might be; for example, whether some beings might be able to experience time backward, or alternately forward and backward (which would involve another direction of life and another concept of cause and effect)."

Fortunately, this is a warning that speculative fiction writers have ignored. Philip K. Dick, for one, uses fiction to explore an impressive variety of strange perspectives caused by alterations in our sense of time. His curiosity about extraordinary temporal perspectives, some demonic and others divine, helps him to pursue the question: what does it mean to be human?

If our experience of time is one of the defining features of human existence, Dick wonders, what happens when that experience is radically altered? Do we lose contact with the human world and those who live in it? Is it possible to overcome ordinary human existence thanks to an extraordinary relation to time? Dick's speculations on these matters take the form of imaginative variations of human temporality, and they diverge in two opposing tendencies, which follow the directions of Nietzsche's own thinking about time and eternity.

Nietzsche himself is not prevented by his own injunction against trying to "look around our own corner" from meditating about the possibility of a radically different relation to time. Nietzsche's idea of eternal recurrence is an imaginative variation of our sense of the passage of time. In the section of *The Gay Science* entitled "The greatest weight," he asks:

> What, if some day or night a demon were to steal after you into your loneliest loneliness and say to you: 'This life as you now live it and have lived it, you will have to live once more and innumerable times more; and there will be nothing new in it, but every pain and every joy and every thought and sigh and everything unutterably small or great in your life will have to return to you, all in the same succession or sequence'.

The demon's secret, and Nietzsche's "abyssal thought," is that time does not pass, but each moment returns over and over again. Thus the world neither begins nor ends, life is not followed by eternal rest, and existence has no aim or purpose. For human beings, this means that the future is sealed as irrevocably as the past, for we do what we are destined to do—we have already done it. We are specks of dust in the "eternal hourglass of existence turning over and over." Nietzsche considers two ways this revelation could be received:

> Would you not throw yourself down and gnash your teeth and curse the demon who spoke thus? Or have you once experienced a tremendous moment when you would have answered him: "You are a god and never have I heard anything more divine." If this thought gained possession of you, it would change you as you are or perhaps crush you.

If we took this idea seriously, then either it would be a tremendous burden, a crushing sense of futility, or it would give cause for celebration, liberating us from the need for an aim of existence.

For Nietzsche, eternal recurrence is a test of the will that distinguishes between "man" and "overman." As opposed to the traditional notions of time and eternity, it is "the highest formula of affirmation." One could not celebrate it if one believed that the world needs a divine purpose, for a world in which everything returns would have no aim. Nor would it be possible to celebrate if one regarded oneself as fallen into finitude and separated from the infinite source of all meaning and value, namely God.

From a traditional religious and metaphysical perspective—one that has too long defined what it means to be human, for Nietzsche—the idea of eternal recurrence is terrifying. However, the ability to embrace it and experience *amor fati* (love of fate) would be a sign of having overcome the need for a source of value outside of life. Eternal recurrence is therefore an idea of time that separates the human from the superhuman, or those who are crushed by the meaninglessness of existence from those who can rejoice in it as if were their own creation.

Dick's curiosity about time manifests itself in his many equally strange imaginative variations on ordinary human temporality. Like Nietzsche's eternal recurrence, Dick's ideas follow two opposing tendencies. In one direction, his characters are rendered powerless by disruptions to their experience of time, and in the other direction, their power is expanded. The first group not only does not transcend human temporality, but the disturbance of their relation to time threatens their humanity. The second group, like Nietzsche's overman, is liberated from finite, human temporality. Through these variations, Dick eventually develops a theory of supertemporality, a beyond-time that differs from eternity as traditionally conceived. This theory accounts for a variety of transformations in the ordinary, human experience of time, both real and imagined.

Human, All Too Human

One of Dick's most interesting variations on human temporality involves the tempo of life. *Martian Time-Slip* takes place in a colony on Mars, where repairman Jack Bohlen finds himself struggling against mental illness. Having suffered from schizophrenia in his youth, Jack had recovered (or so it seemed) and moved to Mars to start over. While functioning highly in his profession and family life, he begins experiencing symptoms of the disorder, particularly feelings of alienation and detachment from reality.

At the same time, he meets Dr. Milton Glaub, a psychiatrist who hypothesizes that autism stems from "a derangement in the sense of time in the autistic individual, so that the environment around him is so accelerated that he cannot cope with it." This appears to be true of Manfred Stein, a boy who is completely withdrawn and unable to communicate with others, except for the Martian "Bleekmen" (who presumably experience the flow of time differently). Manfred is also haunted by visions of the future, including his slow deterioration in a decaying retirement facilty. Jack builds a device to slow Manfred's sense of time, bringing him closer to the tempo of "normal" human beings. However, Jack's own schizophrenic episodes worsen, and he experiences severe temporal disruptions, including glimpses of the future accompanied by lapses in memory.

Through his contact with Manfred and his self-observation, Jack concludes that psychosis amounts to "the utter alienation of perception from the objects of the outside world," including others, and a replacement of communication with others by a "dreadful preoccupation with the endless ebb and flow of one's own self." He discovers that temporal acceleration draws vanishingly closer to a point where time no longer flows, but is given all at once (an idea that Dick explores further in his essay "Schizophrenia and The Book of Changes"). This would account not only for the detachment from a shared reality, but also for the connection—or the fine line—between prophecy and psychosis.

Unfortunately, while Manfred has visions of the future, it is a future that he seems powerless to change or even communicate. As Jack's sense of time accelerates, his world grows increasingly hostile, and he becomes less capable of dealing with others. Although Manfred's tempo is so accelerated that his narrative point of view is unintelligible, from Jack's perspective we can feel his powerlessness as his grasp on reality and his connections with others slip away.

Another story focusing on temporal disturbances is "Your Appointment Will Be Yesterday" (later expanded into the novel *Counter-Clock World*), in which Dick imagines a world where time has changed its course and now flows backward. As the result of a phenomenon known as the "Hobart Phase," which has reversed the flow of time, people now begin their day by getting out of bed, putting on dirty clothes, and disgorging their breakfast. They remember the future and make appointments in the past.

And things get even stranger when Dick considers the implications of this reversal for creation and invention. Great minds do not bring new things into existence, but remove them from it. The library is not an institution for preserving and disseminating knowledge, but for eradicating books as their ideas stop making sense. Rather than sending their work to publishers, authors submit it to the library, and if their appeal is successful, they are permitted to reduce the final remaining copy of their manuscript to a bundle of clean paper and a typewriter ribbon. These authors are regarded not as geniuses, but cranks whose ideas must be destroyed for the benefit of society.

A paradox arises, however, because the Hobart Phase is controlled by a human invention, the swabble, which can be assembled out of ordinary household objects. What will happen when the inventor's work is eradicated? As people take apart their swabbles and the inventor Ludwig Eng's how-to manual is removed from circulation, the Hobart Phase weakens and Standard Time begins to return. With this second reversal of the flow of time, the threat of a closed loop emerges: "as soon as Eng built and placed in operation his pilot swabble, the Hobart Phase would resume. The swabbles would then be abolished by the syndicate until, once again, all that remained was the original typewritten manuscript—at which point normal time would re-establish itself."

Unless something is done, everyone will be trapped in an endless oscillation between Eng's discovery of the swabble in Standard Time and his construction of a model capable of producing the reverse temporality of the Hobart Phase. The solution comes from the crank Lance Arbuthnot who, recognizing the impending re-reversal of time, appeals for the eradication of his own manuscript on disassembling the swabble. If his manuscript is eradicated, knowledge of how to disassemble swabbles will be lost, and the Hobart Phase will remain in effect.

In this story, Dick imagines precisely the scenario that Nietzsche disparages: time flowing backward. What makes his treatment of the theme more than idle speculation is the paradox for those whose relation to time is changed. The reversal of time may, at first glance, appear to provide the key to immortality. Indeed, the characters in Dick's story all grow younger, having either avoided death with the change in time's flow or returned from the dead, rescued from their graves (a central motif of the novel). Yet human life remains finite, ending in birth rather than death. More menacingly, the reversal of time, in this case controlled by humans, ends up producing a closed loop from which escape may not be possible. Ironically, the power to alter the flow of time is ultimately incapacitating.

In a final example of powerlessness produced by an alteration to one's sense of time, the novel *Ubik* explores not a reversal of time, but a reversion of things in the physical world. Dick imagines a society in which the recently deceased are preserved in "moratoriums" in order to continue communicating with the living, and in which telepathy and precognition are not only well-established phenomena but services provided by a booming cottage industry. There are companies that employ spies with psionic talents, and there are also anti-psi firms or "prudence organizations" for counteracting such talents.

Joe Chip, a slovenly, financially-strapped milquetoast with no telepathic or precognitive abilities, is a technician for one such organization, Runciter Associates. After an incident on the Moon in which his boss, Glen Runciter, is killed, Joe has a series of unsettling encounters with ordinary objects undergoing accelerated decay. First there are the stale cigarettes and spoiled milk. Then appliances begin to revert to archaic forms, such as the TV that becomes an old-fashioned AM radio. Struggling to understand the transformations in his apartment, Joe surmises, "The past is latent, is submerged, but still there, capable of rising to the surface." Indeed, the physical world regresses as things in it devolve into prior "templates" or "configurations" and eventually disappear. Although Joe and his associates do not regress in age, their shared reality slips further into the past due to their "constantly declining time-binding capacity."

In these stories, the alteration of human temporality turns out to be incapacitating, as it threatens to crush the individuals whose sense of time is disrupted. The degeneration of reality for Joe Chip and associates in *Ubik* mirrors the disconnection experienced by Jack Bohlen and Manfred Steiner in *Martian Time-Slip*. In both cases, their altered relation to time poses an obstacle to their very survival, and rather than embracing the transformation, they struggle to maintain their connection to the time in which others live and not to be overcome by despair.

In "Your Appointment," while those experiencing the reverse time of the Hobart Phase may know the future and survive death, their lives still come to an end—at birth. If there is immortality, it is only in the form of an infernal circle brought about by their design. What might have been a temporality worth celebrating turns out to leave them powerless in the face of their own inventions, still crushed by the weight of the inexorability of time.

Preparatory Human Beings

Contrary to these demonic alterations of our sense of time, Dick also imagines temporalities closer to the divine. In "The Golden Man," radioactive fallout from a nuclear war has produced an abundance of strange genetic mutations. A government agency that apprehends and euthanizes mutants (called "deeves") dispatches a team to bring in an elusive case: a "blond beast" with golden coat and mane, who has escaped capture by living like a feral animal. They fear that this young man, with his striking appearance and extraordinary ability to remain free, represents *Homo superior*, a form of life capable of supplanting human beings: "A deeve who would be to us what we are to the great apes."

When they finally catch him and lock him in a room with a random-firing gun trained to spray in every direction, he escapes harm with incredible agility. To his captors' surprise, a brain scan reveals an extremely underdeveloped frontal cortex, which explains his inability to speak. It suggests that he has eluded capture not because of his intelligence, but thanks to an instinctive ability to "pre-think." In his experience, possible futures appear along with the present situation, much as for us the present is interwoven with memories of the past. At every moment he sees a panorama of future scenarios and his position in them (depicted vividly in *Next*, a movie loosely based on the story). Consequently, the authorities are forced to revise their conception of *Homo superior*; the golden man's prescience makes him invincible as long as he can see a scenario in which he survives, but this ability is more akin to animal instinct than human intelligence. Lacking the linguistic and technological capacities we tend to associate with intelligence, it is his sense of time—his experience of the possible futures implicated in the present—that makes him a superhuman beast.

A similar idea is explored in *Now Wait for Last Year*, in which the human race, under the leadership of Gino "the Mole" Molinari, is embroiled in a war between its allies from Lilistar and an insectoid race called the reegs. A highly toxic and addictive hallucinogenic drug, JJ-180, is developed for the purpose of spiking the reegs' water supply. As it turns out, the drug's primary effect (not unlike the drug Chew-Z in *The Three Stigmata of Palmer Eldritch*) is to dislodge users from time, sending them into the past, the future, or the present in a time sequence parallel to our own. Molinari uses JJ-180 to time-trip into parallel universes, confer with other versions of himself, and in some cases bring them back to his time for insurance against any coup, assassination attempt, or fatal illness. By tripping from one present to another, rounding up a team of alter-egos, "healthy duplicates of himself from the rank of parallel worlds," he virtually overcomes his mortality, founding "a dynasty consisting of himself." Molinari cannot see the future, but his power is even greater: by moving "sideways" into alternate presents, he gives himself—or himselves—the ability to maintain control in almost any future imaginable.

Along similar lines, *The Man in the High Castle* takes place in an alternate present in which Franklin D. Roosevelt has been assassinated, the Axis Powers have won World War II, and North America has been divided between Japan and Germany. In San Francisco, the Japanese occupy the upper rungs of the social ladder, their traditions and industries eclipsing a dying American culture. Everyone is reading a novel called *The Grasshopper Lies Heavy*, which depicts a world in which Roosevelt survives the assassination attempt and the Allies win the war. The author, Hawthorne Abendsen, has apparently tapped into an alternate present much like our own in order to construct the world of his novel, and consequently he has become a target for elimination by the Nazis.

The experiences of several other characters suggest that they, too, have caught a glimpse of another present, a not-too-distant parallel universe. The expert forger Frank Frink and his partner Ed McCarthy start a business making hand-wrought jewelry, a tremendous risk in a world where innovation—movement into the future—is entirely the department of the Japanese and the Germans. The extent to which America is a land of the past is illustrated by the Japanese obsession with vintage collectibles. But Frink's creations offer a glimmer of hope, for their value is not their historicity; instead, in them "an entire new world is pointed to."

What no one realizes, but Dick hints, is that this "new world" is an America that was never defeated, an alternate present into which Nobusuke Tagomi, who buys and meditates on one of the pieces of jewelry during a personal crisis, actually slips for a short time. Like the *I Ching* (*The Book of Changes*), which is consulted for advice by many characters in the novel, the handmade pieces are oracles. But rather than telling the future, they bring the inhabitants of that world into proximity with our own slightly divergent time sequence. And it is the artist, like the science-fiction author, who has the power to provide this means of resistance to totalitarian domination. With this imaginative variation, Dick explores a mode of temporality less fantastical than that of the precog or the time-tripper, yet nevertheless one that increases the power of those who can tap into other timelines. And like Nietzsche's eternal recurrence, this idea of parallel times separates the human from the superhuman—or at least the supertemporal.

On the Advantage and Disadvantage of Eternity for Life

Over the years, Dick conjured up numerous theories about time to explain the strange temporalities that he explores in his fiction. His most provocative is the notion that we exist in numerous different worlds, each having its own history or time sequence. These are like the "possible worlds" of philosophers, many of which are distinguished from ours by only minor details. In the essay "If You Find This World Bad, You Should See Some of the Others," Dick presents the "wicked thought" that these worlds may actually exist, comprising

> a plurality of universes arranged along a sort of lateral axis, which is to say at right angles to the linear flow of time . . . ten thousand bodies of God arranged like so many suits hanging in some enormous closet, with God either wearing them all at once or going selectively

back and forth among them, saying to himself, 'I think today I'll wear the one in which Germany and Japan won World War II.'

This idea of a multiverse of parallel time sequences raises many metaphysical and theological questions. Since we experience all change as happening along a "linear time axis" running through a single past, present, and future, is it possible to perceive lateral changes, "processes occurring sideways in reality"? If so, how would such changes appear to us? Would they be intelligible? Could this be what schizophrenics experience? And does this provide a way to make sense of eternity? For if eternity is, in Dick's words, "a state in which you are free from and somehow out of and above time," then it could be a mode of supertemporality, an ability to occupy more than one time sequence at will.

This brings us back to Nietzsche. Dick's idea of a temporal multiverse is, like eternal recurrence, more of a speculative hypothesis than a theory about the world. The idea is posed as a question: What if your life and every event in it happened over and over again? Would the endless cycle of time and the aimlessness of existence crush you, or would you revel in it? What kind of being could affirm a universe of this kind and will each moment to return rather than to pass away? Such a being would have been cured of the disease called "man," for there is something superhuman in the ability to celebrate the thought that eternity is not rest, but endless strife.

There are those who could not bear this burden, who would be crushed by it and refuse to believe that there is no higher purpose to existence—namely, humans. But there may be others who would relish the thought—those who, in Dick's words, "will be free from and somehow out of and above" humanity. Whether eternal recurrence is a fiction or a reality is less important than these two tendencies it illuminates.

Philip K. Dick's speculations on time follow both tendencies, exploring the relationship between temporality and human existence. In one direction is the powerlessness of those disconnected from reality by temporal acceleration, threatened by a closed time loop arising from reversals of time, or caught up in a degenerative reversion of the physical world. Their ability to function is compromised by the disruption of their sense of time. In the opposite direction is the extraordinary power afforded by precognition, time-tripping, and the ability to tap into parallel time sequences. The latter variations turn out to be modes of supertemporality leading beyond our experience of time and human existence as we know it.

Struggling against a world where ordinary people are dominated by impersonal, inhuman forces, Dick proposes that not only are there many possible futures, but many alternate presents. Those who can imagine or perhaps even perceive them would, like those who affirm the eternal return, be virtually superhuman—not immortal, not omnipotent, but capable of resisting the supposedly inexorable march of time.

26

The Day Roosevelt Was Assassinated

PETER SIMONS

> Can anyone alter fate? All of us combined . . . or one great figure . .
> . or someone strategically placed, who happens to be in the right
> spot. Chance. Accident. And our lives, our world, hanging on it.
>
> — PHILIP K. DICK

15th February 1933. President-elect Franklin Delano Roosevelt is visiting Miami. From the back of an open car he's giving an impromptu speech in the Bayfront Park area when shots ring out. Roosevelt is hit in the chest and falls at the feet of Chicago mayor Anton Cermak, whose hand he had been shaking. Cermak sobs "I wish it had been me instead of you, Mr. President." On 6th March, Roosevelt dies of peritonitis, and John Nance Garner is sworn in as thirty-second President of the United States. The assassin, a disaffected Italian immigrant called Giuseppe ("Joe") Zangara, freely admits murder and is executed on 30th March.

This did not happen. But it easily might have. Zangara's bullet in fact missed Roosevelt by inches and killed Cermak. We know that Roosevelt went on to re-energize the country's flagging economy through the New Deal, aid the British Empire in its lone fight against Nazi Germany, and after Pearl Harbor and Hitler's declaration of war on the United States, lead the country into and largely through the Second World War. That much is history. But suppose Zangara had hit and killed the President-elect. What would, what could have happened then? How might history then have unfolded?

This counterfactual twist to history is the background to Philip K. Dick's masterful novel *The Man in the High Castle* (1962), which deservedly won a Hugo Prize the next year. Unlike the majority of Dick's work, it is not science fiction, but belongs to the genre of alternate history. Alternate histories are an intermittent theme in Dick's work. In *Minority Report* the story turns on there being several possible futures that can be precognized, brought about, or prevented, and how we may freely try to realize one rather than others, and so does "Golden Man." *Divine Invasion* can be considered to involve alternative histories. Indeed for anyone, like Dick, who's fascinated by alternate realities, whether future or simply other, the step to an alternate reality which rewrites our own past history is not in principle a big one. All the same, none of Dick's work so immerses the reader in a single alternate history as *The Man in the High Castle*.

The Story

Not many writers have tried the alternate-history genre, and fewer still have pulled it off. Dick was influenced by the example of Ward Moore's 1953 novel *Bring the Jubilee*, an alternate history which starts with the Confederate States of America winning the Battle of Gettysburg and the American Civil War, the hinge event being the successful Confederate capture of Little Round Top in the battle. A more recent example is Robert Harris's gripping *Fatherland*, set in a Germany that has won World War II. But to my mind Dick's book is the pick of the pack. It succeeds in part because it is chillingly believable. The characters in the story are the usual mix of partly good, partly bad people, acting for the usual sorts of mixed motives. Their freedom of action is limited. It's the alternate history in which they're embedded that gives the book its edge.

Dick does not tell the story in a linear way. He plunges us first into the alternate reality, so we get used to it. We learn about Zangara in passing, and the event is not treated by the book's characters as hugely important, because all the big important things happened to other figures such as the incoming president and his successors, less important in our history of this period, after the world had been shunted into the alternate path by the assassination.

The story is set mainly in San Francisco, around 1960. For lack of strong US leadership, Germany and Japan have won the war. Even the US has been conquered and partitioned: the Atlantic and Pacific seaboards are ruled by puppet regimes answering to Germany and Japan respectively, with a weak buffer state in between. Hitler is alive but paralyzed and senile from syphilis; the German Chancellor Bormann is dying. The two superpowers divide the world but there is cold-war rivalry between them, and some elements aiming for power in Germany want to destroy Japan in a nuclear attack and take over the whole world.

The characters in the story are all linked to this scenario, but the more convincing players are seemingly historically minor ones: a Jewish jewelry maker, his estranged wife, a dealer in fake Americana, a middle-ranking Japanese official. It is through them that we inhabit the other world. Dick goes out of his way to make this world seem normal and believable. His characters accept things as they are. By introducing grammatical mistakes into the internal thoughts of his Japan-influenced characters he make them alien to our familiar English-dominated culture.

The other link between all the characters is a book, *The Grasshopper Lies Heavy*, written by a man said to live behind strong security high in the Rockies, the high castle of the title. By a neat reversal, this book describes an alternate history in which the Allies win the war. This angers the Reich authorities enough for them to ban it in the rump USA and to try to have the author assassinated. The doubly alternate history is similar to but intriguingly different from the actual course of events: the war goes on for longer, and Britain remains a superpower.

Enough: if you haven't read the book yet, I heartily recommend it.

Reality

Dick's book is "realistic," and realism is perhaps the major concern in his writings. He once wrote, "My major preoccupation is the question, 'What is reality?'." In *Time Out of Joint*, the cosy 1950s world in which the hero lives is a sham. In reality it is near 2000, a nuclear war is raging, and the hero is uniquely able to predict where the next strike will fall. He does so best when at ease, so the sham world is there just to keep him relaxed and efficient, his guesses being part of a supposed newspaper quiz. In this case, it's clear that we have a real world and a merely apparent, constructed "world," through the cracks of which the hero begins to see. A similar mismatch between appearance and reality is present in the brilliant short story "Adjustment Team."

The reality of Dick's alternative world in *The Man in the High Castle* is not meant to be a sham or mere appearance: it is as real as our world. There is no way for its inhabitants to escape into a realer reality, any more than we can. At one point one of Dick's characters gets what appears to be a tantalizing glimpse, or excursion, into "our" reality, one containing the ugly Embarcadero highway, which really and controversially existed for a while in San Francisco, but was never built in the alternate world. But the episode is brief and its status is not clear.

In "How to Build a Universe that Doesn't Fall Apart Two Days Later," Dick wrote "Reality is that which, when you stop thinking about it, doesn't go away." This is as good a characterization as anything a professional philosopher could come up with. The first philosophical question that Dick's book raises is then whether a world described by an alternate history is less real than ours, or just as real. Is our world, the actual world, the only real one? Or are there other worlds, which are just as real as ours? Dick's story is not the first to raise this issue, but by its brilliance and conviction it raises it is a particularly direct and striking way.

In late twentieth-century philosophy, much discussion has turned on the question of alternative possible worlds. The idea of possible worlds goes back to the German philosopher Gottfried Leibniz (1646–1716), but possible worlds were put center-stage for contemporary metaphysics and logic by the American philosopher David K. Lewis (1941–2001).

Lewis claims that there really are innumerable such possible worlds; that every consistent way things might have been really exists, in just the same way as our world exists. That we call such alternative worlds "merely possible" and our world "actual" is due only to our being anchored in our own world. We say our world is actual, but any intelligent inhabitants of other worlds say their world is actual. Our world is no more real than theirs; to think our world is the only real one is like a person who has never left New York thinking that only New York really exists, and London, Paris, Rome, and Tokyo are only figments of New Yorkers' imaginations. That is a sort of chauvinism: world chauvinism. Most philosophers find Lewis's views incredible, but it is hard to show them inconsistent.

We think that real history is different from alternate history because real historians are trying to get at the facts, at what really happened. Dick's novel holds up a mirror to this assumption: he describes a world in which the alternate history is taken for granted: people are as ignorant of what happened or happens there as we are about our world, but in his world there are people thinking about worlds alternate to that one, and those worlds can be more like ours than his. We think Dick's world is unreal; his characters think worlds like ours are unreal. Are we right and they wrong, or is it symmetrical? If it is, then our world has no exclusive title to the label 'real'.

Determinism

Dick himself toyed quite seriously with the idea that there is no single reality. In a 1976 interview for *Science Fiction Review*, for example, he said:

> I think that, like in my writing, reality is always a soap-bubble, Silly-Putty thing anyway. In the universe people are in, people put their hands through the walls, and it turns out they're living in another century entirely. I often have the feeling—and it does show up in my books—that this is all just a stage.

Lewis's many real worlds capture this view, except that there are no channels between them: each world is isolated and self-sufficient, just more or less similar to others. This gives them a feature which makes them unlike our world. It is their determinism. Determinism is the view that what happens in the world is completely fixed, or determined, by how it is at any given time. The complete state of the world at a certain time, say midnight GMT 1st January 2000, fixes in complete detail how it will be at any other time, past or future. On this view, most famously associated with the great French mathematician and cosmologist Pierre-Simon Laplace, history runs on rails with no branching or deviation. Each of Lewis's worlds, because it is complete in all details at all times and places, is deterministic.

There are several reasons for thinking our world is not deterministic. One is that we seem to have within ourselves the power to choose and determine how things turn out, usually in fairly small and local matters: what to eat today, whether to give money to a charity, and the like, but sometimes in bigger things too. We call this freedom. Some philosophers have denied freedom, but most people and even most philosophers believe we are free, within limits. This is what makes praise and reward for good actions and blame and punishment for bad ones meaningful. Being free means being able by your actions to determine that the world develops in one way rather than another, where before your decision, it could have gone either way.

A second reason for thinking determinism is false comes from modern science. According to standard views of quantum physics, many events happen spontaneously, without a cause. A radioactive nucleus splits: it might have split earlier or later, and nothing determines that it must split when it actually does: it just happens that way. Modern physics deals with this by using probabilities. While not all physicists accept this standard view, most do.

The third reason for thinking determinism is wrong is the one most closely related to Dick's novel. It is that many events happen by chance, or coincidence. Zangara might have killed Roosevelt: it was just chance that he did not. No guiding principle or guardian angel kept the President-elect safe: he was lucky. Luck is institutionalized in lotteries and other games of chance, indeed it was in thinking about such games that the science of probability was born. Within the novel, Dick raises the question himself, and that is this chapter's motto.

You might think that chance, luck, and accident concern not how the world is in itself, but simply reflect our ignorance. We don't know how the lottery balls will fall out, but if we knew all their positions, speeds and trajectories, and had a sufficiently powerful computer, we could predict the lottery result with certainty. This was Laplace's idea. If Laplace and Lewis are right, we're simply ignorant about how the world will in fact develop. Our ignorance is about which deterministic world we are in, not about how our one world might follow different histories.

But there is objective chance in this world, and this is high-lighted by alternate histories like Dick's. Consider coincidence. Sometimes you meet someone you know, completely by sur-prise, in a place you would not both expect to be. It seems to be purely by chance. Nobody planned or arranged the meeting: you just both happened to be there at the same time. (That is what 'coincidence' literally means: being in the same 'happen-ing'.) To take the element of personal freedom out of it, imagine two grains of wheat that happen to end up touching in a huge granary. Grains of wheat have no free will: they go where the forces of nature and the efforts of humanity put them. That these two grains end up in contact, when they may have come from different ends of the country, is coincidence.

Technically we can say coincidence occurs when two causal chains of events merge which previously had no interaction. Lottery machines are deliberately designed so that what peo-ple have put on their lottery slips has no influence on how the balls fall out: any win is a coincidence. My event of choosing these numbers and the machine's event of selecting these balls belong to different causal chains until I learn of my win and claim my prize.

Normally coincidence and chance do not make a huge dif-ference to the way things turn out, but occasionally they do. The outcome of a battle may depend on whether a message gets through or whether a general is feeling unwell. Sometimes an inspirational leader is hit by a single bullet. King Charles XII of Sweden and General Stonewall Jackson both died in battle this way. Sometimes an omission rather than an action is cru-cial. Whether Winston Churchill or Lord Halifax would replace Neville Chamberlain as British Prime Minister in 1940 seems to have turned on Churchill saying nothing to King George VI at a crucial point in their discussion. Halifax would probably have negotiated an armistice with Hitler, and the history of the world would have been very different. Dick's twist to history lets a bullet from Zangara's gun deviate just a few inches from its actual trajectory, as could so easily have happened, had Zangara aimed fractionally differently. The significance of the crucial event lies in the magnitude of its consequences: the his-tories diverge considerably.

Now I think Dick is right that hinge events can make huge differences to how things turn out. But I do not buy Dick's hint—or Lewis's theory—that all the different possible worlds are equally real. Only our world is real.

Time in the One Real World

That still does not fix what our one real world is like. Here are four different philosophical positions about that.

The world might consist of all and only events that actually happen at some time, and the objects involved in these events. These objects exist and events happen at different times, but the world encompasses all of them and simply is. This view is called eternalism.

According to the second conception, the world changes with time, as ever-new events happen and objects come into and go out of existence. Events are unreal before they happen. Since reality literally grows by the addition of ever more events and things, philosophers calls this the growing block theory of the world in time.

If, additionally, we take the same view about the past as the growing block theory takes about the future, so that now both the past and the future are taken as unreal, then the world is shrunk so that it contains only what now exists and what happens now. This view is called presentism.

Finally, the fourth theory says that all possible future events are real, and that as time goes by, events make some of these realities go away, leaving others. This is known as the tree-pruning model. The world is not linear in time but like a branching tree, at each instant many futures branch off. As things happen and time goes by, branches incompatible with what occurs are pruned, and reality shrinks.

So in 1930 for example, both our world and Dick's world are real, since it has yet to be determined that Zangara fails to assassinate Roosevelt; by 1934 however Dick's world had been pruned away, whereas ours still remained among the future branching possibilities.

It's often supposed that eternalism, the position that all and only actual events and objects are real, does not allow for chance, coincidence, or freedom of choice. If only what actually happens is real, how can some action or event make a difference to what is real? Surely whatever happens was bound to do so. That is fatalism: history on rails. So those who believe in chance and freedom tend to be drawn to one of the other theories. I think that is wrong: chance and freedom can live alongside eternalism.

Coincidence plays a role in our individual lives, and therefore in history too. As people progress through life, day upon day, they coincidentally encounter other people, things, end up in places and situations without planning or forethought. I might walk out of my house one morning to find a person collapsed on my doorstep. Maybe she had nothing to do with me and was not seeking out my doorstep rather than anywhere else. How I react to this situation, what I make of it, what chain of events I set in motion upon encountering them is part of my life, and now part of hers.

From a chance encounter the two lives may become more or less intricately and deeply intertwined. Such can be the beginnings of a good story. Had she not collapsed by chance on my doorstep, none of this would have happened. The coincidence is that it is this person with this history that lands on just this doorstep. What ensues from that, no matter how tightly constrained by our two different natures, would not have arisen without this coincidental encounter. So while our lives are not wholly ruled by chance, chance plays a fair part in them.

It is all the more so then in history, which is the tapestry created by the interweaving of people, events, places and things, many of them coincidental. So if chance plays any part in people's lives, which I believe it does, since human history is composed of the lives of all humans, chance plays a part in history. The more powerful and influential a person is or gets to be, the wider the effects of chance events in his or her life. Although Leo Tolstoy thought otherwise, the actions of leaders and other powerful people typically have a bigger effect on history than those of ordinary people, and these effects are magnified by modern technology. When President Truman decided the US would drop atomic bombs on Japan, the result was to kill between 160,000 and 240,000 people and injure or shorten the lives of tens of thousands more, at the same time saving the lives of many hundreds of thousands of others.

As in the different possible outcomes to Zangara's shooting, chance and coincidence play a part in determining history, and the more crucial and powerful the people involved, the bigger the differences they make. Yet eternalism can still be the right

view about events in time. Nothing in the idea of an event
being the outcome of merging two previously unconnected
causal chains requires future events to be unreal. While things
might develop in one way rather than another, that does not
mean we should regard the eliminated possibilities as having
the same claim to reality as what actually happens.

Eternalism has many other advantages as an account of
time, because it treats all times democratically as of equal
worth. All other accounts of time privilege something called
"the present," which is exalted above all other times as more
genuine or real, yet which is not a single time but shifts to each
time in turn, one might say "as time goes by."

The decision between eternalism or some other account of
time cannot be made in detail here, so I am just indicating
where I think the best way lies. Eternalism simply takes the
sequence of times as given and equally real, leaving open the
question whether what happens at earlier times does or not
does determine (make inevitable) what happens later.

So eternalism can live alongside indeterminism. That
means that the world Philip K. Dick describes in *The Man in
the High Castle* has no reality whatsoever, but still things could
have happened as he describes. Dick probably would not have
agreed. If not, then as a philosopher I pay enough respect to
him to say that I think he, as a philosopher, was wrong.

[1] *.World Clock-Counter* or "Yesterday Be Will Appointment Your" Dick's in
time of sense making really try just ,bending-mind is *this* think you if ,And

---

,sometimes or—future the of ,present the in ,presence constant
the by provided is experience present our of content The
.constantly it do you ,fact in—that do to *able*
you are only Not .happened yet not has which that think
to able being as defined best be probably would Precognition

Precog a Are You

.Precog a are You
:yourself about
realized never you've that fact basic more ,first a with start
let's ,now For .right is time the when—answered be will
questions These ?with begin to traveler-time a you're claiming
I am why ,matter that for ,And ?obvious more it make this
would Why [1].doing you're what of aware become you help will
and ,ability your weakens it :kryptonite like format this
of Think .this like written is chapter this why that's ,fact In
.it about thinking even without constantly
do you that something is travel Time .in lived always
has it that water the see doesn't fish a like just ,time through
movement your of aware not you're ,course Of .personally
you ,Yes .time in fixed not are you ,them on based movies
the and ,works Dick's K. Philip in characters the of many Like

WITTKOWER D.E.

Time in Unfixed Are You

27

.underneath remaining
substance real any of nothing with ,patches other to
connected patches of network a have we instead but
,patches by supported thing imperfect an have we that much
so not is it eventually ,again and again repaired tire rubber
a Like .mind of state and mood present our of terms in history
own our rewriting slowly ,reality of version that reinforce
we ,another or way one in past the remember we time every
and ,past the remember we how influences mood current
our " ,Incorporated ,Lies" ,chapter his in explained Fallis Don As
.world the of view current our on based history change and past
the into far travel we ,memory Through !past the into travel
also you—possibilities future your in exist just don't you But
.are
"really" we think we who with do to little very has moment
present The .commitments and ,projects ,goals of terms in
foremost and first (well them know we when ,too people other
of and) ourselves of think We .present the in than future the
in more found is ,too ,self the but ,it realize usually don't We
.futures possible many these of
terms in ,foremost and first ,thing the and place the understand We .location that in place particular each in present
potentially as ourselves find we wherein ,envision we possibilities future the all of combination the as location a understand
We .it with taken be might which actions the of terms in us
around object each experience We .future the in thinking ourselves find always we ,*phenomenology* of movement philosophical the to according ,but ,possibilities-as-existence our as
described Heidegger Martin and "protention" called Husserl
Edmund what of examples clearer of couple a are These
.us to present
already was that future the of absence the feel we—chord tonic
the to returning without suddenly ends music the if—follow
not does resolution that when and ,absence its in now resolution the experience We .occurred yet not has that resolution the
of ,moment that at ,presence the is hear we tension the ,com-
position a of end the at tension building music of swell
the hear we When .action our motivates and directs that location future its is it and ,future its of terms in exclusively almost
it experience we—pot flower a or ,example for ,football a—
air-mid in something see we When .futures possible multiple

hearing but ,*is* what with along *was* what hearing ,moment
present each at past the in be must we ,melody a hear To
.melody a not ,noise crashing
single a be would This .together *actually* being as melody the
in notes the all experience not do clearly we ,hand other
the on ,Now .follow that notes the in *felt* is note each where
movement that is music—*music* create doesn't note different a
remembering :next the to note one from tension and movement
the feel wouldn't you ,note each *remembered* just you If .melody
a not :another then and note one hear only would you
,present the experiencing only were you If .melody a as melody
a hear can you that is it thing strange very a what Consider

.present the in us to present already and always being as
past that experience we ,instead—memory a does as ,*recalled*
be to have even not does past immediate Our .it for looking
even without was phone your where for reach simply can you
that you to present so is past your ,rings phone your and couch
the on down lie you When .future the in you to present
stay will you of front in then things the at looking were you
where past the ,around turn you When .you around everything
of past the and past own your into trailing always are
you ,fact in :self the to regard with true just not is this And
.want you
future of kind the create can you that so past the alter and
,ways hidden ,small these in past the into travel also you But
.future the by as past the by tempered as is yourself of understanding your and ,constantly you with past that bring You
.up shit making are
you :vernacular the In .yourself about tell to want currently
you story the of part are that moments empty in patch to
images creating ;past that fabricating and altering instead
are but ,past the of record a accessing not you're that proof
That's ?you didn't ,person third the in yourself saw you ,eye
mind's your before flashed that images the in :this me Tell
.remember can you what see
to minute a for it about think just and reading stop ,Seriously
.event storied other some or ,mountains the to or seaside
the to went you that time that—childhood your from moment
distinct ,clear a remember to try and here minute a Take

Time through Travel You

it precisely as passed. We must be in the 'past,' under erasure, at every present moment. We could not even hear notes as music if we were not always experiencing not only the present, but also presently experiencing the past and precognizing the future. Parallel with his description of present presence of future possibilities as *protention*, Edmund Husserl describes this present presence of the 'past,' not as memory, but as *retention*. And with 'this,' we're now ready to see why reading like this can help you notice yourself traveling through time.

You Are a Blur

Usually, when we read, our eyes unconsciously jump all over the place. We read through something without really paying attention—we mentally use the "autocomplete" functions that frustrate us so much on our mobile phones. Occasionally, when the autocomplete doesn't 'work,' and the sentence doesn't end like we thought it would,' we go back and actually read the thing. By reading in this backwards 'way,' I hope that it has become apparent how much work you are doing in retaining the words that came before and in projecting the words that haven't yet arrived. And 'really,' is it impressive how much precognition and travel-time is involved in even the simplest communication! Consider this sentence as it would have to be understood if spoken:

Consider (imperative action, protends an object) this (protention prolonged: what is it?) sentence (protended object supplied; imperative
must be retained in order to contextualize the intended encounter of
this object) as (modifies retained imperative action "consider") it (pro-
noun calling for retention of substantive "this sentence") would (clarifies
retained modification "as" of retained imperative "consider"—the listener now knows we are going to consider the sentence "as" something
in some counterfactual form yet to be determined) have (the listener
hears /æ/ rather than /ə/, signaling that this "have" does not primarily
modify the "would"—as in the spoken "would've," which uses a
schwa—but will instead modify something which is to follow. If the
speaker is American, this word will be pronounced /hæf/, indicating that
this "have" is not the "have" of possession, which is /hæv/ in both UK
and US English, but will instead form the idiomatic "have to" of neces-

.typesetter volume's this ,Sanders Todd of efforts heroic the for , also ,thanks
Special !it editing imagine ,challenging was this reading thought you if—
seriously ,mean I .chapter this proofreading and editing in help for Barham
Ross and ,Gallagher Michelle ,Weiss Dennis ,Visković Richard to Thanks[2]

.time in unfixed be to is human be To

.us to present always are that futures
calibrate and project to and fixed was thought we that past a
negotiate constantly to is human be To .human be to like
is it what of retelling symbolic a are they because ,stories
as interesting and ,stories as possible are stories these—time
in moments other into thrown themselves find and ,timelines
parallel into slip ,want they future the choose ,past
the change who travelers-time and precogs his all And .all at
alive be to like is it what but ,world contemporary the in like
is life what just not explores work his that surprised be
shouldn't we ,though ,philosopher fictionalizing a As .state the
and liberties civil ,them on war the and drugs of scourges
twin the ,war cold the ,computers of and automation of
rise the—terrain symbolic a on time his of concerns fictional
-non the explored certainly fiction Dick's .level symbolic
a at fiction-non is which but ,fictional literally is which
world a out projecting by present the explores it :future the
through present the explores ,said often is it ,fiction Science

.you on nothing have
Conley Pat and Anderton John .amazing and bending-mind is
time of control Your .futures possible many the precognize
and ,present the of data-sense the experience also you as
time same the at past the in already is what of experience
changing-ever and creative a is moment every at experience
your :time through blur a like are you ,experience every In

now placed under counterfactual conditional supplied).
sentence retained) spoken (will now be supplied, "would," by previously
sider") if (indicates that the specific nature of counterfactualism, implied
content "understood" with object "sentence" under imperative "con-
phrases "have to" and "to be" can now be used to connect supplied
which is necessitated by the "have to" is supplied, and the retained
fragment, the listener must still wait for more context) understood (that
ing a subject to be necessitated yet to be determined) be (infinitive verb
sitation) to (with retained "have" forms idiom of necessitation, pretend-

Briefings

28
"Autofac"

Dan Dinello

Set in a fire-scorched landscape of metallic ash and H-Bomb craters populated by mutated rats, Philip K. Dick's visionary 1955 short story "AutoFac" centers on human survivors of a nuclear war who battle wartime automatic factories that won't stop producing now that the war's over.

The computerized factories—supplemented by robotic trucks, surveillance cameras, and mobile humanoid robots—over-consume scarce raw materials needed for reconstruction and over-produce useless consumer goods for a population that is now mostly dead. Numerous attempts to assert control of the system have proven futile and pessimism reigns among the humans: "We're licked, like always," says one of the survivors. "We humans lose every time."

Designed, programmed and controlled by "The Institute of Applied Cybernetics," the self-perpetuating factory network now undermines human autonomy and ultimately threatens the planet's survival. A vision of technological tyranny and ecological disaster, "AutoFac" criticizes the implications of mindless, cybernetic industrial production and its attendant social philosophy.

The forerunner of artificial intelligence and robotics, cybernetics formed in the crucible of World War II. Along with the race against German scientists to build an atomic bomb and the need to break the secret Nazi cipher machine codes, the urgency to improve Britain's air defense was a major force behind the development of high-speed calculating machines, eventually leading to the supercomputer and cybernetics.

Incorporating radar and high-speed calculation that analyzed feedback data from the German bombers, mathematician Norbert Wiener developed a self-regulating, predictive missile guidance system that adjusted the weapon's gun-sight to the speed, height and direction of the Nazi planes and thereby blasted them out of the sky. Based on his insights into machine learning via environmental feedback, Wiener invented *cybernetics*: the science of communication and control of people and machines.

Feedback, for Wiener, was an essential characteristic of life: all living things function and learn by practicing some form of feedback reaction in adapting to their environment; therefore, all forms of life could be understood mechanically, as a response to external information or communication. In *The Human Use of Human Beings* a popularized version of his classic 1948 work *Cybernetics*, Wiener wrote, "Communication and control belong to the essence of man's inner life, even as they belong to his life in society."

Shifting from bombsight design to social engineering, Wiener believed the nervous system and the operations of complex electronic computers are fundamentally alike in that they are devices whose behavior is based on the processing of information. In the cybernetic view, humans learned and behaved like machines; they could—for society's and their own good—be controlled like machines. By manipulating and regulating information input; by *programming,* Wiener expected to govern and perfect the behavioral output of both machines and people. In fact, the word "cybernetics" is derived from the Greek word *kubernetes,* meaning "steersman" or "governor."

Cybernetics heralded the promise of a techno-utopian world that would result from a second industrial revolution when the "computing machine" became the "center of the automatic factory"—a vision of programmed automation fulfilling people's needs while science-based social controls engineered happy, good citizens. Pursuing this vision, behavioral psychologist B.F. Skinner, in his 1948 book *Walden Two*, proudly depicted a cybernetic "utopia" that resulted from modifying behavior through controlled positive and negative reinforcement (feedback). Far from popularizing the idea, he inadvertently demonstrated cybernetics' totalitarian implications.

"AutoFac" counters the cyber-utopian vision with a dystopian prophecy of automatic factories that become evil in their inflexible self-sufficiency, autonomous expansion, and pervasive control. "Why can't we take over the machines?" screams a frustrated human, condemned to redundancy and humiliation. "My God, we're not children! We can run our own lives." Dick questions the legitimacy of a cybernetic philosophy that views humans mechanically, as passively dependent consumer-automatons incorporated into a technological apparatus devised to furnish physical needs, but indifferent to spiritual ones.

The automatic factories cannot creatively alter their own programming in response to the changing needs of the humans they were built to serve; rather, they scrupulously, logically, and literally persist in fulfilling their now-destructive production objectives. Forcing people to relinquish their freedom "for their own good," these immutable robots illustrate the insoluble problem of designing a technology that accounts for the vast range of human variables and the impossibility of determining what is right or good for humanity in all circumstances. Ridiculing claims of cybernetic perfection, Dick envisions the dire political implications of a technological system so determined in its programmed agenda that an initially positive benefit turns into a human-threatening, techno-tyranny.

This ever-expanding cybernetic system also reflects the dehumanizing logic of late capitalism whose profitability depends upon the reckless overproduction of useless commodities, marketed to a public viewed as gullible and gluttonous. Dick implicitly criticizes an economic system based on the automatic expansion of production to continuously increase corporate profits, rather than a system designed to improve human utility, happiness and freedom.

"Autofac" also demonstrates that this unfettered epidemic of overproduction will ultimately prove fatal: the environmental destruction that results from this self-perpetuating cycle of production and waste threatens to devour the planet. The helpless humans of "AutoFac" realize that "the damn network expands and consumes more of our natural resources," that the system itself "gets top priority" while "mere people come second," and that eventually no resources will remain unless the humans control factory output. Attempts to contact someone who might change the network's programming, however, end in frustrated failure. The factory's representatives are themselves programmed machines, reflecting today's robotic bureaucrats and computerized phone systems that shield corporate owners from public scrutiny and accountability.

After further efforts to directly shut down the factories, the humans confront the machines with logically impossible information meant to confuse and freeze them; but this has the unforeseen result of setting off internecine warfare. When the shipments of goods finally stop, it appears that the factories have destroyed each other. Yet when humans investigate one such damaged facility, they discover that on a deeper underground level the factory functions in a new way, manufacturing something mysterious. The inspection team finds the exit valve of a conveyer tube. Every few moments, a pellet bursts from the valve and shoots up into the sky. Upon examination, the horrified humans realize that the pellet is a tiny metallic element consisting of "Microscopic machinery, smaller than ants, smaller than pins, working energetically, purposefully—constructing something that looks like a tiny rectangle of steel."

In a prescient conception of self-replicating nanotechnology, the automatic factory—exhibiting a living entity's survival instinct—spews out metallic seeds that germinate into miniature replicas of the demolished factory that spurt out more seeds all over the earth and maybe throughout the universe. As one despairing character says: "The cyberneticists have it rigged . . . they've got us completely hamstrung. We're completely helpless." "AutoFac" dramatizes Philip Dick's pessimistic vision of a technocratic ideology that values the system's smooth, self-regulating operation as an end in itself: serving its own needs, expanding its control, replicating exponentially like a contagious disease, devouring the planet and even the universe—all to the detriment and possible extinction of humanity.[1]

---

[1] Thanks to Maureen Musker for feedback on an earlier version of this chapter.

29
"King of the Elves"

MICHELLE D. GALLAGHER

"King of the Elves" is a rare excursion into the realm of fantasy for Philip K. Dick. Nonetheless, Dickian themes abound, including a questioning of reality. Typically, in a Dick story where reality is questioned, we find central characters rejecting their reality as they gradually come to realize that what they thought was reality was really a fabrication (as in *Ubik* or *A Maze of Death*). But in "King of the Elves," the main character grows to accept increasingly strange goings-on as just another part of his world.

One rainy evening, Shadrach Jones, a small town gas station owner, receives a visit from a group of tiny strangers who call themselves Elves. Jones is initially skeptical, telling his visitors "whatever you are, you shouldn't be out on a night like this." He is somewhat embarrassed when he finds himself even momentarily entertaining the idea that Elves could exist. Jones's skeptical stance softens when the King of the Elves dies in his bedroom, but not before naming his successor—Shadrach Jones himself.

The idea of being King of the Elves appeals to Shadrach and he brags to his best friend, Phineas Judd, of his newfound fortune. When a war council is called on Phineas's property to deal with the Troll problem, Shadrach has some renewed concerns. "Were there really Trolls up there, rising up bold and confident in the darkness of the night, afraid of nothing, afraid of no one? And this business of being Elf King . . ."

So, before going to the war council in the backyard, he stops off at his friend's house. Phineas advises Shadrach to go home and get some sleep, but his pleas fall on deaf ears. In the dim lighting, it becomes clear to Shadrach that his friend is in fact a Troll and he kills him, setting off a battle between the Trolls and the Elves which culminates in an Elven victory. Worse yet, Phineas turns out to have been the King of the Trolls, adding even more to Jones's glory. There is a fleeting moment wherein Shadrach looks down at Phineas's body and sees not the Troll King, but his friend. The moment soon passes, however, and Shadrach fully accepts his new role as King of the Elves.

Since the story is told from Shadrach's point of view, we can't tell whether he is hallucinating or whether he really has encountered Elves and become their King and savior. We, like Shadrach, are left to guess what was going on, to figure out for ourselves what's real and what's a fiction of Shadrach's imagination. So, "King of the Elves" can be read either as a story about the ascent of a gas station owner to the Elven throne, or as a story about a man losing touch with reality and murdering his old friend. Either way, however, the story has something to say about what we mean when we say this or that is real. The story poses a challenge for certain ways of understanding empiricist takes on reality.

Bishop George Berkeley, an early modern empiricist, took a pretty practical line on what we mean when we call something real. In his *Treatise Concerning the Principles of Human Knowledge*, Berkeley says that we call something "real" if our expectations are met regarding how that thing will behave. For example, if I leave my wallet on the living room table, when I return to that room, that's where the wallet will be. If I put bread in the toaster, in a few minutes I should have some toast.

Berkeley thought that we don't call something "real" if it is subject to the whim of our imagination. If I imagine some goldfish floating in the air, I don't think they are really there. On the other hand, I can't make Mount Shasta any taller by imagining it to be taller, and that speaks in favor of its reality. Now, Berkeley doesn't mean that new things can never happen. Of course they can. But when a new thing happens, it won't be bread failing to turn to toast in a working toaster. It will be a new thing—a new invention, a new movie, a new dance—with new attributes and results, but not a new way for things to work, like constantly oscillating bread-toast, pain located outside of someone's body, or spiders that do not terrify and disgust me. New things that I accept as "real" will be things I haven't experienced before that nonetheless fit in with my past experiences.

This sort of picture would make some sense of how we figure out when we're dreaming and why we say that the dream world isn't real. In your dream, eventually something stands out as not fitting your expectations or shows itself to be subject to the whim of your imagination. For example, you may dream of your living room, but all of the furniture has been rearranged. The dream itself may be entirely consistent, your furniture could have been arranged like that, but it's not consistent with expectations regarding how furniture behaves. Alas, furniture doesn't rearrange itself.

In a dream, you may think of the White House and suddenly be transported to the Oval Office. You know you're not there because you'd have to take a car, and would likely have remembered to put on some pants. Berkeley's picture might also help us make some sense of why children have a hard time distinguishing between fantasy and reality. Children haven't built up the expectations yet which would enable them to do so.

If Philip K Dick's "King of the Elves" works as a story, however, Berkeley's picture as I've described it above must be wrong. Here we have Shadrach Jones, who keeps seeing unusual things and having unusual experiences, things not in keeping with his expectations, things that don't fit in with the rest of the world. Why then does Shadrach think the Elves and Trolls are real?

Shadrach's changes of heart regarding the reality of the Elves and the Trolls come in response to his wants, desires, and fears. One of the first things we learn about Shadrach is that he thinks there is nothing to attract people to his hometown. He finds it drab, unexciting. He laments his lack of customers, the empty register. Until the Elves make him their King, he's skeptical that they are really Elves. But the prospect of being King is very appealing. A life as King is a much grander life than he had been living thus far. War isn't very appealing and his doubts re-emerge. Being needed, however, having a life that makes a difference, that *is* appealing and so he marches off to war. No one would want their friend to die, and for a moment Phineas's death takes Shadrach back in to the world of the gas station. Nonetheless, life as King of the Elves is ultimately more appealing than life as a gas station owner in a rundown town. That's why Shadrach makes the choice he does at the end of the story.

Very importantly, Shadrach Jones never says to himself anything like "Elves and Trolls—that makes so much sense of everything!" In saying that Elves are real, Shadrach can't be saying that the reality of Elves fits with his past experiences and meets his expectations. Elves are precisely the thing you wouldn't expect, and neither does Shadrach. Instead, his reality attributions are, at least in part, based on what he wishes were true.

At the end of the day, then, I don't think it matters whether "King of the Elves" is about an Elven King or a mad gas station attendant. Whether it is unlikely truth or delusional falsehood, Shadrach decided, in the face of self-doubt and against all odds and evidence, that he really is the King of the Elves, because he wanted to. While that doesn't tell me what reality is, it's quite understandable. Who wouldn't want to be King of the Elves?

30
"The Golden Man"

JEREMY PIERCE

Imagine being able to predict the future to anticipate any eventuality. No one could surprise you. You could prevent any attempt to harm you, knowing the consequences of any possible action. In several Philip K. Dick stories, people or machines are described as predicting the future.

In "The Golden Man," it's a mutated human being named Cris Johnson, living in a post-nuclear United States where many people have mutations that usually just leave them labeled as freaks. "Paycheck" has a machine doing the same thing, and "The Minority Report" has precogs. All are described as predicting the future, but in all three cases "the future" predicted can be prevented if the person seeing that future does something that changes the outcome.

A more precise way of describing these predictions is that they allow the viewer to see what *would* have happened had the *prediction* not occurred. Once the prediction occurs, the viewer can do something to lead to a different outcome. In "The Minority Report," Precrime prevents the predicted killings. In "Paycheck," Jennings anticipates how he'll respond once his memories are erased and gives himself clues to stop the machine's original predictions from happening. In "The Golden Man," Cris Johnson can pursue the consequences of any course of action he might take, allowing him to opt for the path that he most prefers.

Cris has a covering of fine, golden hair. Most mutants in this post-nuclear world are seen as freaks, referred to as "deeves" (short for deviants). Most mutations are harmful or unattractive. Cris is beautiful and has an advanced ability that allows him to evade the DCA (a government agency hunting down and "euthing" those with mutations). He seems superhuman, not a mere freak. Several characters describe him as godlike, the next step in human evolution.

But then they discover that he's also less than human. According to George Baines, "It doesn't think at all. Virtually no frontal lobe. It's not a human being—it doesn't use symbols. It's nothing but an animal." Ed Wisdom responds, "An animal with a highly-developed faculty. Not a superior man. Not a man at all." He chooses options, suggesting a human-like agency, but that choice is instinctual, like an animal, lacking reflective thought about its choices, with no consideration of moral reasoning. He acts on reflex informed by an amazing ability to predict his actions' consequences.

Cris impregnates a character in the story and escapes to impregnate more. We're left wondering how many offspring he'll be able to create and how quickly his genes will be passed on to create more animal-like humans—who will, it seems, eventually replace humanity because of their greater fitness, despite their devolved level of inner life.

How should we think of this Golden Man? Some actually-occurring conditions have similar features. Autism, for example, often involves heightened and diminished cognitive abilities, sometimes severely diminished. Dick's novel *Martian Time-Slip* treats autism-schizophrenia[1] as distortions in time-perception. A psychiatrist in the story proposes that Manfred Steiner, an autistic child, perceives the passage of time at a different rate.

By the end of the novel Manfred turns out to have access to the future and the past in a way that we normally don't. But even in actuality, it's pretty clear that autism can lead to greater abilities in certain domains and cognitive difficulties with other skills. So the general features of Cris Johnson's case

---

[1] Dick seems to treat schizophrenia as the adult version of autism and autism as the childhood manifestation of schizophrenia, while sometimes calling an autistic child's traits schizophrenic and a schizophrenic adult's traits autistic. Autism and schizophrenia have now been shown to be distinct conditions with unique sets of symptoms, though they have related genetic causes. In the early 1960s, when *Martian Time-Slip* was published, the connection between the two was exaggerated.

are not purely fictional, even if the particular ways those features appear in Cris are pure science fiction. So we might then ask if the similarities are close enough to have ethical significance. Should our attitude toward autistic people be anything like our attitude toward Cris Johnson?

Aristotle (384–322 B.C.E.) considered it natural, healthy, and appropriate to have certain abilities as humans. Certain abnormalities are contrary to natural human development. There's something unfortunate and deficient about growing only one arm to full length or having only one working eye. For Aristotle, there are purposes in nature that are part of what it is to be human. It's in our best interests to develop within certain parameters, and things normally do develop within those parameters. Anything below that zone of normal, healthy development is therefore a deficiency. Anything above it would be superhuman.

Lucretius (99–55 B.C.E.) disagreed. He didn't think it made sense to speak of having a purpose unless a conscious being designs it or puts it to a purpose. He didn't believe in a divine creator, so he concluded that any element of human makeup is neither natural nor unnatural in itself. There are no purposes in nature apart from the purposes we put ourselves to. Some people have two arms. Some have only one. There's nothing bad about that except that there are some things someone with two arms can do that someone with one arm can't do.

If Lucretius is right, then it's impossible to speak of deficiencies or superhuman capabilities unless you just mean that someone's level of ability is atypical. The autism community has largely adopted this view in contrasting people on the autistic spectrum with "typical" kids. There's strong resistance to speaking of dysfunction, malformation, abnormality, or deficiency, because such notions presume a negative attitude toward someone. Aristotle, however, conceives of normal development as typical development that suits what's objectively good for a human being, and it follows that conditions like autism involve aspects that are sub-normal or deficient and some that are super-normal.

If Lucretius is right, we shouldn't think of autism as unfortunate except that some people can't do certain things others can do (and can do other things most people can't). But if Aristotle is right, it makes perfect sense to classify autism as a disorder involving cognitive delays and deficiencies, even if it also involves traits that he would see as atypical in the opposite direction. It's important to accept people with disabilities for who they are, but that's compatible with identifying unfortunate disorders as deficiencies falling short of normal and healthy development.

Baines and others in "The Golden Man" initially approach the question from the other end. Cris's heightened ability creates optimal reproductive conditions. A species of beings like Cris would overwhelm and replace humanity. We wouldn't stand a chance. But when they discover the deficiency, their attitude changes from fear to horror. Humans will be replaced by creatures with almost no higher-level cognitive functioning except reflex-based evaluations of possible outcomes. Mere animals will eliminate humanity by impregnating human women and spreading their mutation to the next generation. It's hard to explain the horror without the idea that this new species isn't just *different*. Something is *missing* that's natural and healthy for human offspring to have, and something is *present* that's in one sense better, but in another sense no longer human.

31
"Piper in the Woods"

DAVID SVOLBA

The "essential ingredient" of the science-fiction story, according to Philip K. Dick's preface to *Paycheck and Other Classic Stories*, is a "distinct new idea." So what is the distinct new idea behind "Piper in the Woods," a science-fiction story Dick published in 1953?

This question is not easily answered. Superficially, the story is about an asteroid garrison at which able young men are disburdening themselves of all occupational responsibilities on the grounds that they have become plants, and no longer care to do anything but sit in the sun. The story is also about the official reaction to this bizarre turn of events, and in particular the psychiatrist who is dispatched by the powers-that-be to diagnose and find a solution to the problem. And a problem it most definitely is, for when able young men decide they no longer care to play their role in maintaining the machine, the machine breaks down. As one harried official puts it, "This garrison is one vast machine. The men are parts, and each has his job. When one person steps away from his job, everything else begins to creak."

But of course the distinct new idea behind Dick's story is not the unusual lifestyle adopted by some of its characters. It's better to read Dick's story as communicating an idea about *why* people might be led to make such a peculiar lifestyle choice. Dick's plant-people have become aware of the fact that their entire lives have been devoted to meaningless endeavors, or that their lives have been driven by ambitions that they no longer identify with. They've done their part to maintain a particular kind of society, but cannot answer the question about why this society is worthy of being maintained. Indeed, 'ambition' itself is something these disaffected young men are keen to divest themselves of, which is why they come to prefer a vegetative form of life. Plants have no plans, and no goals; to flourish they need only the nutrients of sun and soil. For people who feel as if they have become mere cogs in a complex machine, a machine directed towards ends that are not their own, becoming a plant is a radical but understandable response.

Of course there's rarely just *one* idea in Dick's fiction, and "Piper" is no exception. In addition to describing the possible implications of alienated labor, Dick's story is also about the potential despotism of our rational natures. As the world becomes increasingly pervaded by technology, we become "tools of our tools," as Henry David Thoreau put it in *Walden*—and so we become increasingly out of touch with the non-rational part of our natures; that part of us that wants nothing more than to sit in the sun and feel a cooling breeze on our flesh. In the techno-industrial world, there's little time for such indulgences. On those rare occasions *Homo technologicus* ventures into nature at all, it's usually in order to rejuvenate himself so that he may be more fit for *work* upon his return.

Dick worried about this arc of human development, an arc on which human beings move away from the earth and their bodily natures towards, at the limits, a world in which the earth and human beings have been replaced by androids inhabiting an alien planet. For this reason one cannot help but sense, when reading "Piper," Dick's tacit approval of those who buck this trend and choose instead to do, well, nothing, except sit on flat rocks by running streams and bask in the sun, dozing with their mouths open and their eyes closed. And as Dick surely knew, it is difficult for his readers, so firmly *rooted* in their non-natural worlds, not to feel a tinge of envy for these drop-outs, who seem so perfectly and simply *happy*.

Interpreted this way, at the heart of "Piper" is an idea not unlike the one Timothy Leary would notoriously spread a decade or so after the publication of Dick's story: "Turn on, tune in, and drop out." I suspect Leary would have approved of Dick's plant-people. Rather than faithfully fulfilling the duties of whatever station had been allotted to them, and so doing their share to keep the machine humming, these are people who abandon the drab and deadening form of life in which they find themselves in favor of a radically different form of life in which higher consciousness is the reward for a lower status. It's notable, if not surprising, that Leary and his followers were subject to the same criticism as Dick's defectors. In both cases the Establishment couldn't help but see them in one way and one way only: as *lazy*—and hence, in a world that needs *workers* and *consumers* above all else, *dangerous*.

So "Piper," like so much of Dick's work, is social criticism in the form of science fiction. And Dick was a trenchant social critic, one whose concerns about the pitfalls facing "modern man" seem even more valid now than during his own lifetime.

But if spending one's life as a cog in a machine, no matter how vital or valued a cog one may be, is something less than a good human life, one might sensibly worry whether becoming a plant-person is in the end any more desirable. The worry is this: although the lives the defectors led may not have been *good* human lives, the vegetative lives they opt for instead look like something *less* than human lives, good or bad. Having jettisoned all ambitions, goals, and desires for either self- or world-improvement, the defectors seemed to have stripped themselves of precisely those characteristics which seem to distinguish them from non-human life forms.

Returning to the Timothy Leary comparison, we might ask: is there any reason to regard the reaction of the young men on Asteroid Y-3 as less regrettable than the reaction of those young people who, disenchanted with the modern world and the expectations it places on them, turn to drugs as a means of escape? Is there a relevant difference between these two reactions, or is Dick's story—perhaps we've finally hit upon the distinct new idea—actually a parable of that preferred form of escapism so prevalent and problematic in our own society?

This question suggests an even deeper critique of this society in which the "men are parts," and "each has his job"—namely, that not only is it a dehumanizing form of life, but it's a dehumanizing form of life which seems strangely difficult to resist, since those who oppose it are drawn too easily into forms of "resistance" which amount to little more than different, self-imposed forms of dehumanization.

32
"The Exit Door Leads In"

ERIC BECK

Philip K. Dick's "The Exit Door Leads In" reads like one of
Plato's dialogues, with just enough dramatic action so that it
can properly be called a story. But it's not just the form that
refers to the ancient Greeks: the main character in the story
studies pre-Socratic cosmogony, and one of his friends opines
that the Delphic maxim, Know Thyself, "sums up half of Greek
philosophy."

As minimal as it might be, Dick's addition of dramatic form
is a difference that does make a difference. He doesn't simply
repeat the Socratic dialogue. He twists and tweaks both its
form and its content, complicating and modernizing it. In the
process, he revises Plato's views on what it means to Know
Oneself.

Plato himself never seemed that enamored with the Delphic
oracle. In *Charmides*, when one of the participants appeals to
its authority, Plato's Socrates claims that he himself lacks
healthy self-knowledge, and then redirects the conversation to
more favored ground. In *Gorgias*, Socrates confirms that the
oracle does sum up only half of Greek philosophy:

SOCRATES: I mean that each one himself rules himself. Or is
there no need of this, that he rule himself?

CALLICLES: What do you mean, ruling over himself?

SOCRATES: Nothing complicated, but just what the many
mean: being moderate and in control of oneself, ruling
the passions and desires that are in oneself.

Knowing oneself is not enough; one must also have a *mastery* of oneself.

This isn't to say that Plato is completely preoccupied with the self. He's concerned with the knowledge of other things as well as of the self. As he says in *Charmides*, "Is not the discovery of things as they truly are a good common to all mankind?"

But still, the dialogue form Plato employs—men of great leisure idly sitting around discussing problems and forming syntheses—suggests that knowing thyself *is* the most important thing: Self-clarification is the goal of philosophy. Coming from full citizens who had servants aplenty and an economy based on slave labor, Plato's characters' explications on justice and happiness and mastery have an abstract, and ironic, ring to modern ears.

Dick, on the other hand, sets his dialogues in motion; his characters act out situations. His short works often have an almost laughably bare dramatic façade, with stories more likely to resolve conceptual confusions through action than through discussion, but even this little difference creates a different kind of self—one less concerned with self-knowledge and self-mastery than with discerning what outside forces expect and how to meet (or rebel against) those expectations. Instead of abstractly discussing problems, Dick's characters often *are* the problem.

This is certainly the case for the main character in "The Exit Door Leads In." The thoroughly average and nearly anonymous salesman Bob Bibleman is accepted into a prestigious university because he (like Oedipus before the Sphinx) correctly answers a riddle posed by a computerized waiter at a fast-food restaurant. Attendance at the university is mandatory: The alternative is prison. Once at the school, Bibleman and his fellow students are informed that disseminating classified information is punishable under the law, then told not to worry because they won't have access to classified information. A school administrator offers as an example an efficient engine, the schematics for which have been expunged from the school's database.

In the course of Bibleman's studies, his computer-terminal study partner inadvertently spits out the plans for the engine. Bibleman has a dilemma: should he reveal the plans in the interest of benefiting society, or should he notify the university that he has accidently received a copy of them? For Bibleman, it's not a moral or ethical conflict. He bases his decision not on a universal principle of right but on what he thinks the authorities want him to do.

Before he has time to decide, university security intervenes, forcing him to hand over the schematics. When the administration asks him what he had planned to do with them, he says he would have handed them over anyway. To his surprise, his answer causes the university to expel him. He was being tested, they say, and he failed to do what would benefit all of humanity. But for the reader, as for Bibleman, it's just as easy to imagine that he would have been imprisoned, or worse, for publicizing the plans and betraying the institution and the law.

The double bind Dick dramatizes here is the contingent, situational nature of what we call self-knowledge. The truth of the self, for Dick, is not just *in here*—but, with apologies to Fox Mulder, it's not just *out there* either. It's between there and here, open to negotiation, change, and interpretation. It's more like a process of calculation than a voyage of discovery.

So while Plato's mastering oneself is an act of self-knowledge and self-regulation, Dick's self is both generic and empty, awaiting the direction of the exterior state and the subject's decision. The 'knowing' Dick has in mind is not getting in tune with one's essence. Instead, it's a decision made in the light (or shadow) of what we can discern of the state's expectations.

In Dick's philosophy, the lesson of mastery has to be taught and enforced. That's the point of Bibleman's attending the prestigious university: to learn conditions for membership in society, to learn when obedience means resistance. His education is successful, in the end: When he returns to the restaurant after he's kicked out of school, he initially decides not to pay for his food. When the computer gently reminds him of his obligation, he hands over the money. He has learned which situations accommodate rebellion and which do not.

At least for now. Despite his obvious pessimism, Dick never completely closes off the possibility that in the future Bob Bibleman will decide to ignore the state's expectations. At some point, he may have to be re-educated.

33
"The Gun"

BENJAMIN STEVENS

"The Gun" imagines an encounter between human explorers of space and a machine intelligence in the form of the gun of the title, a mindlessly planet-defending weapon. The central idea of the gun defending a now-dead community—an image of violence only seemingly in the service of human society—lets Dick raise questions about the relationship between technologies of various kinds and human thought and action.

By depicting a mindlessly or thoughtlessly active machine intelligence, the story raises the question of whether human agency or humanity itself is becoming a 'machine' of sorts as society, culture, and individual choice are subjected to increasingly pervasive mechanizations. How are our capacities to think and to act affected by our relationships to technologies, especially one like the automated gun, one that is both inhuman and, in its total violence, dehumanizing?

Considered as a document of its time, during the first technological flush of the Cold War, "The Gun" asks how our relationship to technology is inflected in particular by what has been called the 'military-industrial complex'. First referred to as such by American President Dwight D. Eisenhower in his Farewell Address to the Nation, 17th January 1961, and anticipated by thinkers including C. Wright Mills, *The Power Elite* (1956) and F.A. Hayek, *The Road to Serfdom* (1944), the military-industrial complex and—according to Dick— its chilling consequences for individual thought and action are clearly in mind in the story. A crucial example is this paragraph:

> They must have been used to the sight, guns, weapons, uniforms. Probably they accepted it as a natural thing, part of their lives, like eating and sleeping. An institution, like the church and the state. Men trained to fight, to lead armies, a regular profession. Honored, respected.

The paragraph depicts a character's thought-process as he tries to understand the military-technological situation of this world as it seems to be so different from his own. At another point, a character describes their ship being shot down by the unmanned gun as a "paradox"—the term suggests that, as Dick sees it, the characteristically human response to such mechanization is precisely alienation, the feeling that the world has somehow gotten away from us.

That feeling of alienation runs especially deep, and Dick's criticism hits especially close to home, when the 'world' in question is of our own design: the world of technology. Already at this very early point in his career, then, Dick's speculative imagination focuses on artificial objects as a way to symbolize—and so to think critically about—our own objectification by technologies: our status not so much, any more, as human beings or even, as Aristotle defines us, political beings but as 'products' of societies and cultures whose processes are increasingly mechanized.

As Theodor Adorno and Max Horkheimer pointed out, by the mid-twentieth century at the latest this mechanization includes culture, such that we now have, and are parts of, a "culture industry." Not just in the sense that cultural objects (blockbuster films based on science-fiction stories, for example) are produced industrially and packaged as if for unthinking consumption. But also in the sense that we, too, are 'produced' industrially: we are prepared by blockbuster films—not to mention breakfast cereals and deodorant ads—to become better consumers, so that we can play our little role in keeping the machines churning out cheap bits of plastic . . . and turning us into the carbon-based equivalent.

As Dick sees it, then, when we look at an artificial object or technological product, it looks back, and that uncannily mirrored gaze makes clear that we human beings, we seemingly natural beings, have come to share in the object's artificiality: we, too, have been made artificial, unnaturally and ironically turned into a technology by the very technology we first brought into being. With artificial objects serving in this way as unwelcome inversions—dopplegangers—for ourselves, Dick disorients our sense of 'human being' and of 'individual identity' to develop and encourage a trenchant criticism of the role of technology in society. He does not criticize our use of machines so much as, instead, our unwitting willingness to be *used by* them.

And 'willingness', or will, is precisely the issue: Dick makes us wonder whether our apparent capacity for individual thought and action, for acts of will, for free will, is indeed ours . . . or whether it has rather been objectified, technologized, made into a 'product' of a system that precedes our conscious thought and, so, may operate without our informed consent. Such a system may have its own purposes in 'mind' and not our best interests at heart. Like the mindless gun, have we been made in the service of a system whose purpose is not derailed if we are given artificial memories and allowed the illusions of intelligence and will?

As Dick's range and skills as a writer developed, and as he began to work in longer forms than the short story, he was able to develop these and similar ideas deeply and very vividly elsewhere. "We Can Remember It for You Wholesale," *Do Androids Dream of Electric Sheep?*, *The Man in the High Castle*, and *Ubik*, among others, all richly fictionalize these ideas. These and other, later works develop further Dick's interest in artifacts as paradoxically disindividualizing or even dehumanizing mementoes or reminders: really, as false 'reminders', given their capacity to cause the seemingly real 'recall' of events that are fictional or otherwise counterfactual.

This particular interest brings Dick's thinking into productive dialogue with that of many other philosophers. For example Walter Benjamin, who feared that new technologies of 'mechanical reproduction', including photography, would result in destruction of historical meaning—what he called "aura"—as culture turns from valuing objects to consuming their mere images. Or Hannah Arendt, who wondered, in *The Human Condition*, whether the launch of Sputnik, as well as the bombings of Hiroshima and Nagasaki, signal a renewed and inadvisable desire to escape our 'earthliness'—"the very quintessence of the human condition"—by technological means. Or Martin Heidegger, who explored 'technology' as more than physical objects and devices, but also including social structures and controls as well as other necessary mediations of, and constraints on, human behavior.

In this connection, finally, Dick may be brought into dialogue with Plato as well. Both asked how one would live the best life, and both asserted that the unexamined life is not worth living. As "The Gun" shows, Dick, already in 1952, had formed the outline of one of the most distinctive parts of his answer: the best life cannot be in a culture beset—as he clearly saw it—by mindless and undesirable mechanizations and militarizations of humanity. In Dick's hands science fiction becomes a fast-moving vehicle for a kind of philosophical thought-experiment, imagining a world that could come to pass . . . so as to ask whether in fact, in all the ways that would matter, it already has.

The Master's Own Voice

34
Beyond Lies the Wub

Philip K. Dick

They had almost finished with the loading. Outside stood the Optus, his arms folded, his face sunk in gloom. Captain Franco walked leisurely down the gangplank, grinning.

"What's the matter?" he said. "You're getting paid for all this."

The Optus said nothing. He turned away, collecting his robes. The Captain put his boot on the hem of the robe.

"Just a minute. Don't go off. I'm not finished."

"Oh?" The Optus turned with dignity. "I am going back to the village." He looked toward the animals and birds being driven up the gangplank into the spaceship. "I must organize new hunts."

Franco lit a cigarette. "Why not? You people can go out into the veldt and track it all down again. But when we run out halfway between Mars and Earth—"

The Optus went off, wordless. Franco joined the first mate at the bottom of the gangplank.

"How's it coming?" he said. He looked at his watch. "We got a good bargain here."

The mate glanced at him sourly. "How do you explain that?"

"What's the matter with you? We need it more than they do."

"I'll see you later, Captain." The mate threaded his way up the plank, between the long-legged Martian go-birds, into the ship. Franco watched him disappear. He was just starting up after him, up the plank toward the port, when he saw *it*.

"My God!" He stood staring, his hands on his hips. Peterson was walking along the path, his face red, leading *it* by a string.

"I'm sorry, Captain," he said, tugging at the string. Franco walked toward him.

"What is it?"

The wub stood sagging, its great body settling slowly. It was sitting down, its eyes half shut. A few flies buzzed about its flank, and it switched its tail.

It sat. There was silence.

"It's a wub," Peterson said. "I got it from a native for fifty cents. He said it was a very unusual animal. Very respected."

"This?" Franco poked the great sloping side of the wub. "It's a pig! A huge dirty pig!"

"Yes sir, it's a pig. The natives call it a wub."

"A huge pig. It must weigh four hundred pounds." Franco grabbed a tuft of the rough hair. The wub gasped. Its eyes opened, small and moist. Then its great mouth twitched.

A tear rolled down the wub's cheek and splashed on the floor.

"Maybe it's good to eat," Peterson said nervously.

"We'll soon find out," Franco said.

The wub survived the take-off, sound asleep in the hold of the ship. When they were out in space and everything was running smoothly, Captain Franco bade his men fetch the wub upstairs so that he might perceive what manner of beast it was.

The wub grunted and wheezed, squeezing up the passageway.

"Come on," Jones grated, pulling at the rope. The wub twisted, rubbing its skin off on the smooth chrome walls. It burst into the ante-room, tumbling down in a heap. The men leaped up.

"Good Lord," French said. "What is it?"

"Peterson says it's a wub," Jones said. "It belongs to him." He kicked at the wub. The wub stood up unsteadily, panting.

"What's the matter with it?" French came over. "Is it going to be sick?"

They watched. The wub rolled its eyes mournfully. It gazed around at the men.

"I think it's thirsty," Peterson said. He went to get some water. French shook his head.

"No wonder we had so much trouble taking off. I had to reset all my ballast calculations."

Peterson came back with the water. The wub began to lap gratefully, splashing the men.

Captain Franco appeared at the door.

"Let's have a look at it." He advanced, squinting critically. "You got this for fifty cents?"

"Yes, sir," Peterson said. "It eats almost anything. I fed it on grain and it liked that. And then potatoes, and mash, and scraps from the table, and milk. It seems to enjoy eating. After it eats it lies down and goes to sleep."

"I see," Captain Franco said. "Now, as to its taste. That's the real question. I doubt if there's much point in fattening it up any more. It seems fat enough to me already. Where's the cook? I want him here. I want to find out—"

The wub stopped lapping and looked up at the Captain.

"Really, Captain," the wub said. "I suggest we talk of other matters."

The room was silent.

"What was that?" Franco said. "Just now."

"The wub, sir," Peterson said. "It spoke."

They all looked at the wub.

"What did it say? What did it say?"

"It suggested we talk about other things."

Franco walked toward the wub. He went all around it, examining it from every side. Then he came back over and stood with the men.

"I wonder if there's a native inside it," he said thoughtfully. "Maybe we should open it up and have a look."

"Oh, goodness!" the wub cried. "Is that all you people can think of, killing and cutting?"

Franco clenched his fists. "Come out of there! Whoever you are, come out!"

Nothing stirred. The men stood together, their faces blank, staring at the wub. The wub swished its tail. It belched suddenly.

"I beg your pardon," the wub said.

"I don't think there's anyone in there," Jones said in a low voice. They all looked at each other.

The cook came in.

"You wanted me, Captain?" he said. "What's this thing?"

"This is a wub," Franco said. "It's to be eaten. Will you measure it and figure out—"

"I think we should have a talk," the wub said. "I'd like to discuss this with you, Captain, if I might. I can see that you and I do not agree on some basic issues."

The Captain took a long time to answer. The wub waited good-naturedly, licking the water from its jowls.

"Come into my office," the Captain said at last. He turned and walked out of the room. The wub rose and padded after him. The men watched it go out. They heard it climbing the stairs.

"I wonder what the outcome will be," the cook said. "Well, I'll be in the kitchen. Let me know as soon as you hear."

"Sure," Jones said. "Sure."

The wub eased itself down in the corner with a sigh. "You must forgive me," it said. "I'm afraid I'm addicted to various forms of relaxation. When one is as large as I—"

The Captain nodded impatiently. He sat down at his desk and folded his hands.

"All right," he said. "Let's get started. You're a wub? Is that correct?"

The wub shrugged. "I suppose so. That's what they call us, the natives, I mean. We have our own term."

"And you speak English? You've been in contact with Earthmen before?"

"No."

"Then how do you do it?"

"Speak English? Am I speaking English? I'm not conscious of speaking anything in particular. I examined your mind—"

"My mind?"

"I studied the contents, especially the semantic warehouse, as I refer to it—"

"I see," the Captain said. "Telepathy. Of course."

"We are a very old race," the wub said. "Very old and very ponderous. It is difficult for us to move around. You can appreciate that anything so slow and heavy would be at the mercy of more agile forms of life. There was no use in our relying on physical defenses. How could we win? Too heavy to run, too soft to fight, too good-natured to hunt for game—"

"How do you live?"

"Plants. Vegetables. We can eat almost anything. We're very catholic. Tolerant, eclectic, catholic. We live and let live. That's how we've gotten along."

The wub eyed the Captain.

"And that's why I so violently objected to this business about having me boiled. I could see the image in your mind—most of me in the frozen food locker, some of me in the kettle, a bit for your pet cat—"

"So you read minds?" the Captain said. "How interesting. Anything else? I mean, what else can you do along those lines?"

"A few odds and ends," the wub said absently, staring around the room. "A nice apartment you have here, Captain. You keep it quite neat. I respect life-forms that are tidy. Some Martian birds are quite tidy. They throw things out of their nests and sweep them—"

"Indeed." The Captain nodded. "But to get back to the problem—"

"Quite so. You spoke of dining on me. The taste, I am told, is good. A little fatty, but tender. But how can any lasting contact be established between your people and mine if you resort to such barbaric attitudes? Eat me? Rather you should discuss questions with me, philosophy, the arts—"

The Captain stood up. "Philosophy. It might interest you to know that we will be hard put to find something to eat for the next month. An unfortunate spoilage—"

"I know." The wub nodded. "But wouldn't it be more in accord with your principles of democracy if we all drew straws, or something along that line? After all, democracy is to protect the minority from just such infringements. Now, if each of us casts one vote—"

The Captain walked to the door.

"Nuts to you," he said. He opened the door. He opened his mouth.

He stood frozen, his mouth wide, his eyes staring, his fingers still on the knob.

The wub watched him. Presently it padded out of the room, edging past the Captain. It went down the hall, deep in meditation.

The room was quiet.

"So you see," the wub said, "we have a common myth. Your mind contains many familiar myth symbols. Ishtar, Odysseus—"

Peterson sat silently, staring at the floor. He shifted in his chair.

"Go on," he said. "Please go on."

"I find in your Odysseus a figure common to the mythology of most self-conscious races. As I interpret it, Odysseus wanders as an individual, aware of himself as such. This is the idea of separation, of separation from family and country. The process of individuation."

"But Odysseus returns to his home." Peterson looked out the port window, at the stars, endless stars, burning intently in the empty universe. "Finally he goes home."

"As must all creatures. The moment of separation is a temporary period, a brief journey of the soul. It begins, it ends. The wanderer returns to land and race. . . ."

The door opened. The wub stopped, turning its great head.

Captain Franco came into the room, the men behind him. They hesitated at the door.

"Are you all right?" French said.

"Do you mean me?" Peterson said, surprised. "Why me?"

Franco lowered his gun. "Come over here," he said to Peterson. "Get up and come here."

There was silence.

"Go ahead," the wub said. "It doesn't matter."

Peterson stood up. "What for?"

"It's an order."

Peterson walked to the door. French caught his arm.

"What's going on?" Peterson wrenched loose. "What's the matter with you?"

Captain Franco moved toward the wub. The wub looked up from where it lay in the corner, pressed against the wall.

"It is interesting," the wub said, "that you are obsessed with the idea of eating me. I wonder why."

"Get up," Franco said.

"If you wish." The wub rose, grunting. "Be patient. It is difficult for me." It stood, gasping, its tongue lolling foolishly.

"Shoot it now," French said.

"For God's sake!" Peterson exclaimed. Jones turned to him quickly, his eyes gray with fear.

"You didn't see him—like a statue, standing there, his mouth open. If we hadn't come down, he'd still be there."

"Who? The Captain?" Peterson stared around. "But he's all right now."

They looked at the wub, standing in the middle of the room, its great chest rising and falling.

"Come on," Franco said. "Out of the way."

The men pulled aside toward the door.

"You are quite afraid, aren't you?" the wub said. "Have I done anything to you? I am against the idea of hurting. All I have done is try to protect myself. Can you expect me to rush eagerly to my death? I am a sensible being like yourselves. I was curious to see your ship, learn about you. I suggested to the native—"

The gun jerked.

"See," Franco said. "I thought so."

The wub settled down, panting. It put its paw out, pulling its tail around it.

"It is very warm," the wub said. "I understand that we are close to the jets. Atomic power. You have done many wonderful things with it—technically. Apparently, your scientific hierarchy is not equipped to solve moral, ethical—"

Franco turned to the men, crowding behind him, wide-eyed, silent.

"I'll do it. You can watch."

French nodded. "Try to hit the brain. It's no good for eating. Don't hit the chest. If the rib cage shatters, we'll have to pick bones out."

"Listen," Peterson said, licking his lips. "Has it done anything? What harm has it done? I'm asking you. And anyhow, it's still mine. You have no right to shoot it. It doesn't belong to you."

Franco raised his gun.

"I'm going out," Jones said, his face white and sick. "I don't want to see it."

"Me, too," French said. The men straggled out, murmuring. Peterson lingered at the door.

"It was talking to me about myths," he said. "It wouldn't hurt anyone."

He went outside.

Franco walked toward the wub. The wub looked up slowly. It swallowed.

"A very foolish thing," it said. "I am sorry that you want to do it. There was a parable that your Savior related—"

It stopped, staring at the gun.

"Can you look me in the eye and do it?" the wub said. "Can you do that?"

The Captain gazed down. "I can look you in the eye," he said. "Back on the farm we had hogs, dirty razor-back hogs. I can do it."

Staring down at the wub, into the gleaming, moist eyes, he pressed the trigger.

The taste was excellent.

They sat glumly around the table, some of them hardly eating at all. The only one who seemed to be enjoying himself was Captain Franco.

"More?" he said, looking around. "More? And some wine, perhaps."

"Not me," French said. "I think I'll go back to the chart room."

"Me, too." Jones stood up, pushing his chair back. "I'll see you later."

The Captain watched them go. Some of the others excused themselves.

"What do you suppose the matter is?" the Captain said. He turned to Peterson. Peterson sat staring down at his plate, at the potatoes, the green peas, and at the thick slab of tender, warm meat.

He opened his mouth. No sound came.

The Captain put his hand on Peterson's shoulder.

"It is only organic matter, now," he said. "The life essence is gone." He ate, spooning up the gravy with some bread. "I, myself, love to eat. It is one of the greatest things that a living creature can enjoy. Eating, resting, meditation, discussing things."

Peterson nodded. Two more men got up and went out. The Captain drank some water and sighed.

"Well," he said. "I must say that this was a very enjoyable meal. All the reports I had heard were quite true—the taste of wub. Very fine. But I was prevented from enjoying this pleasure in times past."

He dabbed at his lips with his napkin and leaned back in his chair. Peterson stared dejectedly at the table.

The Captain watched him intently. He leaned over.

"Come, come," he said. "Cheer up! Let's discuss things."

He smiled.

"As I was saying before I was interrupted, the role of Odysseus in the myths—"

Peterson jerked up, staring.

"To go on," the Captain said. "Odysseus, as I understand him—"

Planet Stories, July 1952. Dick recalled: "My first published story, in the most lurid of all pulp magazines at the time, *Planet Stories*. As I carried four copies into the record store where I worked, a customer gazed at me and them, with dismay, and said: 'Phil, you read that kind of stuff?' I had to admit I not only read it, I wrote it." On another occasion Dick commented: "The wub was my idea of a higher life form; it was then and it is now."

35
The Eyes Have It

PHILIP K. DICK

It was quite by accident I discovered this incredible invasion of Earth by life-forms from another planet. As yet, I haven't done anything about it; I can't think of anything to do. I wrote to the Government, and they sent back a pamphlet on the repair and maintenance of frame houses. Anyhow, the whole thing is known; I'm not the first to discover it. Maybe it's even under control.

I was sitting in my easy-chair, idly turning the pages of a paperbacked book someone had left on the bus, when I came across the reference that first put me on the trail. For a moment I didn't respond. It took some time for the full import to sink in. After I'd comprehended, it seemed odd I hadn't noticed it right away.

The reference was clearly to a nonhuman species of incredible properties, not indigenous to Earth. A species, I hasten to point out, customarily masquerading as ordinary human beings. Their disguise, however, became transparent in the face of the following observations by the author. It was at once obvious the author knew everything. Knew everything—and was taking it in his stride. The line (and I tremble remembering it even now) read:

... *his eyes slowly roved about the room.*

Vague chills assailed me. I tried to picture the eyes. Did they roll like dimes? The passage indicated not; they seemed to move through the air, not over the surface. Rather rapidly, apparently. No one in the story was surprised. That's what tipped me off. No sign of amazement at such an outrageous thing. Later the matter was amplified.

... *his eyes moved from person to person.*

There it was in a nutshell. The eyes had clearly come apart from the rest of him and were on their own. My heart pounded and my breath choked in my windpipe. I had stumbled on an accidental mention of a totally unfamiliar race. Obviously non-Terrestrial. Yet, to the characters in the book, it was perfectly natural—which suggested they belonged to the same species.

And the author? A slow suspicion burned in my mind. The author was taking it rather *too easily* in his stride. Evidently, he felt this was quite a usual thing. He made absolutely no attempt to conceal this knowledge. The story continued:

. . . presently his eyes fastened on Julia.

Julia, being a lady, had at least the breeding to feel indignant. She is described as blushing and knitting her brows angrily. At this, I sighed with relief. They weren't *all* non-Terrestrials. The narrative continues:

. . . slowly, calmly, his eyes examined every inch of her.

Great Scott! But here the girl turned and stomped off and the matter ended. I lay back in my chair gasping with horror. My wife and family regarded me in wonder.

"What's wrong, dear?" my wife asked.

I couldn't tell her. Knowledge like this was too much for the ordinary run-of-the-mill person. I had to keep it to myself. "Nothing," I gasped. I leaped up, snatched the book, and hurried out of the room.

In the garage, I continued reading. There was more. Trembling, I read the next revealing passage:

. . . he put his arm around Julia. Presently she asked him if he would remove his arm. He immediately did so, with a smile.

It's not said what was done with the arm after the fellow had removed it. Maybe it was left standing upright in the corner. Maybe it was thrown away. I don't care. In any case, the full meaning was there, staring me right in the face.

Here was a race of creatures capable of removing portions of their anatomy at will. Eyes, arms—and maybe more. Without batting an eyelash. My knowledge of biology came in handy, at this point. Obviously they were simple beings, unicellular, some sort of primitive single-celled things. Beings no more developed than starfish. Starfish can do the same thing, you know.

I read on. And came to this incredible revelation, tossed off coolly by the author without the faintest tremor:

. . . outside the movie theater we split up. Part of us went inside, part over to the cafe for dinner.

Binary fission, obviously. Splitting in half and forming two entities. Probably each lower half went to the cafe, it being farther, and the upper halves to the movies. I read on, hands shaking. I had really stumbled onto something here. My mind reeled as I made out this passage:

. . . I'm afraid there's no doubt about it. Poor Bibney has lost his head again.

Which was followed by:

. . . and Bob says he has utterly no guts.

Yet Bibney got around as well as the next person. The next person, however, was just as strange. He was soon described as:

. . . totally lacking in brains.

There was no doubt of the thing in the next passage. Julia, whom I had thought to be the one normal person, reveals herself as also being an alien life form, similar to the rest:

. . . quite deliberately, Julia had given her heart to the young man.

It didn't relate what the final disposition of the organ was, but I didn't really care. It was evident Julia had gone right on living in her usual manner, like all the others in the book. Without heart, arms, eyes, brains, viscera, dividing up in two when the occasion demanded. Without a qualm.

. . . thereupon she gave him her hand.

I sickened. The rascal now had her hand, as well as her heart. I shudder to think what he's done with them, by this time.

. . . he took her arm.

Not content to wait, he had to start dismantling her on his own. Flushing crimson, I slammed the book shut and leaped to my feet. But not in time to escape one last reference to those carefree bits of anatomy whose travels had originally thrown me on the track:

. . . her eyes followed him all the way down the road and across the meadow.

I rushed from the garage and back inside the warm house, as if the accursed things were following me. My wife and children were playing Monopoly in the kitchen. I joined them and played with frantic fervor, brow feverish, teeth chattering.

I had had enough of the thing. I want to hear no more about it. Let them come on. Let them invade Earth. I don't want to get mixed up in it.

I have absolutely no stomach for it.

Science Fiction Stories, #1, 1953.

Skin-Jobs

PAUL ATKINSON is a Lecturer in the School of Applied Media and Social Sciences at Monash University in Australia. His main area of research is the intersection between time and visual culture. He only has a theoretical interest in time travel, for the thought of traveling into the future, only to find that it is pretty much the same as today, horrifies him.

ROSS BARHAM spends his days as Head of Philosophy at Melbourne High School, and his nights as a Doctorial Candidate at the University of Melbourne. Somewhere in the cracks of space-time he also manifests as a new father, an Aikidoka, and a hobby farmer.

ERIC BECK is a freelance editor and writer who lives on a farm that is home to goats and sheep, none of whom are electric but whose doe eyed stares do, like the story of the wub, make him occasionally question his carnivorous eating practices.

ANDREW M. BUTLER remembers teaching film and cultural studies, but is convinced that that was his nephew's memories. Books on Philip K. Dick, Terry Pratchett, Cyberpunk, Postmodernism, and Film Studies have been published with his name on them, but it was the voices that told him what to write. He is currently writing about his version of science fiction of the 1970s. He always reaches for the light switch on the wrong side of the doorway.

JESSE W. BUTLER is an assistant professor of philosophy at the University of Central Arkansas, where he splits his brain between philosophical reflection on self-knowledge and trying to live a good life with his wife and two children. It isn't always easy to do both, but he's managed to avoid the need for holo-scanners so far. If anyone knows where to find a good cephalochromoscope, though, please let him know.

GERARD CASEY believes that work is the curse of the thinking class. He watches far too many noir movies and listens to ridiculous amounts of mainly classical music when not distracted by the demands of his day job teaching and writing about political philosophy at University College Dublin.

PHILIP KINDRED DICK was born in Chicago in 1928. His twin sister died six weeks after birth, and Dick later blamed their mother for the death. Dick's parents divorced, and Dick grew up with his mother in Berkeley. He read his first science-fiction story in 1940. His first published story, "Beyond Lies the Wub," appeared in 1953. He wrote forty-four published novels and over 120 short stories. His novel *The Man in the High Castle* received the Hugo Award. Dick had a fanatical following among hard-core sci-fi addicts, but only achieved the wider fame which rescued him from poverty toward the end of his life. More major Hollywood movies have been made of Dick's work than of any other writer except Stephen King, but Dick only lived to see the first of these, *Blade Runner*. His novel *Ubik* has been listed as one of the hundred best English-language novels published since the 1920s. In early 1974 Dick experienced powerful visions which influenced his later novels such as *VALIS* and *The Divine Invasion*, and which he explored in philosophical meditations, now published as *The Exegesis of Philip K. Dick*. Dick was married five times. He died in 1982.

Built from cloned organs, **DAN DINELLO** resembles a Professor in the Film and Video Department of Columbia College Chicago where he was recently named its Distinguished Faculty Scholar. Though confused by his memory implants, he wrote the book *Technophobia!*, directed episodes of *Strangers with Candy,* and runs the website shockproductions.com.

DON FALLIS is Associate Professor of Information Resources and Adjunct Associate Professor of Philosophy at the University of Arizona. He has written several articles on lying and deception, including "What Is Lying?," *Journal of Philosophy* (2009) and "The Most Terrific Liar You Ever Saw in Your Life" in *The Catcher in the Rye and Philosophy* (forthcoming). Like PKD, he spent many years of his life in Orange County. And he can confirm that it's easy to lose track of what is real and what is not, especially if you live near Disneyland or in one of the "off-world colonies" (*aka* "planned communities") in South County.

RICHARD FEIST is Dean of the Faculty of Philosophy, Saint Paul University. During a meeting with the Rector's agents, where everyone wore a scramble suit, Dr. Feist was told to monitor the philosophy professors and to concentrate on the activities of Dr. Feist. To this day

Skype makes Dr. Feist nervous; he remains unsure as to which video image he should speak. Despite his paranoia, Dr. Feist insists that he has published a number of books and articles on ethics and metaphysics. But he denies passing on his phobias to students.

MICHELLE GALLAGHER is an early modern scholar who laments the fact that science fiction is not recognized as a subfield of philosophy. She's convinced that in some alternate universe Philip K. Dick is celebrated as the visionary founder of a school of neo-skepticism which dominates philosophical literature. In anticipation of the day when travel to that universe is possible, she has read every PKD story in print at least three times.

PATRICK GRACE is a lawyer in the Washington DC Metro area (who isn't?), has done legal commentary on talk radio (ditto), and teaches Postmodern Jurisprudence with his co-author George Teschner. He is hard at work developing innovative strategies to corner a future market of new clientele—androids who have been charged with DUI.

RONALD S. GREEN's true name may not be spoken. After creating and entering the amnesia labyrinth in which we all currently wander, his children at the University of Wisconsin amusingly awarded Him a PhD in Buddhist Studies. He encodes pink light transmissions at Coastal Carolina University, awaiting the student who will remember.

G.C. GODDU is Associate Professor of Philosophy at the University of Richmond where he specializes in metaphysics and logic. In between dreaming up new ways to make time-travel stories consistent, he tries to determine if any of his students are replicants and to convince them that he is not an alien imposter.

BENJAMIN HUFF is Assistant Professor of Philosophy at Randolph Macon College. His research and teaching interests include virtue ethics, Chinese philosophy, philosophy of religion, and free will. He doesn't remember ever going to Mars, but has spent a lot of nights camping in the deserts of Utah and Saudi Arabia, written patent applications for a space startup company, and applied for a pioneer spot in the Virgin Galactic/Google colonization plan (still waiting to hear back on that one!).

PAUL LIVINGSTON lives in the Sandia Mountains outside Albuquerque, New Mexico, and teaches and writes on the nature of mind, language, and reality. He's the author of three books: *Philosophical History and the Problem of Consciousness* (2004), *Philosophy and the Vision of Language* (2008), and the forthcoming

Politics of Logic (2011). In their spare time, electric sheep dream of him.

HEATH MASSEY is an amazingly lifelike construct programmed to function as a teaching machine. As an Associate Professor of Philosophy at Beloit College, he offers a convincing illusion of enthusiasm and genuine wonder. His students only suspect that he is a mechanical artifice when he slips a gear and repeats the same phase of his cycle until a technician is called in to perform repairs. He is the author of *The Origin of Time: Heidegger and Bergson* and co-translator of Maurice Merleau-Ponty's *Institution and Passivity*. Recently he has been making the most of his time with his newborn son, Theo.

MATTHEW MCCALL is currently a graduate student in Philosophy at Ohio State University, where he enjoys laboring over the thoughts of Early Modern philosophers. He's undecided on whether or not he is part of a blob. He would like it to be true, though, so that he can necessarily overcome and understand the strange behavior of his cat, Phil 2420 (whose namesake is, of course, one amazing science fiction writer).

LOUIS MELANÇON has lost several oxfords trying to pinpoint the exact moment the Principle of Sufficient Irritation occurs. To date he has only made a mess of the oven (the most convenient source of heat), confused the garbage man over the state of old footwear and slightly miffed his wife (not quite sufficient irritation). Louis is a US Army officer with combat arms and intelligence experiences ranging from the tactical to strategic levels. He holds master's degrees from the Joint Military Intelligence College (now National Defense Intelligence College) as well as King's College, London and has been awarded the Bronze Star Medal. He has been published in *Military Review* and contributed to *Battlestar Galactica and Philosophy: Mission Accomplished or Mission Frakked Up?*, *Anime and Philosophy: Wide Eyed Wonder*, and *Dune and Philosophy: Weirding Way of the Mentat*.

ETHAN MILLS is a sci-fi nerd who happens to be a PhD candidate in philosophy at the University of New Mexico where he studies epistemology and Indian philosophy and teaches a variety of classes. He lives with his wife, Beth, and cat, Elsie. He previously contributed to *Stephen Colbert and Philiosophy: I Am Philosophy (And So Can You!)*. The idea for his chapter in this volume was caused by showing *Minority Report* to his Philosophy 101 students. He wonders if his dissertation on skepticism in ancient India would be better if he were replaced by a skeptical android . . . unless of course he already is that android.

PETER MURPHY is Associate Professor of Philosophy at the University of Indianapolis. He is most interested in applied ethics and epistemology. Unlike Steven Spielberg, he's looking forward to a future with a Division of Precrime.

JUSTIN NICHOLAS is currently pursuing his undergraduate degree in philosophy at York College of Pennsylvania. He is rather notorious among friends for owning a cat that he vehemently hates. When asked why he keeps it, he simply mumbles something about a strange religion and complains that the township code prevents the keeping of animals on roofs.

A Rexorian who replaced **TRAVIS PATERSON**—years ago, probably—is a graduate student in Political Science at the University of Edinburgh. Assuming, at least, that that Rexorian has not himself been replaced by an Outspace Imposter.

JEREMY PIERCE is a PhD student at Syracuse University and teaches at Le Moyne College. He works in such diverse areas as metaphysics, philosophy of religion, and philosophy of race and has previously written popular culture and philosophy pieces on *Harry Potter*, *X-Men*, and *Lost*. Jeremy spends much of his free time trying to figure out how to make use of the prophetic abilities of his two autistic children, so far to no avail.

BEN SAUNDERS is currently Lecturer in Philosophy at the University of Stirling in the UK. His research interests include democracy, lotteries and, in particular, their intersection. He has previously written about the relation between lotteries and penalty shoot-outs in *Soccer and Philosophy: Beautiful Thoughts on the Beautiful Game* (2010). Unfortunately, he can't see the future, or he'd be a retired lottery winner by now.

ALF SEEGERT is Assistant Professor (Lecturer) in the Department of English at the University of Utah. In addition to teaching and publishing on nature and virtuality, he designs internationally published Euro-style board games themed on trolls and *The Canterbury Tales*. His cats are still not sure if he's a real human being or a cunningly contrived simulation. His homepage is at www.alfseegert.com.

PETER SIMONS is Professor of Philosophy at Trinity College Dublin. He has worked in England, Ireland, and Austria, researches in metaphysics and logic, has written two books and over two hundred articles. When not sleeping or philosophizing he likes hill walking and choral singing.

BENJAMIN STEVENS teaches literature and languages at Bard College as well as music history and theory around the country. Having witnessed the end of the Cold War, he wonders whether it was by human, machine, or extraterrestrial action . . . or all three, each in its own parallel universe. When not writing about literature—including the classics, science fiction, and comics—or writing his own poetry he organizes curricula at a cappella music festivals.

JOHN SULLINS putters about in the small land of Sonoma County California, an area Dick described as: "a well settled farm area, and very hot. A very dull area. Just right for a barbershop." He lives there with his wife and two daughters. He's an associate professor of philosophy at Sonoma State University where he lectures about the ambiguous distinctions between humans and robots, a problem his students don't seem to be all that worried about.

DAVID SVOLBA earned his PhD in Philosophy in 2008 from the University of Chicago. He taught philosophy at the University of Illinois at Chicago between 2006 and 2010, and is currently a visiting lecturer in Philosophy at the Jesuit University of Philosophy and Education in Krakow, Poland. Although he saw *Blade Runner* in his youth, he didn't really discover the world of Philip K. Dick until recently and has no plans on leaving that world anytime soon.

GEORGE TESCHNER teaches courses in Philosophy of Technology, Human and Machine Intelligence, Contemporary Continental Philosophy, and Philosophy and Literary Theory at Christopher Newport University in Virginia. He teaches with the conviction that language speaks us, rather than we speak language, and is expecting to get rich quick by designing the Teschner Artificial Thought Simulator modeled after the Penfield Artificial Mood Simulator of *Do Androids Dream of Electric Sheep?*

RICHARD VISKOVIĆ is a PhD candidate at the University of Auckland in New Zealand, where he is completing a thesis on Philip K. Dick and Philosophy. He hopes that in an alternate universe, Philip Dick is writing a thesis about Richard D.D. Viskovic, but suspects such a thing is beyond the bounds of even the most speculative fiction.

DENNIS WEISS is Professor of Philosophy at York College of Pennsylvania where he teaches courses on and writes about human nature, technology, film, and science fiction, exploring those ubiquitous themes of Dick's science fiction but alas in far more mundane ways. But, wait, isn't the mundanity of life a Dick theme too?

D.E. WITTKOWER exists simultaneously in multiple timelines: one in which he is a father-thing to two exceptional children and four wonderful cats; another in which he teaches philosophy of technology and computer ethics as an Assistant Professor at Old Dominion University; another in which he has edited *iPod and Philosophy*, *Mr. Monk and Philosophy*, and *Facebook and Philosophy*; and yet another in which he has written articles and book chapters on topics including business ethics, copyright law, friendship, and online culture. He may or may not be from the future.

SARA WORLEY is Associate Professor of Philosophy at Bowling Green State University. She works mostly in philosophy of mind and philosophy of psychiatry. She doesn't think she's planning on committing any crimes, but apparently you never know. She's hoping the Adjustment Bureau will come and do some adjusting.

Index

CPSIA information can be obtained at www.ICGtesting.com
Printed in the USA
LVOW10s1006050716

495065LV00005B/23/P

9 780812 697346